AND I'LL NEVER LOVE HIM LESS

"Real, raw, relatable … Candy's new book will make readers laugh and cry, and most of all it will give them a renewed sense of hope that they can get through even the toughest challenges and hardships of life with a little more grace, peace and joy."

Michele Chynoweth
Bestselling Author of The Faithful One
and other contemporary Bible-based suspense novels

Caring for Mr. Drew was such a blessing. I looked forward to my Friday visits with him, and Candy too! I admired how stoic, classy, collected and loving she was during the hardest time of her life. Alzheimer's disease has no mercy on anyone, and Candy carried that burden with ease. On good days, but most importantly on the worst of days, Mr. Drew's face would light up at the slightest glimpse of Candy. He would say to me, "Oh my, she is beautiful, isn't she?" It was a love in the purest form, one he couldn't control. Alzheimer's disease may have taken over his brain, but never his heart. Memories of his witty personality and the silly tricks he liked to play on me bring a smile to my face every time I pass by Elizabeth Street. Thank you, Candy, for trusting me to care for someone so precious to you. It was an honor and I am forever grateful God allowed us to cross paths.

Jena Wilkins, RN
Delaware Hospice

This beautiful memoir is a testament to faithful and faith-filled marriage. It also teaches us all how to find and nurture the human soul in one who happens to have Alzheimer's Disease. It was my privilege and my joy to provide spiritual support for Drew and Candy. I will never forget the look in Drew's eyes the day I provided Communion for them. He said not one word out loud, but his look spoke volumes about his faith and the presence of God in his life. In her beautiful prose, Candy has given us all a glimpse of how we can continue to love and nurture the sacred in all who struggle with this disease.

Rev. Marjorie Egger, MDiv
Hospice Chaplain, Delaware Hospice, Inc.

And I Will Never Love Him Less is the beautifully written sequel to *I've Never Loved Him More*. Candy Abbott is a gifted writer who has chronicled her beloved husband's journey through Alzheimer's disease. Alzheimer's affects everyone who is close to the person that has the disease. Candy vividly shows the effect on herself and on others close to Drew. Her faith shines through the darkness of the Alzheimer's disease journey. If you have a loved one with dementia, you need to read both of these books. "And now these three remain: faith, hope and love. But the greatest of these is love" (1 Cor. 13:13, NIV). Thank you, Candy, for showing us all three.

Dave Kelly, BSW, CDP, CVP
Alzheimer's Support Group Facilitator

Spellbinding. The way Candy writes, you can't wait to see what Drew is going to say the next day or what is going to happen. It's hard to imagine what Candy was going through and what her emotions were, yet she explains them so well you feel like you're right in the house with her. In fact, I was. During the last year-and-a-half, as a hospice volunteer, I stayed with Drew to give Candy some much-needed respite, which gave me a chance to witness their interaction firsthand. The devotion that she had to Drew and Drew to her is a testament to the kind of love people long for. I found this book not only interesting but useful as I work with clients with Alzheimer's. Of course, each day is different and each client is different, but there's always something in these pages that you can use. Just be creative, be patient as Candy demonstrates here, and it will work.

Tom Beach
Delaware Hospice Volunteer

Rarely can a person write a book in diary form that holds the reader's attention. Candy is one of those exceptional authors who has mastered the skill to do so. *And I'll Never Love Him Less,* is filled with resources and helpful tools. For example, Candy learned how to practice therapeutic fibbing and the value of the word "tomorrow." Her book would be a useful resource for professionals, caregivers, spouses, families, prayer partners, and people interested in going into the help profession regardless of the field.

M. Wayne Clark, D.Min.
Retired United Methodist Minister,
Licensed Marriage and Family Therapist,
AAPC Diplomat, and author

I loved reading every word of this book. Every word, every emotion, every struggle and every insight. This isn't just a book for caregivers and family members. It is a book for everyone on how to live a life with God.

Nancy Rue
Best-selling author

And I'll Never Love Him Less is such a good read that it's difficult to put down. Candy shows unbelievable love, courage, strength, determination, faith, and an unwillingness to give in to self-pity or despair, even when Drew's situation gradually got worse and her own health took a toll. I was anxious to get to the end to see what happened to her and with her. I was not disappointed. There was a sense of gratitude, relief, calmness, peace, undying love, and sorrow, yet a calm determination to move on into the future. The journey was so difficult and challenging, and yet she showed strength and a feeling of contentment that she had done the best she could, and everything was going to be okay. This book is such an important witness. Everyone in a similar situation needs to have it.

Margery Mayer
Author of Repairers of the Breach
Brentwood, Tennessee

Copyright © 2020 Candy Abbott
ISBN 978-1-938796-64-7
Library of Congress Control Number: 2020903539
SAN 920-380X
ISNI 0000 0000 5048 9968

Health/Diseases: Alzheimer's Disease • Christian/Family & Relationships
• Christian/Inspirational

Nancy Rue, Content Editor
Michele Chynoweth, Copy Editor
Fran D. Lowe, Copy Editor

Cover photo by Dana Abbott Painter (Drew's daughter)
taken in Bermuda on John Smith's Bay

Published by Fruitbearer Publishing, LLC
P.O. Box 777 • Georgetown, DE 19947
302.856.6649 • FAX 302.856.7742
www.fruitbearer.com • info@fruitbearer.com

Printed in the United States of America

And I'll Never Love Him Less

BOOK 2
THE REST OF THE STORY

SEQUEL TO
I'VE NEVER LOVED HIM MORE
A HUSBAND'S ALZHEIMER'S, A WIFE'S DEVOTION

CANDY ABBOTT

FRUITBEARER PUBLISHING LLC

To My Children

DANA, TROY, AND KIM

WHO ARE BONDED CLOSER TO ME
AND TO ONE ANOTHER
THAN WHEN WE BEGAN THIS JOURNEY
WITH THEIR DAD.

"This disease might hide the person underneath,
but there's still a person in there
who needs your love and attention."

— *James Calandriello*

Contents

D

"Of course, you'll encounter trouble.
But behold a God of power
who can take any evil
and turn it into a door of hope."

— *Catherine Marshall*

Foreword

"I do." A lifetime commitment in two words. The romance that leads to speaking those two words is often mesmerizing, euphoric, and light-hearted. As the marriage unfolds, there are trying moments and challenges in the seasons of life that put this commitment to the test. At times, it can look and feel as though love is failing. But true love endures. That endurance can produce greater strength and an increased desire to remain true to those two words. This is what Candy and Drew Abbott have done. They have remained true to their love, even throughout the season of Alzheimer's.

I've Never Loved Him More, Candy's first book about the beginning stages of the disease in her beloved's life, led to this sequel. *And I'll Never Love Him Less* chronicles the second half of their journey with day-to-day complexities, nuances, and dramatic shifts. While Candy's writing is fresh and penetrating, she threads her words with colorful yet needful dependency on her faith. That vulnerability lends itself to the authenticity of her writing. Candy's honest depiction of the navigation by them both is captivating as much as it is informative. Her portrayal of the difficult emotional changes in Drew is not veiled as she gives her audience an open door to the Abbott home and heart and turbulence. There is no shield for the reader from the pain of the disease and what it takes from life.

One need not have read Candy's previous book to be encouraged and inspired by this volume. Both yield value that applies to younger and older readers alike. What is most telling about this book is the agitation of Drew and anger in him in latter sections. This is not uncommon with Alzheimer's patients; however, from a spiritual perspective, it is striking. The Bible teaches that every person who follows Jesus and accepts Him as their Savior has an adversary, Satan. Satan's goal is to kill, steal, and destroy. That includes a marriage where illness agitates feelings and identities.

But the faith Candy had in Christ to shepherd their marriage toward the end, as at its beginning, remained firmly in place. It is as though the love of Jesus Himself surrounded and undergirded their marriage as a protective hedge. This is faith, which Candy points to steadily as the reason she has been able to press on with love and gratitude.

"I thought I trusted God all my life," Candy told me, "but I barely knew anything about trust. This ordeal brought me to a place of maturity, to a place where I *had* to trust Him because I came to the end of myself. Now, I know what it means to *truly* trust God."

Her willing utterance of "I do" forty-four years ago became love-in-action during these difficult years and an inspiration to family, friends, and all who witnessed the tenderness she and Drew exchanged right to the end.

Read this book as a reminder of the precious gift of time. Time is measured by how we spend it with those we love and even those who are unloving toward us. When illness enters lives and relationships, love is still present. However, it is newly expressed as it provides an opportunity for the surrender of self to care for the needs of another. Doing so brings with it the reward of a job well done and the satisfaction of a life well-lived.

And I'll Never Love Him Less furthers the expansiveness of love and gives deeper credence to "I do." Hope will meet the readers of this book as love reveals new diamonds in the rough. The key is to accept the challenge of going the distance in love to mine for the diamonds. Candy and Drew Abbott have done just that. Let us read their example and apply it to discover what love has to give us. May God's blessing of an open heart lead the way.

Chris Ann Waters
Author of *Transitions*
and *Seasons of Goodbye:*
Working Your Way Through Loss
Hospice Chaplain

"When we dwell on God's provision,
His promises, His presence,
authentic joy is the natural overflow,
which inspires us to praise and worship Him
through our hardships.
In so doing, we can experience His peace
through any circumstance."

—*Kim Meeder*

Preface

"I've told you these things for a purpose:
that my joy might be your joy,
and your joy wholly mature.
This is my command:
Love one another the way I loved you.
This is the very best way to love.
Put your life on the line for your friends."

Jesus (John 15:11-13, MSG)

Whoever thought Alzheimer's could be a source of joy? I never did. Until now. This relentless journey contains hidden gifts. With the right perspective, *any* adversity has the capacity within it to contain joy at its core. The worse the situation, the more reason to cling to the One who is the source of joy—mature joy, sustaining joy. When we sacrifice ourselves for the sake of someone else without expecting anything in return, we step beyond the trials of this world and into the kind of love Jesus spoke of in John 15:9-10:

"I've loved you the way my Father has loved me.
Make yourselves at home in my love.
If you keep my commands,
you'll remain intimately at home in my love.

> *That's what I've done—*
> *kept my Father's commands*
> *and made myself at home in his love."*
> —Jesus (John 15:11-13 MSG)

That's what I've been trying to do—make myself "at home in His love." It can be done. I've found that safe place—a place that has a purpose larger than myself—a place where joy catches you by surprise when you face a crisis and come through it victoriously.

I wasn't always this way. No, not by a long shot. But I've practiced the presence of God long enough now that it's become a way of life, overshadowing my whiny, fearful, fleshly nature. On my best days, I go through the ups and downs with an awareness of how things might look through the eyes of the Holy Spirit. Some days are harder than others, of course. But I want it all: the good, the bad, the ugly—whatever God has for me. That's a dangerous prayer because sometimes the Lord sends us into prickly territory to make us stronger and draw us closer to Him.

With Alzheimer's, the crisis is so long and drawn out that it sometimes doesn't feel like it will ever be "over," and joy and victory are illusive. But Isaiah 30:15 (NIV) provides a cushion for us:

> *The Sovereign Lord, the Holy One of Israel, says:*
> *"In repentance and rest is your salvation,*
> *in quietness and trust is your strength,"*
> and then there are seven terrible words:
> *"but you would have none of it."*

If you are grappling with the many questions and challenges of caregiving and feel like you would rather "have none of it," I'm hoping the Lord will meet you between the lines of this book.

Book One, *I've Never Loved Him More: A Husband's Alzheimer's, a Wife's Devotion,* carried us from the discovery, adjustment, and acceptance of Drew's Alzheimer's into the moderate stage. These pages pick up where those left off. *And I'll Never Love Him Less* continues our journey through the moderate to late stages of the disease, right up until "death do us part."

As I share how I cling to my safe place of "quietness and trust" during the upheavals of Alzheimer's caregiving, may you find comfort and, yes, even joy in the journey.

"Blessed are the flexible,
for they shall not be bent out of shape."

— *Robert Ludlum*

CHAPTER ONE

The Dreaded Words

October 1, 2016

This morning at ten o'clock, with the aroma of freshly brewed coffee wafting through the kitchen, I padded into the bedroom, shook Drew's shoulder, and kissed him on the cheek. "Rise and shine, sleepyhead—your breakfast is just about ready."

Minutes later, he made his way to the table, and I placed his fried egg and toast in front of him. FOX News droned in the background about the upcoming election as I prepared my own plate and joined him.

I was about to take my first bite when he said softly, "I'm so sorry, but I can't recall who you are or why you're here."

I've been dreading these words. The sound of them reverberated in my ears like the dut-dut-dut of an automatic rifle. In reflex motion, my hand flew to my chest as if to protect my heart. Nothing prepares you for this no matter how prepared you think you are. *He doesn't know me.* I plastered a smile on my face to hide the pain and said, "I'm Candy I'm your wife. And I live here with you."

My prayer from the beginning has been that Drew would always know me, but I see I'm getting a *No* on that.

The second half of my prayer was that he would keep his sweet disposition and not get combative. So far, that part is intact as well as his sense of humor. Although he no longer initiates hugs and kisses, he's quick to respond when I do and is still his sweet, gentle self.

October 11, 2016

I find it interesting that for someone who was never too keen about travel, he thinks we're away somewhere. Several times a day, he'll ask, "We're leaving tomorrow, right?" or other things that make it clear he doesn't know he's at home. When I ask where he thinks we are, he can't come up with an answer, so we laugh, and I say this is a no-hassle way to travel. "No packing or flight delays," and "Maybe we'll take a train next time."

We went to dinner with Dana tonight, and when we got home, Drew said, "Where are we?" I've learned to take questions like this seriously, but Dana laughed and said, "You're kidding, right? Come on, Dad; you know where we are. Where are we?"

He paused long enough for his brain to wrap around the question being fired back at him and came up with, "In my house?"

"See, Dad? I knew you were joking around."

He wasn't.

Later, when we kissed goodnight, he said, "We've had fun on this whole trip—gotten to know each other a little bit."

He's right about one thing: this journey into the world of Alzheimer's is like taking a trip together. We have, indeed, had fun on "this whole trip" (our marriage), and even now, the vibes between us continue to be enjoyable in spite of the challenges. Besides, each day he sees me as if for the first time, and how much fun is that!

October 18, 2016

We saw Dr. Kemp, the neurologist, for the second time, and I told him that driving is no longer a concern. Because I couldn't talk freely in front of Drew, I didn't explain that I no longer see any hint that he is interested in getting behind the wheel. I considered hiding his car keys but decided against it because he would be upset if they weren't in his pocket. Besides, he's content to let me drive.

In the MMSE (Mini-Mental Status Exam), the neurologist asks the patient to write a sentence, any sentence. The first time Drew had that exercise, he wrote, "I love my wife," which pleased me to no end. Today he wrote, "Help me."

Those two words went right through me. Even though Drew is still in denial that anything is wrong with him, something inside tells him that he's in trouble. Which means I'm in trouble, too. How much more can I help him? I'm giving it all I've got already.

It was a brief, pleasant visit except for "help me" echoing in my ears. When I asked Dr. Kemp how Drew scored, he said twenty-one, which is the same as last time. He confirmed that this is the end of the mild stage and the beginning of the moderate stage.

Stepping outside into the parking lot, cool air smacked me in the face, and I felt like it was the hand of God. Words pierced my spirit. "Did I not see you through the mild stage? Will I not see you through the moderate stage?"

By the time I got behind the wheel, I could smile like I meant it. I drove us to The Blacksmith in Berlin, Maryland, where we had an enjoyable lunch and then headed home. The weather was gorgeous— crisp autumn air with low humidity—so Drew and I took a short walk. He started a little wobbly but soon got into a steady stride and then began walking too fast for me to keep up. It wasn't until I asked him to slow down that I realized he was walking with his hands in his pockets.

"That's something new," I said. "If you fall with your hands in your pockets, you won't be able to catch yourself."

"I could, too," he said. "I'm quick."

"Well, just humor me and swing your arms as you walk, okay?"

He didn't know what I meant by "swing your arms," so I demonstrated. We wound up making a game of it to see who could swing their arms the highest as we walked. I'm sure we must have looked comical if any neighbors were watching, but we had a good time and got home without any mishaps.

October 25, 2016

My mammogram looked suspicious, so they did a second one, which wasn't a big deal, but when the radiologist said I needed a biopsy of my right breast because they saw a "cluster" that wasn't there last year, my hands suddenly felt clammy, and I felt dizzy. I sat down and collected my thoughts. I reminded the Lord that He knew the responsibilities I already faced and reminded myself that He would give me strength for whatever might come. Normally, I would have confided in Drew and turned to him for compassion and comfort; instead, because I didn't want to worry him and he probably wouldn't understand anyway, I turned to family and friends for prayer and support. I even looked at wigs online in case I should need one.

October 28, 2016

I got the results today of the biopsy, and everything is fine, praise the Lord! I sat in Dr. Spellman's parking lot and couldn't call Drew to share my joy, so I sent a text message to my daughter Kim, called my stepdaughter Dana during the drive home, and sent emails to others when I got to the computer. My friend Elizabeth called, and we shared tears of relief over the phone.

The priority for Drew today was seeing how loud and how often he could belch.

October 29, 2016

I walked into the bathroom as Drew was painting his face with stick deodorant. Very matter-of-factly, I opened the can of shaving cream that was sitting on the counter and squirted some of it in his hand. "This will feel better to you, hon."

"I guess I need you to watch me every minute," he said with a smile.

I guess I do.

November 2, 2016

Drew has a new habit of standing at the bar in the kitchen and drumming his fingernails, so it sounds like galloping horses. A little of that is tolerable, but it goes on and on for two and three minutes at a time. I told him, "That's irritating, you know—like nails on a blackboard," and he said, "Is that right?" and continued. I tell myself that it's just a phase that will pass, and I should be happy he's found a way to entertain himself. This rationale is shallow, and the irritation continues, so I cope by leaving the room. This morning, when the galloping horses returned, he said, "Here they come." To which I responded, "Let's hear how they sound when they go." And, don't you know, he faded the phantom hoof -beats until the horses were gone. *Ahh*, blessed relief.

I'm finding it more and more difficult to concentrate on my work because Drew feels an increased need to be with me. While I'm at the keyboard, he parks himself behind me in the swivel rocker and continually asks questions which, of course, I'm supposed to answer. If I don't say anything, he says, "Why won't you talk to me?" This would not be a problem if I were playing a mindless computer game, but when I'm trying to concentrate on editing where *every* comma counts, it brings my work to a screeching halt.

Michele Fletcher, my beautician, offered a temporary solution. "I'm in the shop all day, and we have a room upstairs with WiFi if you want to bring your laptop. There's a bed and bathroom there, too, if you need an undisturbed nap." Her offer is very appealing and may give me a couple of hours of productive or at least stress-free time. If I leave Drew a note on the marker board, he's still okay to stay alone for two hours. Now, the trick will be finding a couple of clear hours on my calendar to reserve for myself. He takes naps during the day, but I use that time to run errands. I could look into having a volunteer do the banking and grocery shopping, but scheduling someone and explaining it seems like it would take more time than doing it. *Sigh*. Thinking about all this makes me just want to park myself in front of the TV and zone out.

November 7, 2016

At 9:45 p.m., while I was in my office paying bills, Drew said, "Come here when you get a chance. I need your expert opinion."

I kept writing the check and trying to stay focused so I wrote the right amount. "In a minute, hon." My minute grew into several more as I tried to get closure on at least one thing I'd started today.

"I need your help on this," he said. And something in his voice drew me to my feet.

"I'm coming, hon."

When I got to the kitchen, the first thing I noticed was our chubby blonde Cocker Spaniel, Buttercup, panting and looking up at the counter where her sixteen-foot leashes were rolled up.

"Sorry, girl," I said. "You're not going for a walk at this hour." Grabbing the leashes to take them back outside where they're supposed to be, I scolded Drew. "These need to stay hooked up so we can let her out at night."

"That's not it," he said. "I need you for something else. Where do we put this?" He opened the sliding glass door to the deck, and I gasped.

He had dismantled the clay statue-fountain that my stepson Troy had so carefully repaired and recently filled with several gallons of water. The cord was unplugged, and Drew had lifted the heavy thing and tried to bring it in the house along with several outdoor cushions.

"You dumped the water out?"

"Yeah, over there, but where can we put this thing?"

"It belongs right where it was," I said, trying to keep my voice as calm and pleasant as possible while I hooked up Buttercup's leashes.

"But, won't somebody steal it when we're gone?"

Ahhh. With those words, I understood the "why" without having to ask. He thinks we're leaving "to go home," and he's working hard to secure everything. I dragged the fountain back into place and returned the cushions to their rightful places, chatting with him the whole time. I was able to convince him (for the moment) that this is our home, that we haven't been anywhere, and that we're staying put.

He gave me a sheepish look as we stepped back into the house and closed the sliding glass door. "I guess you'll just have to watch me every minute."

He said the same thing a few days ago. This time, I was ready. "Watch you every minute?" I gave him a hug, a lingering kiss, and broke into an off-key version of the Four Seasons' song. "Can't take my eyes off of youooooh . . . you're just too good to be trueooooh." We laughed ourselves silly, and he didn't mention anything about "going home" the rest of the night.

After finishing up the bills around 11:00 p.m., I bowed my head and turned my thoughts to God.

Thank You, Lord, that Drew still has a good sense of humor and responds well to mine. Thank You that he cares about protecting the things that belong to us, that he is strong enough to lift heavy objects, and that he didn't get hurt in the process. Thank You that we are home and don't have to pack anything. Thank You that he can still talk and move and reason, whether it makes sense or not. Thank You that, although he's confused, he's not combative or argumentative. Thank You for being my peace no matter what the circumstances.

Praising God for the little things changes your perspective on the big picture.

November 21, 2016

Last night when we were getting ready for bed, Drew couldn't find the sweatpants he sleeps in.

I pointed to the chair by the desk in the bedroom. "Look on the seat. Maybe you have something piled on top of them."

He insisted they weren't there, so I strolled over to prove him wrong. "There were two pairs, folded up right here on this cushion yesterday morning," I said with confidence. I picked up two sweaters, a pair of jeans, and two long-sleeved shirts. No sweatpants.

I looked in the hamper.

I looked in the closets.

I looked in every dresser drawer, under the bed, in the washing machine and dryer . . . in short, everywhere they could be. *Two pairs of sweatpants can't just disappear!*

Correction. Oh, yes, they can. After forty-five minutes of searching every conceivable hiding place, I called it quits and found something else for him to wear to bed. *Tomorrow,* I told myself, *I'll get him new ones at Walmart.*

It was cold and windy today, so we stayed in all day. Dinnertime came, and I didn't feel like cooking or going to a restaurant, so I ordered a pizza online. I told Drew that I would drive him to the store, give him the receipt, and all he had to do was hand it to the guy at the register and bring the pizza to the car.

We bundled up, told Buttercup we'd be right back, locked the front door, and stepped off the front porch. I clicked the key fob in my purse to unlock the car doors and then looked at the car for the first time. All four windows were down!

Drew was alarmed. "Why would you put the windows down?"

By then, we were at the end of the walk where we could look into the car, and there in the back seat were two pairs of sweatpants, neatly folded!

Two mysteries solved themselves in the time it took me to ease into the front seat. When Drew got dressed yesterday morning, he must have been thinking that we'd be "going home" and had packed up his PJs, pressing all kinds of buttons to get the car unlocked. No doubt, the windows went down in the process, and he didn't know how to get them back up. By the time he got back into the house, he would have forgotten all about it. So, all day yesterday and all day today, the car must have sat in the driveway with the doors unlocked and the windows rolled down.

This is my cue that it's time to take the Cadillac key fob off his key ring.

December 1, 2016

Thanksgiving was a week ago, and I'm still thinking about what happened. We kept our usual tradition of bringing the mashed potatoes to Dana's for dinner. No sooner had I handed over the casserole dish and exchanged hugs than Drew spied a love seat with two folding tables and claimed them for us. He sat down, so I sat with him as others milled around in happy conversation.

When I stood up to speak with our grandson, Trevor, and his wife, Jill, Drew grabbed my hand and said, "Where are you going?"

"Right over here, behind you," I said. "I'll be right back."

Normally, we would have sat in the dining room with Dana, John, and Troy, but the short conversation I had with Trevor and Jill was about the extent of any meaningful interaction I would have with the family that day. Our meal was delicious, as always, but as soon as Drew finished eating, he was ready to go.

Today, I had lunch with friends and shared my frustration. As the four of us were leaving the restaurant and walking to the parking lot, Carol stopped. "Candy, there's something I feel I need to say before we go."

"Whatever it is, I want to hear it!"

"About what happened at Thanksgiving—remember, you're the caregiver, and you can choose where you sit. You don't always have to do what Drew wants. You have to think of yourself and your needs, too."

"I hear you loud and clear," I told her. Carol made her point. But it's natural for me to defer to Drew because now he derives more of his identity from me than from himself. His comfort is having me by his side, so I stay there. Everybody says the caregiver needs to take care of the caregiver. I'll work on that. I'll learn how to detach long enough to care for myself. *But how?*

The things that matter most in our lives
are not fantastic or grand.
They are the moments when we touch one another,
when we are there in the most attentive or caring way."

— *Jack Kornfield*

CHAPTER TWO

All You Have to Know

December 3, 2016

Every day, Drew asks where he is. It used to be only after sundown that he became confused, but now he doesn't recognize his home even in daylight.

Nothing looks familiar to him, and when he gets up in the night to go to the bathroom, he asks me for directions.

I'll say, "Go to the end of the bed, turn left, and go straight," and then open one eye to be sure he goes through the bathroom door. Sometimes, in the wee hours, I'll hear him roaming through the house and know he's trying to find something that looks familiar; most often, he'll lie in bed obsessing over it, unable to remember what I've just told him.

Last night, every time I was about to doze off, he would say, "Where am I?" and I would tell him, once again, that this is his home, and I am his wife. If I say that our house is across the street from Aunt Fannie's, that seems to give him a landmark. He can also get his bearings if I tell him that the alley past Fannie's house leads to the house where he was born and raised. The best thing I've come up with to say is, "All you have to know is this: You're in a safe place with someone who loves you."

He'll laugh and say, "Well, then, that settles it. Goodnight, darlin'."

At that point, I fall asleep, and his questions don't come again until morning.

December 6, 2016

This morning's breakfast conversation made for a more interesting discussion than usual.

"Where did the world come from?" he asked matter-of-factly.

"God spoke it into existence," I said. "In six days, He made the earth and everything in it."

"Where did God come from?"

On days like this, I appreciate Drew's childlike thought process. "God has always existed," I said. "It's hard for humans to understand because we're finite humans, and God is infinite."

"What's infinite?"

"No beginning and no end. Nobody made God. We are earthbound, restricted by time and space, and God isn't, so it's hard for us to understand."

He paused and smiled. "So, what you're saying is you don't know the answer."

I laughed. "That's exactly what I'm saying. I don't know the answer. Nobody does. So, you know what that means? You've asked a really good question."

December 7, 2016

Last night, Drew was more confused than usual, and we didn't get to bed until 1 a.m. because he couldn't settle down. As soon as I was about to drift off to sleep, he would say, "Where am I?" or "Who owns this place?" I began looking at the clock each time he punctuated the night with a question:

"Where is this place located?" (1:30)
"Are we going home tomorrow?" (2:15)
"Who's taking care of our dogs?" (2:45)

"Can you tell me where we are?" (3:20)
"Where is this place located?" (4:10)

Off and on it went, all night long, and each question triggered a discussion that lasted a good ten minutes or more.

At 4:30, when he was finally snoring gently, Buttercup needed to go out, so I had to get up with her.

By 6:30, Drew was wide awake and ready for breakfast, and so our day began. I had a line-up of people scheduled to meet with me all day. He could nap, but I'd be operating on energy fumes. To keep my momentum going, I stayed busy by starting a load of laundry, left a message on the marker board on the kitchen counter ("Running errands. Be home in 20 minutes") and dashed out to the post office and bank.

I was feeling pretty buoyant when I breezed into the kitchen at 9:45, in contrast to Drew, who stood in the doorway looking forlorn. "Didn't I have a wife?"

"You sure did. And you still do. Taaa-daaa! It's *me*, your wife!"

He frowned. "No, really. Tell me. Do you know where my wife is?"

He looked serious, but I wasn't ready to be. "I sure do," I said, striking a pose. "And she's right here before your very eyes."

"Don't joke about this. I'm serious," he said. "Did something happen to my wife?"

The verbal slap sobered me up. I blinked and put on my compassionate face. "I'm so sorry, honey. I am your wife. Truly. It's just that your memory plays tricks on you, and now and then you don't recognize me."

His already-slumped shoulders dropped another inch. "That's not normal. What's wrong with me? I need to know. Tell me the truth. Tell me everything."

Was this the moment I should tell him that he has Alzheimer's? Would he even understand what that was? If I put him through the trauma of telling him, would he remember? I needed a stall tactic to think this through.

"I know this is important, and we'll have a nice, long talk in a little bit, but right now—" I elbowed my way past him to get to the washer— "I have to get this laundry under control because I have somebody coming in a few minutes."

I moved the clothes from the washer to the dryer while he watched. "Why can't we talk now?"

I can't handle it right now, that's why. I pushed my thoughts away and said, "Because Gloria will be here any minute, and I need to be ready for her."

"Who's Gloria?"

I pushed past him to gather up another armful of dirty clothes. "Our bookkeeper who helps us get all our tax stuff ready for the accountant." Just as I pressed start on the washing machine, the doorbell rang.

"There she is now. Let me get her settled in, and then you and I will have a good, long talk about what's going on with your memory."

By the time I was ready to sit down with him, I had breathed the prayer, "Lord, give me the right words," a dozen times. I began by telling him about the "incidental finding" of the benign brain tumor the vascular surgeon discovered from a routine brain scan when Drew had his carotid arteries checked. I told him how we met with a neurosurgeon who wanted to remove the tumor right away, but Drew talked him into watching it instead. How every six months for three years, he had MRIs until the edema from the tumor triggered his memory problems. And then came the surgery that we hoped would "fix it," but three years after the surgery, here we are with a memory that short-circuits, so we'll just have to learn to live with it.

"Isn't there anything we can do about it?" he asked. "Is there some medicine I can take?"

"You're already taking the medicine," I said. "But it can only do so much. Basically, there's nothing more we can do. Your memory is shot. We need to enjoy every day and make the most of it."

"Well, I have a pretty good life." He smiled. "But didn't I used to have a wife?"

Back to square one. "You still do. I'm your wife, and I have a marriage certificate to prove it. So, let me ask you a question. Who do you think I am?"

He gave me an offended look. "You're *my mom!*"

Ouch! Punch to the gut. Pretend not to be shocked.

"No, hon, I'm not. I'm the wife who's been loving you for forty-one years, and I'll be loving you right up until the end. Your mom died thirty years ago."

"Oh. That's sad."

Truly.

After I had some time alone to think this through, I wondered if the association with his mom might be because I am doing all the things his mother used to do for him. Or, maybe there is no explanation other than this is what it looks like when a brain deteriorates before your very eyes.

He calls himself "stupid" and "dumb," and I counter it with quips like, "You're not dumb—you're smart. It's just that your memory is shot. But that's okay. That's what I'm here for: to tell you whatever you need to know."

Ten minutes after he had told me, "You're my mom," he pinched my butt and asked, "So, did we have sex last night?"

Looks like Candy's back! I smiled and gave him my usual answer. "We sure did, hon, and it was the best."

"You mean we've made love more than once?"

"Yes, I'm your wife."

"We're married?"

"Yep, that's how I get to be a wife."

"So, we're married, and you're my wife?"

"Yep." I winked. "You catch on quick!"

I wish you could have heard the belly laugh he gave me.

December 12, 2016

My friend, Pam Halter, who has a special-needs adult daughter, is also the primary caregiver for her mother-in-law, who has dementia. Her situation is more intense than mine because her mother-in-law's once-sweet disposition is now filled with outbursts. Unlike Drew's compliant temperament, Pam is caring for someone who is extremely controlling with strong opinions of what she wants and when she wants it. She describes her caregiving experience it this way:

"It's like being on a roller coaster in a dark funhouse. Twists and turns you can't see, so you're always tense, anticipating when you might be jerked into a sharp curve. Things jump out at you, but you never know when. None of it is pleasant. None of it is wanted. But you get it anyway. Having Anna certainly doesn't help, but I am thankful she loves it here so much. And she's very loving with her Mom-Mom."

Another analogy she came up with is, "It's like I'm carrying a heavy weight all the time, and the short breaks I get don't allow my muscles to heal. I have to pick up the weight before my muscles stop hurting, and then it's heavier than ever. You do gain strength because you have to, and that's how muscles work. But man, the process is excruciating!"

She adds, "No way could I do any of it without God's help and the people He's brought into my life."

AMEN, Pam.

December 24, 2016

Ever since our first year together in 1975, Drew and I have hosted a Christmas brunch for the family. We've developed the tradition of forming a circle in the living room and standing face-to-face for a time of reflection before saying grace. This is the Abbott family Christmas devotional I put together for 2016:

*In whatever you do, don't let selfishness or pride be your guide.
Be humble, and honor others more than yourselves.*

(Philippians 2:3 ERV)

At Christmas, it is good to remember that Jesus knows us and, in spite of our missteps and blunders, He is quick to forgive and to reconcile us to Himself and one another.

The success that Drew and I have experienced in our marriage is because we truly consider each other as more important than ourselves. Whenever we have a misunderstanding or disagreement, we don't gloss over the prickly situation but talk it through until everything is out in the open and resolved completely, leaving nothing to fester and no confusion. This way, the slate is always clean.

So it goes with family. The Abbott family is blessed to have a history of practicing love and kindness toward one another, speaking hard truths when necessary, and forgiving quickly and thoroughly. Openness and personal soul-searching are vital. On our best days, we listen to one another—really listen. We work through things together.

No family is perfect. Heaven knows, we've overcome a ton of challenges, and there will be more to come. The goal is to grow closer through our difficulties. Other families allow circumstances to divide them. Some even stop speaking to one another.

Drew said something profound the other day: "The devil likes to walk around in back of us and kick us in the behind." Today and every day, it's important that we have each other's backs! Next year, we will welcome a new member to our family circle. *(Our granddaughter Natalie had our first great-grandbaby, Jaxton, in February; and Trevor and Jill are expecting to present us with our second in August.)* And we don't know how long the rest of us will be around.

Consider what Julie Blair wrote in her blog:

I challenge you on this day to get out of your own self and look at what you have. Sure, you may think your family is dysfunctional and—guess what? It is!

But so what? It is your family of dysfunction. It is your family. Every family has a level of dysfunction. Some just hide it better than others is all. The great news is that you have a family. Don't take that for granted. Ever. Your family needs you. You need them. You all have something to contribute to the betterment of one another for a much larger purpose. See this. Know this. Accept this. Receive this. Live this. Live larger in forgiveness. Live larger this holiday season. Live and forgive.

Of all the gifts we can give one another, family harmony is the greatest.

December 25, 2016

Christmas was great! Everybody pitched in to help with meal preparation and clean-up. Afterward, we sorted through boxes of pictures from the attic, which brought back wave after wave of memories.

Although Drew didn't recognize most of the family members, he still has his sense of humor. He came up with this profound observation: "When somebody asks, 'What have you been up to lately?' Why do people say 'nothing'? They've been doing *something*, so why do they say 'nothing'?" Everybody laughed.

Then, a few minutes later, Troy said something that Drew couldn't hear and asked him to repeat it. Although Troy repeated it several times, Drew still couldn't understand. When he asked again, "What did you say?" Troy said, "It was nothing, Dad."

Without skipping a beat, Drew said, "See? You were talking about *something*, but you said 'nothing.'"

Everybody cracked up all over again.

As soon as the laughter faded, Drew said, "If a doctor came in here right now, he'd say, 'What are you laughing about?' and we'd say, 'Nothing.' Then he'd say, 'Well, you were laughing about *something!*' We'd laugh harder like we're laughing right now, and he'd say, 'You're all crazy.'"

Ahhh, laughter is like medicine to the soul.

Drew's reasoning and humor are still functioning nicely. What a gift.

January 9, 2017

Dana came to the support group for the first time tonight. She talked about how she's been in serious denial about her dad for a long time—wishing and hoping that he would get better or at least level off to retain the abilities he has now. Gradually, she has come to realize that this is a progressive disease that follows a somewhat predictable course of decline.

Dana picked up some brochures and said she's ready to begin learning all she can about this disease. One piece was on End of Life Care, and it made me think that there will come a time when Drew won't be able to articulate if he's in pain. In fact, that's happened already.

Recently, Drew began rubbing his jaw after a meal. It happened about once a week, and then I noticed he was doing it more often. I asked if his tooth hurt, and he said no, but when we went to the dentist for his cleaning, I mentioned it, and an X-ray showed that he had an infection. This resulted in another appointment for a root canal, and the whole time we were driving there, he kept saying, "It doesn't hurt; why do I have to do this?" He even asked the dentist when he got in the chair, and she told him, "Because we want to fix the infection before you're in pain." If I hadn't been alert, he could have had a much more difficult time.

I'll be attending a writer's retreat this weekend, and Dana, Troy, and Kim are taking turns staying with their dad. This will be the first time Drew has had anyone in the house overnight other than me, so I'm a little anxious about how he'll respond. But I need this three-day respite, and it will be good for the kids to spend some quality time with him.

We tend to think of each level of decline as negative, but you can find bright spots if you pay attention. It seems that the moderate stage is easier for me than it was in the mild stage when he more aware. Then, frustration made him argumentative and suspicious. Now, he's compliant, and it's easier for me to change the subject or divert his attention.

Tonight, he began asking questions about one of our rental properties—how much rent the tenants pay, how often I collect the rent, which banks the money gets deposited into—and then he asked to see the checkbook. A year ago, he would have inspected each item in the check register and quizzed me *(ad nauseam);* now, I can say, "Let me get the checkbook," disappear into my office for a few minutes, and when I go back empty-handed, he doesn't even mention it. As a test, I asked, "Do you still want to see the checkbook?"

"Why would I want to do that?" he said.

I'm still smiling.

January 15, 2017

I came home from my three-day writer's retreat refreshed, and all is well at home. Dana and Kim both told me that I should go away more often because they had such quality time with their dad.

Dana took him to dinner on Friday, and they watched TV together. At one point, she thought about how good he used to be with math and asked, "Dad, what's five plus five?"

"Ten," he said immediately. "Why would you ask me that?"

"Oh, it's just a little exercise," she said. "So, what's five *times* five?"

He thought and thought, and she told me she waited because of what she learned at the support group—that it takes a while for Alzheimer's patients to process their thoughts. And then, just when she thought she should change the subject, he said, "Twenty-five. Why did it take me so long to come up with that?"

"The important thing is that you got it!" she said.

She stayed overnight, and the only problem she had, other than her dad peppering her with, "When's Candy coming home?" was that Buttercup woke her up to go out and then barked and pestered her "for something" when she came back in. "I couldn't figure out what she wanted," Dana told me, "but she kept pawing at the closet door in the kitchen." No doubt, she wanted a treat, a habit which I forgot to mention. She'll know for next time.

Troy made sure Drew had his breakfast Saturday morning and was still there when Kim came in the afternoon. She sat in the living room talking with Drew while Troy sat in the dining room around the corner, chiming in occasionally. Every time Troy spoke, Drew would turn his head and lean forward in an attempt to see where the voice was coming from.

The whole time Troy was talking, the topic was about a girl he had met on the Internet from Russia. Kim suggested he might be better off getting on Facebook and finding a local girl, so Troy left immediately to get on his computer.

"Are you hungry?" Kim asked Drew, and he said, "Sure. Where are we going?"

"Pizza King," she said. After helping him into the car, she reminded him to fasten his seat belt. On the way to the restaurant, she knew he would be shocked when he saw the Isaac's farmhouse, which had burnt down the day before, so she mentioned it in advance. He seemed to know what she was talking about. After she made two more turns and came out to the highway, he saw it and said, "Oh, my goodness! What happened there?" Kim was shocked by the quick disconnect from just moments before.

At Pizza King, she asked, "So, Dad, what do you think about Troy wanting to date someone from outside the country?" He paused and said, "I guess, as long as he's happy, that's all that matters."

What a thoughtful, sweet, and unexpected response. After the farmhouse incident, Kim was surprised that he even remembered the conversation from twenty minutes earlier.

Kim placed her order and Drew said he would have the same, which was typical because he had lost the ability to make decisions.

While they were eating, instead of asking questions, Kim began reminiscing about her childhood and telling him about things he did during her growing-up years that meant a lot to her. She told me he was fully engaged. Before finishing the first half of his sandwich, he began wrapping up the other half in a napkin.

"You've always been so good about maintaining your weight," she told him.

"I *am* good at that, aren't I?" he said, and then added, "What else am I good at?"

"You've been Mom's biggest cheerleader, you've supported us, you're a good golfer . . ." She expounded on other things like being a good provider, kind and compassionate, etc., and she concluded with, "and you're so humble."

"Yes, I am!" he said. How wonderful to know they can laugh together.

Little did Kim know that she was doing precisely what the professionals recommend. They call it "validation therapy." The basic principle of the therapy is the shared communication of respect, which lets the person know they are acknowledged, appreciated, heard, and are being treated with genuine esteem. This provides a legitimate expression of their emotions and attributes, rather than allowing them to feel marginalized or dismissed.

Before leaving, Drew reached for his wallet, and Kim told him she had already paid. He insisted until she explained that she had a gift card that would expire if she didn't use it. Then he tried to leave a tip, but Kim told him she had that covered, too.

"Oh, I like going out with you!" he said.

As soon as they got back to the house, Drew went to the bathroom, and Kim told him she was going to the attic to get the Christmas box and undecorate the tree.

She was working on the tree when Drew came back into the living room. "Hey!" he said with delight as if he hadn't seen Kim in a long time. "When did *you* get here?"

Being a quick thinker, Kim said, "I must have slipped in while you were in the back."

"You're putting up my tree?"

"No, taking it down. But you can pretend I'm putting it up if you like."

He began singing, "It's beginning to look a lot like Christmas," and Kim told him he had a really good voice. After he sang it another couple of times, he asked what he could do to help, and Kim gave him a baggie to put the ornament hooks in. When he finished, he wanted to do more; she told him that his job was to supervise.

"I'm good at that," he said.

Troy came to help drag the tree outside and vacuum the pine needles, and Drew said, "I should help, too."

"You are," Kim told him. "You're supervising."

Troy was on overnight duty Saturday night and said he made out fine except that his dad kept asking, "When will Candy be home?" He even woke him up several times in the middle of the night to ask, which was disorienting for both of them.

The kids did okay, after all, while I was gone. It was freeing to be able to go away and come back with a refreshed outlook and validation that I didn't even realize I desperately needed.

February 15, 2017

Kim and I attended an Alzheimer's workshop last night on Effective Communication Strategies, and I realized that I need improvement on slowing down to give Drew time to process things.

I always seem to be rushing from one project to another and scooting past him or talking fast, trying to fit everything into my day. But one day last week, I did it right.

Drew was gazing out the sliding glass door in the kitchen, and I could tell he was pondering something, so I waited for him to speak.

"The trees are so still," he said. "They haven't moved."

He continued to stare outside.

"Mmm-hmm," I said, and I continued to watch him.

"They were here yesterday."

Too funny! Now, that was worth waiting for.

February 20, 2017

When Drew began the habit of asking me questions deep into the wee hours of the night, I called his neurologist and asked if I could give him Tylenol PM, and he said a better, more natural sleep aid is melatonin and to start at a low dose of 3 mg. I picked up a bottle at the pharmacy the next day and tried it that night, and Drew slept just fine. No more inquiries at 1:00 a.m.

But last night and the night before, the questioning began again and went on for several hours.

"Who owns this place?"

I mumbled, "We do. This is your home."

"Where is this exactly?"

"Right across from Fannie's. If you go down the alley, you'll come out to the house where you were born."

"We're going home tomorrow, right?"

"We *are* home. This is where you live."

Then, at 2:15, he woke me with a question I hadn't heard before.

"Candy, can you get up? I want you to look at this picture of us."

Apparently, he had been wandering around the house looking for something familiar and recognized us in a photo. As pleased as I was about that, I was more tired than eager to comply. "I'm trying to sleep here. Let's look at it in the morning."

And so we did. It was our framed wedding picture, and his only question about it was how long ago it was taken.

Last night, I added two 3 mg tablets of melatonin to his P.M. pillbox and enjoyed a glorious, uninterrupted eight hours of sleep.

A new pattern was born.

February 26, 2017

As soon as Drew opened his eyes this morning, he asked, "Is Candy gone?"

"No, hon. I'm right here."

He scoffed. "You're not Candy. When will she be back?"

"I really am Candy," I said gently. "And I haven't gone anywhere."

He scoffed again. "I know who you are, and you're not Candy."

"If I'm not Candy, then who am I?"

"You're . . . you're. I don't know your name, but I know you're not Candy. What aren't you telling me? That there *is* no Candy?"

The depth of his confusion left me breathless. It's one thing to watch him disappear a little at a time. I wasn't expecting myself to disappear with him!

I went into the kitchen, distressed, and when I came back into the bedroom, Drew beamed, stood up, and reached out with both hands. "Candy! Where have you been?"

Ahhh, the pleasure of recognition. I don't know which one of us was happiest. But the joy was short-lived as the clarity didn't last long. I savor the remembrance, though, however brief.

February 28, 2017

Drew hasn't known me now for two days. Yesterday, he turned away when I approached him for a kiss because he doesn't let "just anybody" kiss him. Under normal circumstances, I would have felt rebuffed and rejected, but the ache in my heart wasn't for me—it was for him and how confusing this must be.

He woke me at 1:00 a.m. to take a tour of the house with him. He called me by name and asked me to stay close as we walked from room to room in the dark with night lights to guide us.

"This is the kitchen," he said as we passed through it. The counters gleamed, and I was glad I had cleared the clutter before going to bed. I was seeing the house through Drew's eyes, as if for the first time. Drew moved slowly, allowing me time to take it all in, and led me past the refrigerator and the closet I call the pantry.

It's been a long time since he walked in front of me instead of trailing behind. He paused as he stepped off the laminate floor and onto the carpet. "This is the dining room." The bouquet of silk flowers on the table looked friendly.

Gesturing to the right, he said, "This is the living room." It impressed me that he could identify each area of his home after so many days and nights of not knowing where he was.

We proceeded down the hallway at a snail's pace, and he showed me the doorways at the end. "These are three bedrooms." I didn't correct him that they've been offices for years, which served as a reminder that I'll need to replace his desk with a bed soon and turn it into a guest room. But we still haven't addressed the beams under the foundation that are wet-rotted. Drew knows nothing of that, while the responsibility weighs heavily on me.

Drew spoke and brought my thoughts back to where they belonged. "And here, we have a bathroom."

"It's a nice house," I said.

"It is," he agreed. "Do other people stay here?"

"No, just you and I. This is our home."

"You mean we own it?"

"Yes."

"But this is a two-hundred-thousand-dollar house! How did we swing that?"

"You built it—sixty years ago."

"I built it?"

"Well, actually, Lankford built it, but I'm sure you supervised."

Of course, that only raised more questions, which we discussed all the way back to the bedroom. Tomorrow, we'll both need to take naps.

I wonder if the melatonin isn't working for him after all.

March 1, 2017

Drew is talking less now. For the most part, he seems pleased to sit silently with me wherever I am. This reminds me of what my mom told me about her early days with Dad. They were driving from New Jersey to Pittsburgh for him to meet her relatives and hadn't spoken for miles.

"That's when I knew I loved him," she said. "We were comfortable just being together without having to carry on a conversation. It wasn't forced, and we weren't trying to impress one another. In that instant, I realized that I wanted to be with him for the rest of my life."

In a way, that's what I'm experiencing with Drew, which explains why this journey isn't as painful as some people describe. He's still here with me, a comforting presence, even though he can't respond to me like he used to.

Just as I resign myself to this stage of our relationship, he speaks while I'm folding papers.

"You're pretty to look at."

Those few words will carry me for days.

March 6, 2017

When I went out this evening to spend some time with Kim, I left Drew alone in the house and placed the marker board on the kitchen bar with a note and my phone number as usual. Rarely does Drew call me, but tonight he did. He sounded anxious.

"Are you coming back tonight?"

"Yes, I'm just spending a little time with Kim. I'll be coming back soon."

"You're sure? Because if you're not, I'm going to leave. There's nobody here."

Panic shot through me, and I forced my voice to stay calm. "No, don't leave. You're at home where you belong, and if you leave, I won't be able to find you when I get back."

As soon as I hung up, I called Dana to see if she could drop everything to be with her dad.

"Sure," she said as naturally as breathing. I'll go right away." And she did.

The rule of thumb I've been following is to let him remain as independent as possible, doing as much as he can for himself. I've often wondered how I would know when it was time to do more, and I think tonight's phone call was a clue. It appears we might be getting to the point where I'll have to make arrangements for someone to stay with Drew when I go out, at least at night. During daylight hours, he seems content to sit and take naps, but confusion muddles his mind after sunset (thus, the term "sundowning").

I'll have to start planning more, adding another layer of scheduling— one more responsibility. But it will be comforting for me as well as for Drew to have the assurance of others being nearby.

March 7, 2017

I just realized that I haven't cried in a long time, not even at my dear friend Wilma's funeral on Saturday or her graveside service today. I think my emotions have gone into hiding so I can navigate what each day brings, and the only thing I *feel* is deep, abiding peace. I can't decide if I like this or not.

Ha! I just got a nudge from above. "Yes," the Holy Spirit says. "You like it."

Whether this comes as a command or as confirmation of inner contentment, I cannot tell. But one thing I know: to experience abiding peace is a good thing.

I shared this with my friend, Chris Ann, in an email, and this is her reply:

Candy, the Lord has you in His Shalom. This is answered prayer so you can remain focused, thinking for both you and Drew, and keep both clinical and operational needs met. When Drew is called home, all this will cease, and stillness will come. With that stillness will be resting in that you will no longer need to be on constant alert. When you get to that time, the tears will come. A flood of them. It will be well with your soul, as it is now. Why? Because every ounce of sacrifice was out of love, and Jesus is the One you lean on. Those will be tears of relief and release. I am confident that when that season comes, you will know the peace of no regrets, and the tears will be cleansing. You will feel lighter.

I further believe that your physical weight will come off then. That extra weight is almost a cloak or covering now. You have no time to exercise as you need to nor think of your body because you are devoted to Drew and his body. You take time now and then for you, but it is not structured. But it will come.

All that said, you are right where you are meant to be. The outflow of tears is being stored up, and the living water that is within you is what keeps Drew afloat. Be encouraged, my precious sister. Jesus keeps every promise.

March 8, 2017

I have some good news about Drew's sleep pattern. About a week ago, I stopped giving him melatonin with his nighttime medicine and substituted Benadryl. He's been sleeping all night again, praise the Lord!

March 9, 2017

We met Dana for lunch in Milford and then went to visit with our two-week-old great-grandson, Jaxton, today. He is adorable, of course, and Natalie is such a relaxed mom. It was a very special time for us. Drew didn't want to hold him but was very attentive and kept cautioning me not to drop him. The protector role is ingrained in him, and this reveals his continued gentleness.

"Don't try to escape your trials.
Lean into them."

— *T. D. Jakes*

CHAPTER THREE

The "A" Word and Lighter Side

March 11, 2017

I watched Drew as he shaved this morning because I suspect I will have to take over that responsibility soon. For the past several weeks, he needed coaching about how to get started. I've had to show him how to wet his face, put shaving cream in his hand and spread it over his whiskers, and then place the razor in his hand. Today, he gave me a blank look when I did that, so I wrapped his fingers around the handle of the razor and then wrapped my fingers around his to do the first few strokes. After that, he got the hang of it and finished all by himself.

If I don't catch him in time when he's dressing, he will wear the same underclothes he slept in. We're definitely in moderate or mid-stage Alzheimer's.

March 13, 2017

Troy came to the support group for the first time and talked about how difficult it is for him to watch his dad decline—he knows in his head what's happening, but his heart can't accept it. He opened up for the first time about how he felt in January when he stayed overnight with his dad. Three times during the night (2:00, 4:00, and 6:00 a.m.), he awoke to find Drew standing over him on the couch, asking, "When's Candy coming home?" Each time it startled Troy.

He's come to realize that, at this point, he's fine with being around his dad for short periods (two to three hours at a time) and is always ready to run right over to help out with anything we need, but he wouldn't be comfortable staying overnight again. We talked about how he is working through his grief, and everybody does that at their own pace.

If not for this discussion, I wouldn't have known. Communication is so very important, and it's difficult to find time to talk with the kids when Drew isn't around. Troy assures me that he will continue to attend the monthly sessions.

March 16, 2017

From six to eight p.m., Elizabeth and I sat in my office with our computers on, participating in a Facebook launch party for one of my authors. Pam Halter had fifty guests who were very excited about *Willoughby and the Terribly Itchy Itch*. The posts were coming in at lightning speed, so Elizabeth and I had to pay close attention to our monitors.

Drew appeared in the doorway. "Can I interest you ladies in a Coca-Cola?"

We thanked him but declined, and he left.

About half an hour later, he came back and said, "Would either of you ladies like a Coca-Cola?"

"No, but thank you," we said, glancing away from the screen momentarily before turning back to the online party. Not only did we not want the calories, but we were having too much fun to think about anything else.

Once again, he appeared in the doorway. "How about a nice cold Coca-Cola?" When we said no, thank you, he smiled and tried to persuade us by adding, "No charge!"

As before, we declined and resumed typing responses to Facebook posts. In hindsight, I wish we had accepted his offer. He was being hospitable and so, so sweet. No doubt he was bored, feeling very much alone, and had come up with a good idea to connect with us. If only we had said yes, it would have made him feel needed and appreciated. Even with our consistent refusals, he stayed pleasant.

Later, I was making us a bedtime snack, and he said, "Are you staying the night?" and then added, "Candy will be home tomorrow."

Here we go again. Instead of telling him who I am, I asked, "Who do you think I am?"

He thought for a long time and then said, "A wonderful woman. Thanks for helping me out tonight."

I grinned. "I'll help you out tonight and every night and every day after that. I'm all yours."

He grinned. "That's a wonderful feeling."

We ate our oatmeal, and I could see his mental wheels turning, but neither of us spoke until I picked up the empty bowls.

He gazed into my eyes. "Do you have a boyfriend?"

Ahh, this was fun. Drew was flirting with me. "Nope," I said, "I don't have a boyfriend." I placed the bowls in the dishwasher and added, "I don't need one. I have the most wonderful husband."

His shoulders slumped. "He's a lucky guy."

Moving back to the kitchen table, I touched his hand tenderly. "That lucky guy is you. You're my husband." I thought his disappointment would lift immediately, but not so. It only confused him more.

"Are you sure you're talking to the right person?"

"I am. You're Drew Abbott, and I'm your wife, Candy Abbott. We've been married forty-one years—almost forty-two."

"But you haven't been here before."

And so the discussion continued long into the night. Somewhere around midnight, it morphed into, "Where are all the other people who stay here?" and "How much does this room cost a night?" Through his distorted lens, it must have seemed like a hotel with no other guests but us.

At one point, he said, "I'd ask somebody else, but you're the only one here, and you don't know anything."

On that happy note, we laughed and headed for bed.

As I settled down to sleep, a rerun of the Coca-Cola offers played in my mind, and I realized that he must have thought two ladies had checked in, and he was a single guy being gentlemanly.

March 19, 2017

"Where am I?" This is Drew's typical first remark every morning.

And my typical answer is, "You're in your home in Georgetown with your wife of forty-one years."

Next comes, "Where is this building located exactly?"

And so, our day has begun. "I don't know anything," he complains.

I respond with, "That's what you have me for, to answer all your questions. I know everything about you."

"Everything?"

I wiggle my eyebrows and give him an ornery look. *"Everything."*

He wiggles his eyebrows back at me and begins to sing, "I'm gonna sit right down and write myself a letter . . ." When a cloud comes over his eyes, he continues the melody, "I can't remember the words to this song . . . so I'll make them up as I go along."

How awesome is that?! He can't remember the words to the song that he knew by heart last week, but he's able to keep the melody going and come up with a verse that *rhymes*.

Music means more than ever now. "Through the Years" by Kenny Rogers came on the radio while we were driving home from dinner tonight. The lyrics made me choke up because they fit us so well:

I can't remember when you weren't there
When I didn't care for anyone but you
I swear we've been through everything there is
Can't imagine anything we've missed
Can't imagine anything the two of us can't do

Through the years
You've never let me down
You turned my life around
The sweetest days I've found
I've found with you

Through the years
I've never been afraid
I've loved the life we've made
And I'm so glad I've stayed

Through the years
Through all the good and bad
I knew how much we had
I've always been so glad
To be with you . . .

A friend was talking about *The Notebook* by Nicholas Sparks and said the movie and the book romanticized Alzheimer's. She made a face as if to say that's not how real life is. But I told her that I'm living it out, that romance is alive and well in our world. Even if the memories are one-sided, they're built on shared experiences. If Drew should ever become repulsed by my touch or frightened by my presence, it would be hard to take, but that doesn't mean I would love him any less or that he would love me any less. It only means the disease is turning ugly, making those precious times we had together all the more valuable. The thought of how badly things could deteriorate makes me appreciate how lucid he is now. He may not be able to take out the trash the way I like, but he still wants to help. I love that.

March 20, 2017
Drew turned eighty-one today. Because I procrastinated last week in getting our bloodwork done for doctors' appointments scheduled for

tomorrow and Wednesday, I had no choice but to take him to the clinic this morning. Danielle, the phlebotomist, knows us well and suggested we sit together on the bench to have our blood drawn. What an odd but cozy way to start a birthday.

Shortly after we got home, Bunky Eye, a friend since childhood, called to wish Drew a happy birthday. They spoke for a few minutes, and when he hung up, Drew said, "That was nice. Who was that?"

Another friend, Doris Tingle, surprised us with a box of Dunkin' Donuts, so we shared them with glasses of milk.

Then, Aubrey Hudson, a friend Drew hasn't seen in years, stopped by to reminisce about the track record of 5.6 that Drew had set for the State of Delaware in the 50-yard dash.

"But you were fast, too," Drew said. And they chatted about the time when Ronnie Waller and Aubrey had an impromptu race after a football game in high school.

Several times Drew asked, "Is Ronnie Waller still living?"

And several times, with equal enthusiasm, Aubrey answered, "Yes, he lives in Seaford," and elaborated on the details each time.

Drew seemed engaged, and I could tell he enjoyed the visit, but as soon as Aubrey left, he asked, "Who was that?"

I thought about his once-strong legs in contrast to the shuffle of his feet this morning when I had to loop my arm around his in the Beebe clinic parking lot to be sure he didn't fall. *At least he can still walk,* I *consoled myself, even if he is unsteady.*

Trevor and Jill stopped in to say they had just found out the sex of their baby and will be having a reveal party on Saturday. We talked about Jaxton and how Drew will be a great-grandfather again in August. After they left, Drew said, "That's a nice young couple. Who were they?"

I took him to dinner at the Blue Water Grill in Millsboro, where we dined on jumbo shrimp, broccoli, and a salad with blue cheese dressing.

The mailbox was full of envelopes addressed to Drew, and he had a good time opening a slew of cards.

At six o'clock, Kim, our son-in-law Wyatt, and their children Kade and Saige brought an ice cream cake, and Dana and Troy came over to celebrate their dad's special day. It's been several months since we had family gathered around the dining room table. It felt so good.

Even though Drew didn't know who people were throughout the day, he had a good time with them, and so did I—despite the guilty splurge on calories.

March 21, 2017

Drew and I both got glowing reports from the doctor on this warm, sunny day. We came home happy, and Drew noticed the birthday cards on the bar in the kitchen.

He picked them up. "What are these for?"

"They're for the birthday you celebrated yesterday." And I elaborated on all we did.

"That scares me," he said, and I noticed he wasn't smiling.

"What's scary about a birthday?"

"Am I dying?"

"What?! You just had the best report ever from your doctor, and you think you're dying?"

"Why else would everybody make such a fuss over me?"

You never know how someone with Alzheimer's will view things.

March 30, 2017

For quite a while now, Drew has been doing the "senior shuffle," but lately, his feet rarely leave the ground, and his gait has become more of a "slide and scrape" motion. He routinely kicks the threshold between the bedroom and kitchen out of place, so I've asked Troy to nail it down, and I've removed the throw rug from the back door. Suddenly, everywhere I look, I see a fall risk.

It has become standard procedure now for me to loop my arm in his whenever we're in a parking lot. I act playful when I do it, and he receives the closeness well and seems happy to have the support. Not long ago, he would have told me he didn't need help. We stroll along, wobbly and wonky. Soon, I'll have to help him in and out of the car, but not yet. He also had trouble finding his seat belt yesterday, so I may need to assist with that, too.

I'm always on alert. Always.

April 3, 2017

Today, I used the "A" word with Drew for the first time. He asked this morning why he couldn't remember anything, and the words intentionally and very naturally slipped from my lips.

"You have a disease called Alzheimer's, and it steals your memory."

He frowned, and I held my breath as I braced myself for his reaction out of denial and into reality.

As he spoke, the corner of his mouth lifted slightly. "Stealing. Isn't that illegal? Will somebody pay me back?"

After all my concern about whether or not he'd be able to handle the truth if and when I told him, I guess I can relax. He is drawing on humor and his still-intact quick wit instead of facing the hard facts.

He had other questions, too. "How long have I had it?"

"Oh, several years now, but you're in a safe place, and you have me to help you with anything you need."

"Anything I need? What if I need sex? Can you help me with that?"

"*Anything* you need," I repeated in my sexy voice.

We exchanged meaningful looks as I opened the cupboard and reached for the graham crackers. "Want some milk?"

He nodded, I poured two glasses to go with our snack, and that was that.

April 5, 2017

Drew composed a silly song in the kitchen this morning. It was a sweet, nonsensical tune, and he made up the words as he went along. It was a pleasant song, and the longer he sang, the more he got into it, dipping and swaying. It ended with him sidling up to me and crooning,

"I'm gonna get into your paaants" long pause—"and then I'm gonna daaance" long pause—" all around the room in them."

I'm not sure if this is an X-rated song or just plain comical, but it's evening now, and I'm still enjoying the memory of how hard we laughed together over the mental picture he painted with those words and how surprised he seemed by them.

When I went to my office, I was greeted by a nice email from Kelly, our sister-in-law, as a follow-up to last night's visit when Dana, Drew, and I stopped by to see her and Drew's brother, Howard. She complimented me on how patient I was with Drew while we were there, and I wrote back:

My mom was the epitome of patience, and I don't remember Dad getting upset about much of anything, so I grew up with great role models. And I'm pretty outspoken about the Fruit of the Spirit being my life verse (Gal. 5:22-23), so for years, I've made it a point to "cling to the Vine" in the patience department because I knew people would be watching me and saying, "And she calls herself a Christian?" if I messed up. By now, patience has pretty much become a part of my personality, which can also backfire in an emergency like matters of health, and that's where you come in as the voice of common sense saying things like, "You need to get to a doctor!"

I felt really good about myself the whole day—until now. I didn't remember until midnight that the trash collection was tomorrow, so I scurried outside to take the container to the curb while Drew was watching TV in the bedroom.

I knew that he sometimes puts the wrong bags in the bins, and I was prepared to have to move the ones with eggs and coffee grounds from the recycle container into the garbage container. What I wasn't prepared for was a recycle bin filled with loose trash and smelly garbage with NO bags. I raced into the house and grabbed a garbage bag, ran back outside, opened the bag, and began scooping up yucky handfuls into it. When I realized my arms weren't long enough to reach most of it, I tried tilting the container forward and then almost lost my balance.

Grumbly thoughts began streaming through my mind. *I'm sure he was trying to be helpful. Some help* this *is.*

Bend, lift, toss. *What was he thinking? Conserve trash bags?*

Bend, lift, toss, grunt. *If the garbage collectors emptied this thing, trash would be flying all over the neighborhood. How mortifying.*

Bend, lift, toss, grunt, squish. Ewww! Gross! *Why am I out here cleaning up this mess? He made it; he should be doing this!*

I stomped into the house. "Drew, I need you. I need you out here right now." Was that anger in my voice?

He loves to be needed and came right away. "What is it? What do you need?"

My heart was pounding, and I tried my best to add some sweetness to my words. "Come with me. I'll show you." They came out sour, like a command.

When he saw the mess, he had the gall to say, "Who would do such a thing?" But it wasn't gall. He didn't remember doing it himself. He no longer has any concept of how to organize or how things work in sequence. While I grabbed big handfuls, he picked up one small piece of trash, looked at it, and then gingerly put it in the bag I was holding open for him.

The sickening reality of his declining condition came to me with gunk on my hands and stench in my nostrils. I needed to be kind to him, but the enemy of my soul used the trash to taunt me. *You'll never get this done. And your patience is no better than those nasty, crumpled papers in your hand.*

I stopped fixating on the job in front of me and took a good look at him—so pitiful standing there with a yogurt cup dangling between his fingers. I felt like dirt.

Sadness, guilt, and a wave of compassion collided in my heart and mind.

"It'll be fine, hon. How about if you help me tilt this thing so I can reach in, and then you hold the bag. Teamwork. That's our specialty."

We began to get into a rhythm.

Bend, lift, toss. "Do you remember that song you made up for me this morning?"

"What song?"

Bend, lift, toss. "Let's see. It went something like, 'I'm gonna get into your paaants . . .'"

April 7, 2017

My review copies of book one, *I've Never Loved Him More,* arrived today, as well as the tabletop display banner and bookmarks. It's a strange and empty feeling not being able to share my joy with Drew, the one I've shared every important part of my life with and the very person I've written about. I'm planning to share these first copies with my inner circle—the Alzheimer's support group on Monday night and with the members of Delmarva Christian Writer's Fellowship on Saturday. In this draft edition, the dedication page reads,

> To Drew, of course,
> who will never read this book
> but wouldn't expect anything less than
> how transparent I've been with our lives
> because he knows me so well.

On March 28th, I announced via email and Facebook that *I've Never Loved Him More* is being released in April. Since then, I've been trying to figure out how I'm going to autograph and distribute the books without Drew catching even one glimpse of the cover.

But with the books now in hand, I decided I should be totally honest with Drew about his Alzheimer's. For our forty-plus years of marriage, Friday nights have always been "Date Night," where we go out to dinner and sit across the table sharing the joys and concerns of our week. This is Friday. And it's time to go out to dinner at a restaurant.

I think I'll take one of the books with me and present it to him.

This is a big moment for me. For him. But it's not just about the book. It's about him facing the truth about his condition. After all, he doesn't think there is anything wrong with him. I'll be back later to let you know how it went.

Things did not go well *at all*. At least I had the good sense to present him with a bookmark, not the whole book. He read the words, "struggling with Alzheimer's disease" and looked up at me. "Why would you say such a thing? And why now, here at dinner?"

He wouldn't look me in the eye and ate his dinner in silence with sadness that seemed to dim the lights in the whole restaurant.

I asked for the bookmark back, but he put it in his shirt pocket. "I want to read this later."

I couldn't let that happen. But at least it was no longer in front of him. And so the bookmark taunted me, peeking out from his shirt pocket, the whole time we ate. It was no longer in his line of vision, but I knew another glance at the words would set him spinning into anxiety all over again. I began to plan how I would pickpocket it from him. *He'll need to use the restroom before we leave*, I thought; maybe then I could get up at the same time and practice a little sleight of hand.

People at a nearby table began singing Happy Birthday, and the waitress came to check on us a couple of times. Eventually, I was able to turn his attention to other topics, and the pain in his eyes faded away. By the time the check came and he stood up to go to the bathroom, I was able to reach around him, pretending to get his jacket, and nab the bookmark undetected. *Whew!*

By the time we got in the car, everything had returned to normal, and his happy countenance was back—an answer to my panicky prayer. I drove us home with the blanket of God's peace securely wrapped around us.

As difficult as this exercise was, it served as solid confirmation that my original plan to handle the book in secret is, in fact, the correct thing to do.

April 9, 2017

I have to fine-tune my policing skills in the pet food department as well as trash bag monitoring. No matter how hard I try to keep my ears attuned to the sound of cat food cans popping open, bags rattling, or cupboard and refrigerator doors opening, Drew continues to sneak past me to feed Buttercup whatever he thinks she'll like. Sometimes I'll find cashews mixed in with her dry food or lying next to her bowl. What a waste of good cashews. Or yogurt smeared over her food. What a waste of good yogurt. Or Raisin Bran or—you name it.

A few days ago, I saw that he had put a handful of Juice Plus gummies on the mat next to her bowl.

"Oh, honey," I said. "These aren't for Buttercup. They're vitamins for us, and they're not good for her."

I bent down to pick them up, thinking *what a waste of expensive gummies*. When I stood up, he looked at me with sad, puppy dog eyes and said softly, "Maybe someday I'll be able to please you."

It broke my heart. I mended it by relocating the Juice Plus boxes from the pantry to the office so that he won't reach for them by mistake.

The biggest problem is the canned cat food. Buttercup almost died from bladder stones a few years ago. We learned that cat food, which is high in protein, is dangerous for dogs.

After two surgeries and thousands of dollars, the vet put her on a strict diet of special food to keep the problem from recurring. Of course, that plan went out the window when Alzheimer's moved into our household. I keep Midnight's dry and wet cat food bowls on the counter where Buttercup can't get to them, and—wouldn't you know—I often catch Drew placing them on the floor for Buttercup.

"But she likes it," he'll say.

Of course she does. But it can hurt her. It could even kill her. I can't tell Drew this because it would crush him to think he would do anything that would harm an animal, especially Buttercup. So, I whisk it back to the counter and tell him, "This is for the kitty."

His answer to that is, "What can I feed Buttercup? She's hungry."

She's not hungry. She's just learned that if she stares at him long enough, he'll give her something to eat.

"Let me get her chew stick. That'll keep her busy for a while."

"What's a chew stick?" he asks.

I announce that I'll be right back, scamper into the bathroom, open the closet, push the hangers aside, and reach for the PetSmart bag that hides the Milk-Bone Brushing Chews, SmartBones Chicken Sticks, and Dentley's Rawhide Munchy Logs. Okay, so Drew is not the only one who spoils Buttercup.

I have hiding places all over the house. My most recent one is storing the cat food and dog treats on the floor in the corner of the dining room instead of in the pantry. But it won't be long before Drew or Buttercup (or both) figure that out.

April 10, 2017

The Alzheimer's support group was especially meaningful tonight, with six of us around the table. Dana, Troy, and I joined two others in addition to Dave Kelly (the leader of the group). Dana and I lingered to talk with Dave after everyone else left.

Dave congratulated Dana on the birth of her grandson.

Dana beamed. "Candy told me, 'When you hold Jaxton, it'll be as if all the problems of the world just fade away,' and she was *right*. Whenever I'm with him, I feel a joy I can't describe—like overwhelming happiness that shatters any worries I brought into the room. But the problem is, it doesn't last. Oh, that feeling stays for a little while, but whenever I think of Dad, a wave of sadness like a dark cloud settles over everything. It's like the sun goes dim even though it's still shining in the sky."

"You're experiencing grief," Dave said. "Alzheimer's disease is like death, but the person is still here. Everybody handles grief in their own way. Recognizing that's what you're dealing with is a healthy first step. It's good that you're acknowledging it, and it's important to let yourself grieve."

Dana shifted in her seat. "For a long time," she said, "I was in denial."

"Yes, you were," I agreed. "And denial can provide comfort for only so long before reality forces its way in. When you push things down, they fester and sizzle beneath the surface and eventually come out—usually in some not-so-pretty ways like depression or a nervous breakdown. The cushion of trying to love your dad from a safe distance and holding onto false hope is being pulled out from under you. In facing things as they are, you've placed yourself in a position of moral courage. This is maturity, Dana, and I'm so proud of you. But with it comes the emotional pain you've been trying to avoid."

Dana nodded. "So, how do I handle this grief?"

I smiled. "It helps when you focus on others. When you're with Jaxton, you're focused on him, and when you help others, it takes your mind off yourself."

The conversation ebbed and flowed around the table, and Dave mentioned that Easter would be the next weekend.

"Count it all joy," I blurted out. "Another way to handle your grief is to look for the joy. When Jesus was in the Garden of Gethsemane, He sweated blood, which sounds very much to me like a broken heart. *For the joy set before him, he endured the cross* (Hebrews 12:2). His time in the Garden was where He came to grips with the choice—to do the hard thing or to retreat. He could have easily said, 'Father, let's not do this.' But, despite the ugliness of what He would go through, He focused on the JOY that His sacrifice would bring: having us in heaven with Him.

He did not shrink back. He did the hard thing. And that's right where you are now, doing the hard thing and not shrinking back."

"You're right," Dana said. "I should look for the joy, but seeing Dad like this is so painful. You're always so positive. How do you do it?"

"People tell me all the time, 'I'm so sorry for what you're going through,' but I have such peace about this journey with your dad that there is an actual joy for me as I make the most of every day he's here. Oh, I've had my times of sadness and grieving. But I tell him, 'I'll take you any way I can get you,' and I mean that. He's done so much to bring joy into my life, so the least I can do is offer that joy back to him. The fact that he will be less and less able to respond to me as he declines won't make him any less important to me."

"Your dad is still here," Dave said. "And even though he may not be able to express himself, he knows when you're with him. He feels the love, and he can also feel when love is being withheld. Here in the Alzheimer's unit, I see too many family members who regularly visit at first and then fade away. Some stop coming altogether. The saddest thing is that they could have shared a lot of meaningful moments with their loved ones while they were lucid."

Dana leaned forward. "So, what you're saying is that I should enjoy Dad as he is, whatever state he's in. He may not be the dad he used to be, but he's still my dad."

"Exactly!" I said. "When it's all said and done, you'll want to look back on this with no regrets. You'll have gone through the hard part with him, and you'll be glad. Doing a kindness for someone has a way of building you up."

Before we left, Dana decided she would saturate herself with the Word of God. "If I can't grab a Bible—like when I'm driving—I can write out a Scripture verse on an index card and keep it handy for quick reference." Her face lit up. "I can tape it to my dashboard!"

My takeaway from the meeting was that I should focus on the moment knowing that God is in that moment—and fix my eyes on Jesus so I can love as He loved, sacrificially, not shrinking back, not expecting anything in return.

April 11, 2017

I attended the Delaware Hospice 35th Anniversary Breakfast this morning and was impressed all over again with the wonderful resources they provide. The misconception is that Hospice is for a time when there is no longer any hope. I'm already benefiting from their Transitions program, designed for caregivers, and the step after that would be their Palliative Care Support. After that comes the traditional end-of-life care.

One thing I learned that I never thought about before is that they have bereavement counselors available. I think Dana, Troy, and Kim could both benefit from connecting with Delaware Hospice *right now*.

Another takeaway I gained was that the biggest regret people have after their loved one dies is that they didn't contact Hospice sooner. That will not be the case for the Abbotts as I plan to take advantage of all they have to offer as soon as I'm able to recognize our needs.

April 28, 2017

I took Drew to a matinee this afternoon to see *The Fate of the Furious* because he can follow action movies better than ones that have complicated plots. Of course, I would much rather have watched *The Case for Christ*, which was playing in the same theater complex, but today was about him.

In the middle of the movie, with all the bang-bang-shoot-'em-up going on in living color, he asked, "When does the movie start?" And about fifteen minutes later amid the detonations, fireballs, crashing cars, and bad guys, he said, "Is this the movie?" Toward the end, there were some exaggerated scenes with an innocent baby in the midst of all the blood and gore, and I noticed Drew fully engaged in the action on the screen. His protective instinct was on alert.

I'm glad we went. It put things in perspective for me. The world is not physically exploding around us, and my life at home with the good guy (and his repetitive questions) is better balanced than I realized.

April 29, 2017

I was telling Kim and Wyatt about the movie, and they reminded me of our *Polar Express* experience in December of 2013 when Drew's symptoms were mild. Wyatt drove us to dinner at the Salted Rim in Ocean View, with Drew in the passenger seat of the SUV, Kim and I in the middle seats, and Kade and Saige in the back.

The restaurant has a locomotive car parked next to the building, and in December they offer a special family event: *The Polar Express* movie and buffet dinner. Groups sign up and are urged to come in their pajamas and hop aboard the authentic train car decorated for the holiday season. The conductor, in his classic uniform, punched our golden tickets as we boarded the train to embark on a magical journey to the North Pole. As we watched *The Polar Express* on large-screen TVs, Santa's elves served us hot chocolate and cookies and the evening culminated in a visit from Santa himself.

Drew didn't say much the whole time, but he participated as I guided him through each part and explained portions of the movie over the ruckus of the kids squealing with delight.

Afterward, Wyatt dashed off to warm up the SUV and bring it around to pick us up. We piled in and bubbled over about the highlights of the experience. After about ten minutes, the conversation subsided, and Wyatt asked Drew if he was enjoying the seat warmer.

"Seat warmer?" Drew said. "Oh, thank goodness! I thought my butt had a fever."

We still get tickled over that, even this many years later.

May 1, 2017

Drew needed his toenails cut tonight, something he used to be able to do himself. Rather than grab the clippers and grit my teeth for a grueling experience, I thought we might as well do it up right with the royal treatment and use the bubble therapy foot spa I bought last Christmas.

Excitement built within me as I hunted around the house for a three-prong outlet near a seat that would be comfortable for him. The only suitable outlet I found was in front of the toilet. So much for ambiance. Still, I was not deterred as I filled the plastic spa with warm water, poured in a generous dose of lavender Epsom bath salt, folded a towel as a seat cushion for the toilet lid, and plugged the cord into the socket.

Drew sat on his throne and eased his feet into the water for what I hoped would be a relaxing, luxurious experience. I pressed the buttons for heat and bubbles and kept a close eye on him. After ten minutes, he said, "I've had enough."

So, I toweled his feet dry, looked up lovingly at him, and thought about Jesus washing His disciples' feet. It seemed holy and special.

And then reality hit me. I needed to clip Drew's toenails. After all, that was the whole point. Hmm, how do I *do* that? His toes would have to be positioned at just the right height and just the right angle. I scouted around for something low to the floor to sit on. Ah, the footstool in my office. While he sat patiently on the toilet seat, I collected the clippers and little scissors. I dragged the footstool into the bathroom, pressing myself through the bathroom door, and sat down in front of him, knee-to-knee.

"Okay, hon. how about putting your foot on my knee?"

Well, that was tricky, and I had to keep telling him to relax his toes so they wouldn't point toward the ceiling, but it worked. Five toenails down, the other foot to go.

Success! Mission accomplished. As my reward for a job well done, I decided to treat myself to ten or fifteen minutes of relaxation in the foot spa. In preparation, I took the footstool back to my office, returned the clippers and scissors to the closet, took off my shoes and leggings, brought a book into the bathroom, and settled onto the towel-draped throne. I eased my feet into the warm, lavender-scented water and pressed the buttons. The machine began to hum, the bubbles danced around my ankles and toes, and I opened my book.

Immediately, the lights went out, and the machine stopped working.

Hmm. The circuit breaker must have tripped. I sat there just long enough to feel sorry for myself. With that, Drew came to tell me, "The lights are off," and I was back on duty as the fixer-of-all-things.

Our electrical panel is in the laundry room next to the kitchen at the other end of the house, and the stacked washer/dryer units are in the way. I squeezed my belly through the opening and reached as far back as I could. My tunic allowed the top half of me to slide a bit, but my bare right leg glued itself to the side of the washer. I stretched to flip and reset as many circuit switches as my fingers could reach.

"Are the lights on?" I called Drew. He couldn't hear me. I would have to go to the other end of the house to see for myself.

As I tried to back out of the laundry room, I discovered I was stuck. *Come on, Candy, suck it in and get yourself out of here.* I wriggled and squirmed to no avail.

Just when I was about to panic, Drew came into the kitchen. "Oh, there you are."

I was wedged between the door and the washer/dryer and couldn't move forward or backward. "I'm stuck." My right leg was bearing all my weight, and I was trying not to panic.

"You look sexy," Drew said.

That was the last thing I wanted to hear, but it served to keep my panic at bay. I shifted and scrunched and felt a little relief. All the while, he's making kissy sounds and comments like, "This is some show you're putting on."

At last, I broke free! "Are the lights back on?" I asked.

"Nope," Drew said with a wink. "Looks to me like you're going to have to go back in there and look sexy again."

"No way," I said as I picked up the phone. "Troy, I know it's late, and you're all settled in for the night, but can you come over and fix the circuit breakers? I have them all messed up."

I hung up, and I turned to my foot-spa partner. "We need to put our pants back on. Troy's coming over."

May 3, 2017

Today's theme is Worry. Sometimes a few simple words of wisdom will put things in perspective. Mom had a lot of one-liners that did that for me, and the one that comes to mind right now is, "Everything will work out in the end."

Drew's Mom Mom Phoebe always said, "I never worry until something happens, and when something happens, it's too late to worry; you just have to take care of things the best you can."

I found this on Martine Foreman's blog, and it spoke to me:

"The problem with worrying is that it doesn't change a single thing. It's a wasted emotion that causes stress and anxiety. You can worry until you turn blue in the face; it has no impact on the potential outcome of a situation. And even more concerning is the fact that worrying can make things worse. When we worry, we are letting our emotions get the best of us and admitting that there is absolutely nothing else we can do.

"But you see, you can do something else. You can choose prayer instead. First, let's be clear. Some of the most worrying people I know are also prayerful people. They believe in God and His power. However, when a situation becomes overwhelming, they lose sight. It's happened to me before. I have found myself so worried about how something might turn out, and often it's something I am praying about—failing to recognize that it's counter-intuitive for me to do both."

And these tidbits by Andy Rooney chase worry clouds away:

- I've learned that when you're in love, it shows.
- I've learned that being kind is more important than being right.
- I've learned that I can always pray for someone when I don't have the strength to help him in any other way.
- I've learned that no matter how serious your life requires you to be, everyone needs a friend to act goofy with.

- I've learned that sometimes all a person needs is a hand to hold and a heart to understand.
- I've learned that it's those small daily happenings that make life so spectacular.
- I've learned that to ignore the facts does not change the facts.
- I've learned that love, not time, heals all wounds.
- I've learned that the easiest way for me to grow as a person is to surround myself with people smarter than I am.
- I've learned that life is tough, but I'm tougher.
- I've learned that when you harbor bitterness, happiness will dock elsewhere.
- I've learned that when your newly born grandchild holds your little finger in his little fist, you're hooked for life.
- I've learned that everyone wants to live on top of the mountain, but all the happiness and growth occurs while you're climbing it.

May 15, 2017

While we were on the way to Seaford for dinner, an ad came on the radio that said, "Has anybody ever found a needle in a haystack? Of course not!" The music resumed, and we drove along without speaking. After a few minutes, Drew said, "It's not hard to find a needle in a haystack. All you have to do is get a magnet."

All that time, not only had he been thinking about solving the problem, but he came up with a solution! That part of his brain is obviously in full working order. The mind is a complex and astonishing thing.

May 20, 2017

As I prepared to leave the house to attend Delmarva Christian Writers' Fellowship, Drew was still sleeping. I counted out his pills and put them on a paper towel with a glass of water, put the box of Raisin Bran on the table with his bowl, spoon, and sugar. Last month, he made out fine, but today I had the feeling that he might put the water on his cereal, so I wrote a note, "The milk for your cereal is in the refrigerator."

Since I would be gone from 8:45 to 2:30, I arranged for Troy and Dana to check on him and get his lunch. It's time to begin scheduling volunteer help through the Delaware Hospice Transitions program. They said to call when I'm ready. I'm almost convinced that Drew can handle strangers being here with him, but I've been stalling. This will be a new layer of things for me to plan. But it will be good for Drew, and it will give me more freedom.

I'll think about that another day.

May 23, 2017

Sitting at the kitchen table over breakfast, Drew asked, "Are you dating anyone?" The question jolted me but triggered a memory of when we used to role-play, pretending we had just met.

Once, at Goin' Nuts Cafe in Salisbury, Maryland, we had finished our dinner and stopped by the adjoining bathrooms in the hallway on our way out. We both came out at the same time.

"Going my way?" Drew said.

Recognizing the cue, I slipped into my role. "That depends on where you're going."

"Do you live around here?"

"No. I live in Georgetown."

"Georgetown, Delaware?" he said. "I live in Georgetown, too. Can I follow you home?"

"Why, sure!" I said, looping my arm through his. "I would love to get to know you better."

Until the inebriated man behind us spoke, I didn't know he had observed the whole scene.

"Hey, how'd you do that?" he said to Drew. "I wish I could pick up girls that easy."

Drew and I looked at each other and laughed.

"Ohhh, I see what's going on here," the man slurred. "You two are a couple, aren't you?"

"I'm sorry, buddy," Drew said. "We've been married for twenty years."

We laughed about it the whole forty-five-minute ride home. But that was then. Now, while sitting across from him at the breakfast table with a hopeful look on his face, I could tell Drew was serious when he asked if I was dating anyone. He sincerely wanted to know. I decided to play the game, anyway.

"No," I said. "I don't date."

He looked puzzled. "You don't date? Why not?"

"Because I'm married."

His whole countenance drooped. "You're married?"

"Yes," I smiled and paused. "I'm married to YOU."

He grinned. "You're married to me? You're my wife?"

"Yep, I'm your wife, and we've been married almost forty-two years."

"Forty-two years? But how can that be? We don't live together."

"Yes, we do. We live right here together in your house in Georgetown."

"This is my house in Georgetown? And you live here with me?"

He recognizes me less often now, but he's glad to be with me. In the mornings, his typical questions are, "Where am I?" and "Who are you?" followed by "Why am I so dumb?"

I tell him that he's not dumb—it's just that his "memory stinks." I say it that way on purpose because it has a playful sound, and it's a gentle way of changing the subject. When raising our kids, I was keenly aware that *the mother sets the tone of the household.* In spite of the bumps and bruises that come with blended families and growing-up challenges, this has always been a happy, peace-filled home. It's important to me to keep it that way. I have little control over how Drew behaves as the disease progresses, but I have total control over the tone I set in this place.

It would be easy to worry, to feel sorry for myself, or to feel lonely. But what would that accomplish but depress me?

May 25, 2017

Harrison House of Georgetown and VITAS Healthcare are co-sponsoring a book event for me next month, and we were talking at the planning meeting about how few people come to the support group. Part of it is that family members don't know about the free help and many resources that are available to them. But another problem is that this disease carries a stigma, and people are uncomfortable talking about it. Because their loved one is no longer "normal" and may do embarrassing things in public, some don't even take them out for dinner.

Since eating out is one of Drew's favorite things to do and because I'm not ashamed of him, it never occurred to me to hide him at home.

I received the following letter from Jo Ann Taylor, which warmed my heart and testifies to the positive impact we can have on others in public, even in our unguarded moments.

Candy,

I thought you would be interested in an observation I saw recently. The other night, just as we were leaving Georgetown Family Restaurant's parking lot, I saw you and Drew walking toward your vehicle. I asked Bill to wait because I wanted to ask you when your new book would be published.

As I watched the two of you walking toward us, you with your arm around Drew and Drew walking so erect, it became apparent that Drew was happy. He was smiling, and the expression on his face was so peaceful. It just filled my heart with so much joy. With excitement, I told Bill, "Drew is HAPPY. He is happy with this stage of life." You both looked so in love.

You are definitely on the right course to help Drew and yourself.

Keep up the good work.

Love,
Jo Ann

May 26, 2017

I'm blessed from every angle, so I know the many prayers people are sending up on our behalf are hitting the mark. There is a lot of buzz going on about *I've Never Loved Him More*. Dr. Palekar received his book yesterday and called with excitement in his voice. He said his nurse Angie read the first few pages aloud to him *while he was with a patient.*

"Angie cried when she was reading it, and all my staff went immediately to Amazon to look it up online."

He plans to order more to keep on hand.

I told him about the book signings and events that are pouring in, and he said, "That's very nice. But you don't need them. You have Dr. Palekar. This is a best seller. I'm going to talk it up to everyone I know." I'd never heard him refer to himself in the first person before, which added to my delight about what he was saying.

He hasn't even read it yet, and with his wonderful sense of humor, I'm eager to hear what he thinks, especially about the funny parts.

I've become so accustomed to staying home and out of the limelight that I'm feeling a little intimidated about the back-to-back speaking engagements lined up for me in June. On the other hand, the organizers are giving me such an outpouring of encouragement, I'm relatively calm about it. There was a time when I would write an outline and compose detailed remarks for an upcoming speech. I don't have the energy or inclination to do that now, so I'm planning to speak from the heart as the Lord gives me the words.

Under normal circumstances, I would confide my insecurities to Drew, who would know just the right things to say to build me up. Instead, I'm learning to press on without him—a foretaste of widowhood, I suppose. At least he's still here for me, even if only to be the recipient of my touch.

Last night he said, "If you're not asleep, there's something I want to tell you."

"I'm still awake," I whispered.

"I've been lying here thinking, and I've made a decision. I want to give you some money for all that you do for me."

"That's thoughtful but not necessary, hon."

"I think it is," he said. "I want to pay you. We'll talk about it in the morning."

Of course, he won't remember in the morning. But it's the thought that counts. He may not be able to give me the feedback I need about my daily emotional struggles, but Alzheimer's has not yet stolen his kindness or generosity. Now, that's something to think about in the morning and to savor for days.

June 5, 2017

Dana took us to Abbott's Grill in Milford for my birthday dinner, and our waiter was very tall. I saw Drew staring up at him and, since he has no filter, I figured it was only a matter of time before he said something. Sure enough, he peppered us with: "That guy is really tall." "Look how tall that guy is." "How tall do you think that guy is?"

"I don't know," I said. "Why don't you ask him?"

And, by George, he did as soon as the waiter came back to our table. The young man said he was six-foot-five, so Drew was satisfied for the moment. But it wasn't long before he said, "I wonder how tall that guy is."

Dana and I answered in unison, "Six-five."

"How do you know?"

"Because he told us."

"He told you? When? Where was I?"

Before we could answer, the tall waiter appeared at our table again, and Drew said, "I'm going to tell you something you never heard before."

Dana and I looked at each other, eager to hear what this new thing was going to be, and then Drew followed up with, "How tall are you?"

He answered smoothly as if for the first time. "A lot of people ask that. I'm six-foot-five. Then he winked at Dana and whispered, "My grandmother is the same way."

I read something this morning that I hadn't heard before: "People with dementia can't learn new things, which is why they repeat so often." *Makes sense.* I'm pleased that Drew is still interested in interacting with others. After all, there will come a time when he may not have the desire or ability to ask.

"When I am resting because my body is weak,
I need to remember that
I'm not wasting the day doing nothing.
I am doing exactly what I need to do.
I'm recovering."

— *Author Unknown*

CHAPTER FOUR

Learning to Take Care of Myself

July 6, 2017

During our monthly lunch with my dear friends Carol Lynch and Susan Wingate at The Brick, Carol leaned over her plate and peered into my eyes. "You know what I'm going to ask you." It was a statement, not a question. She paused just long enough for me to do some soul searching, and then said the words I was expecting: "What are you doing for *you?*"

I squirmed a little in my seat. "Once a week, I make sure I have lunch with friends, like today."

"What else are you doing for yourself?"

"I get my hair done, a manicure, and a pedicure. And the book signings have given me a lift—being around people and feeling like I'm contributing."

Susan chimed in with glowing comments about the book and how many pages she dog-eared for future reference.

Carol would not be deterred on her mission to be sure I was taking care of myself. "Do you have someone coming in to give you a break?"

I confessed I had gotten a name and number of the Sussex County Volunteer Coordinator for Delaware Hospice and then launched into my litany of obligations (excuses) that kept me too busy to make the call. I promised to follow through. What I didn't admit (to her or myself) is that scheduling someone to come in adds another layer of things I have to think about and plan. My rationale used to be that Drew wouldn't understand having a stranger in the house while I was gone, but he's not even sure who I am at times. So, I told her, "I will do it. I will make the call." I have a feeling I'll wish I hadn't procrastinated.

"And . . . what else are you doing to take care of Candy?" Carol was relentless.

"What else is there?" I asked.

"A massage. And I have the perfect person to recommend. Alyce has a great set-up in her home, and she has a special going on through August to benefit the Hope Center, so you'll be helping others as well as yourself." *Does this gal know what pushes my buttons, or what?* "A massage will release all those nasty toxins that are hurting your body." Carol not only made the suggestion but fairly commanded it by immediately sending Alyce and me a text message and two emails.

I didn't articulate my feelings but nodded numbly. Right now, scheduling a massage seemed like just one more thing to add to my ever-growing to-do list. As it is, I could barely keep things in balance to stay caught up with my responsibilities. Besides, it felt more like a guilty pleasure than a needed respite.

As the three of us exchanged goodbye hugs, Carol said, "You know I'm only doing this because I love you and don't want you to risk your health in this process."

I smiled sweetly. "I know, and I love you for caring so much. I'll give her a call. I promise." *Lord, help me to mean that.*

So, I left The Brick with happy taste buds from my crab and cheddar quiche, peace from a relaxing visit, joy from our time of meaningful sharing, and the weight of two assignments: Make the call to line up a volunteer to provide respite for me, and schedule a massage. *Lord, help me to do it.*

July 7, 2017

Months ago, Michele Fletcher, my beautician, also suggested that a massage would do me a world of good, but I filed the card away, and it's still buried under one of my paper piles. Now, with Carol's insistence and a number in front of me, I called Alyce and left a message. Carol and Michele are right. I *need* to make time for myself. I think I have forgotten how to relax. Funny, but now that I've taken the initiative to make the call, I'm eager for Alyce to schedule the appointment. What seemed overwhelming to me yesterday feels like an escape hatch today.

The last time I felt this kind of anticipation was our family's Bermuda cruise in June of 2015, which turned out to be more stress-filled than relaxing for me. The fact is, I can't remember the last time I fully unwound.

While I still had the phone in my hand, I dialed Maxine, the Delaware Hospice Volunteer Coordinator. I've had her name and number for almost two months but couldn't bring myself to call until now.

Delaware Transitions is a Delaware Hospice program for caregivers who need assistance. It's a free service and a godsend. Their volunteers not only offer respite care but shop for groceries, do light housework, provide emotional support, and do other things to make the life of a caregiver easier. Delaware Hospice has just celebrated its thirty-fifth anniversary. One Transitions coordinator said, "We often hear from individuals and their caregivers that they wish they had known about our services earlier in their illness. They are amazed that we can customize the level of support, depending on their needs, at no charge."

I explained to Maxine that I needed someone to keep Drew company on Monday evening when I go to the support group and Wednesday night when I meet with ladies at a book club. Maxine noted that Drew was already enrolled in the Transitions program and said she would check to find a volunteer who would be a good match for those two dates. In a few minutes, the phone rang, and Maxine said I could expect a call from a volunteer.

This will be the first time that Drew has had a new acquaintance stay with him when I'm gone. I think this is harder on me than it will be on him, which is probably why I've been stalling.

Carol saw it when I couldn't. Saw what? That I'd been unknowingly crippling myself by slowly, silently, becoming more and more protective of Drew, making excuses so I could have him all to myself. She was right. I need to take care of Candy. I need to pry myself away from him so I can learn to breathe and relax and regain my independence (as opposed to co-dependence). Scheduling a massage and respite care wasn't selfish. It was practical and much needed.

July 10, 2017

Debbie Morrison, the Delaware Hospice volunteer, called to confirm our appointment for tonight. She asked a few questions about Drew's alertness, abilities, and condition to find out where he is in his journey.

My question for her was, "What do I tell him about a stranger being in the house while I'm gone? He thinks there's nothing wrong with him."

Debbie had a ready answer. "It has worked well in the past for me to say, 'I'm new to the neighborhood and stopped by to get acquainted.' Then you can say you have to go out for a little while."

And that's exactly how it played out. Debbie arrived right on time, and her warm personality put me immediately at ease. After introductions, the three of us chatted for a bit, and when Drew began asking her about what kind of work she did, I very matter-of-factly said, "I have to go out for a while, so you keep Debbie entertained, and I'll be back soon."

Two hours later when I returned, Drew was in the bathroom, so I had a chance to speak with Debbie alone. She told me they had some good conversation "about the same things over and over again," but she found Drew delightful and was looking forward to coming back on Wednesday evening. When Drew joined us, Debbie said, "See that? Candy was hardly gone any time at all."

What surprised me most was how relaxed I felt while I was at the support group, knowing that Drew was in the company of a volunteer who derived fulfillment from providing respite care.

July 12, 2017

Debbie came back tonight, and when I was ready to leave, she said to Drew, "I've come to hang out a while with you again. Would that be okay?" I held my breath. She asked for his *permission*. What if he said no? But she knew what she was doing. He returned her smile and said, "Sure. I would like that."

When I got home, Drew hugged me and wouldn't let go as Debbie looked on. We all laughed at his enthusiastic greeting, especially Drew. It was clear he purposely exaggerated the strength and length of his embrace.

July 25, 2017

I was working away in my office and heard Drew's footsteps in the hallway.

"You gotta come and see this," he said, beaming as proud as a little boy who had just hit a home run.

My fingers hovered over the keyboard that was calling me to finish the sentence I had begun composing. "I'm busy, hon. Can it wait?"

"It'll only take a minute. I want to show you something."

I didn't want to go. Not only because I was in the middle of working on something important but because I had a good suspicion of what I was about to see. Dutifully, I stood up and followed him down the hallway, through the kitchen, and into the master bathroom where he stopped at the far end of the room.

"Look!" he said as he stood over the toilet and pointed.

"Wow!" I said as I gazed in the bowl, trying to sound excited as I stared at a perfectly formed turd that had wound around in a circle and sunk to the bottom. "That's a real prize winner!"

This wasn't the first time. We've had several proud poop moments, and we'll probably have several more. It doesn't take much to bring a smile to the face of a person with dementia. I may not be happy about the source of his joy in this case, but it brings me pleasure to see him happy. *Whatever it takes,* I thought.

And then I said, "You'd better flush that whopper before it decides to settle in for good."

August 8, 2017

I've had inertia for the past four or five days. Vegged out with TV and naps. No energy for much of anything, not even checking email. Maybe my body is crying out for a rest, so I gave in. Now I have piles of papers and an overflowing inbox that needs attention. I'm still not up to speed but have appointments, so I have to get dressed.

Drew hovers over me, asking the same questions he asks me multiple times each day. I give him one-liners for answers.

"Where is this place?"

"Your home in Georgetown." I'm in the recliner with my eyes closed.

"This is my home?"

"Yes."

"In Georgetown?"

"Yes." I pull the fringed burgundy throw around my neck.

"Where exactly is it located?"

"On Elizabeth Street." I wave my hand to point behind me. "Across from Fannie's."

"And if I walk down the alley?"

"You'll come out to where you were born and raised."

"So, this is my home?"

"Yes. Where you've lived all your adult life."

"Where do you live?"

"I live here."

"You live here in my home . . . with me?"

"Yes."

"Why is that?"

"We're married."

"We're married?"

I know what's coming next, so I say, "Forty-two years."

"We've been married for forty-two years?"

"Yes." I want to rest, but the poor guy is lost and needs to get his bearings.

"How did we meet?"

"Fannie," I say, with the hope that it will trigger a memory for him.

"Fannie?"

"Yes. She walked me in your back door and said, 'I brought you somebody.'"

"Sure brought me a pretty one!" he chimed in without prompting.

I smile. "Yep, that's when I fell in love with you."

"So how long have we been together?"

"Forty-two years." I need to get some rest.

"Forty-two years?"

I pause before answering. "Yes, and now I need to take a nap. Let's talk about this when I wake up."

"Okay." He pats my foot. "Have a nice nap."

Before I can close my eyes, he asks, "Is my mom still living?"

"No. I'm sorry, hon. She died thirty-two years ago. I'll tell you all about it when I wake up." I close my eyes.

"She died thirty-two years ago?"

I don't answer.

"Who lives in the home place now?"

I concentrate on closing my eyes, instruct my ears not to listen, and keep my mouth shut. As I drift off, I think about my support group leader saying it's not good to confront an Alzheimer's patient with the truth of the death of a loved one because sometimes they grieve all over again as though it just happened. Fortunately, that doesn't seem to be the case with Drew. It just triggers more questions as he tries to find his place in the world.

That's the last I remember before I doze off.

August 16, 2017

I have a fresh appreciation for the phrase "out of sight, out of mind."

Drew hasn't gone into his office in the past several months, not even to sit in the chair behind his desk, so a few months back, I decided it might be time to begin cleaning things out and eventually convert it into a guest bedroom. I gave his computer to Troy and had him remove all the tools that were lying around. When I get motivated, I'll need to sort through everything in the filing cabinets, but the bigger, more immediate challenge would be how to get rid of the desk that Drew had assembled in the room.

When Elizabeth was here several weeks ago, I told her about my plan and said she could use the desk and she offered to buy it.

"You don't have to pay me," I said. "If you and Joe can come some night while Drew and I are out for dinner, you can have it for free." I was just glad that the desk had found a good home and that I wouldn't have to do anything but empty the drawers. This was a win-win deal, for sure.

A few days later, I called Elizabeth to tell her we were leaving (she and Joe had parked their truck around the corner from our house). I followed behind Drew to unlock the front and back doors he had just locked, and off to Salisbury we went for dinner. I purposely chose a place about forty-five minutes from home so Elizabeth and Joe would have plenty of time to dismantle the desk and put it in the truck.

Everything worked as planned.

The next hurdle would be what to tell Drew when he noticed the space in the room. When he and I got home, instead of working in my office (across the hall from his office), we watched TV together at the other end of the house. I hadn't figured out what explanation I would give him, and this was my best attempt to postpone his questions.

Overnight, I still hadn't come up with an explanation, so I just let things unfold the next day. He followed me to and from my office several times and never once noticed the space where his desk used to be. *Maybe he won't ask me at all.*

His question came two days later. "What happened to the bed?"

Ha! He thinks his office is his old bedroom. Quick thinker that I am as a newly experienced fibber, I said, "Oh, it was in such bad shape, I took it to the dump." *Liar, liar, pants on fire.* (Alzheimer's professionals refer to this as therapeutic fibbing and creative communication techniques.) I waited for his outburst.

"How old was it?"

"It was here when I came forty-two years ago, so it was time. I'm cleaning out the room a little at a time to redecorate it. Do you want to help me go through the papers and books?"

"No," he said. "You go right ahead without me."

Ahhh, sweet consent.

A week later, Brandon, of B-Dun Cleaning, shampooed the carpets in my office and Drew's old office and put my chair mat on the floor in Drew's office to give the carpet around my desk a chance to dry.

That night, Drew sat in his usual chair in my office and looked across the hall. "What did you do with my desk?" Having the chair mat in the place where his desk used to be must have triggered his memory.

This time, I confessed the truth about giving it to Elizabeth.

"That was a perfectly good desk. I liked that desk. You gave my desk away and didn't even ask if that was okay with me? I wouldn't do that to you. Don't I have a say about anything?"

I had been caught red-handed. I hemmed and hawed and stammered with apologies that felt hollow at first and then became sincere. I felt bad. He felt mad. We were both sad. As long as that chair mat lay in the bare spot where his desk used to be, the discussion continued.

When I couldn't take it any longer, I turned off my office light and headed to the bedroom. As I expected, he followed me. After watching television for a while, I sneaked back to the other end of the house and dragged the mat back to where it belonged, beneath the chair in my office. Then I hurried back to the bedroom where he was still in his recliner.

It's been two weeks now, and he asks me on occasion, "What happened to the bed?" I revert to my fib about the dump, and he's fine with that.

September 7, 2017

Someone at the post office asked about Drew this afternoon, and I said, "Sometimes, he doesn't know me." Although I'm getting used to him continually asking my name, it's hard to say those words aloud. But it's true. He knows he needs me, wants me around every minute, and is playful and loving toward me, but sometimes he doesn't know my name, or that I'm his wife, until I tell him.

It's not uncommon for him to ask me to write my name so he won't forget. The other day I found one of my notes in his wallet. He's trying so hard to piece all the important pieces of his life together.

Who does he think I am? Sometimes I'm his girlfriend, sometimes his mother, sometimes a stranger, sometimes his wife.

Who am I? I am the face of love. I am a stable presence. I am an anchor in his mental storm. I am the assurance that everything will be okay. I am his security.

When I mention Catherine, his first wife, he doesn't remember anything about her. Our typical conversation goes like this:

"That's just as well," I say. "It was an unpleasant time for you."

"What do you mean?"

"She ran off with another man, and you got divorced, but the silver lining was it opened the way for me to come into your life."

"So that's a good thing, right?" And then adds, "Is she dead?"

"Yes, Catherine died two years ago."

This much of our conversation is standard fare. But today, he looked up at me with a peculiar expression and said, "And I didn't kill her, right?"

I laughed.

"What's so funny?" He didn't laugh with me.

Now, I'm the one wearing a peculiar expression.

After a brief silence, he asked if we had any kids together. I told him about our blended family—that I have one daughter, and he has two children (a daughter and son) who are grown with children of their own. He gave me a puzzled expression.

"Two children, that are mine? My children?"

I assured him that Dana and Troy are his biological children.

"But I never see them," he said.

I explained that he sees them every week (sometimes every day).

"Dana makes it a point to have a meal with you every week, and Troy was here half an hour ago giving you a shave." (He comes every other day, which is one less job for me).

He peppered me with other questions: "How old are they? Who is their mother? Who raised them? So, you know them pretty well? If you saw them on the street, you'd recognize them?" And then he added, "I doubt if I would."

I assured him that Dana is always saying, "You're the best daddy in the whole wide world," and "You're the most important person in the world to Troy."

Drew appears to know who they are when he's with them—at least, he enjoys their company. Whether or not he knows them, he responds to the stimulation of their presence.

Dana enjoys quizzing her dad on the lessons of life, pulling out nuggets of wisdom that still reside within him. She began recording his answers about a year and a half ago.

One of the things he tells her frequently is, "I've had a great life."

Dana often wonders what advice her dad might have given to prepare us for what we're going through if he had known he would be seeing us through the hazy lens of Alzheimer's.

Most of all, Dana asks, "Dad, what is the meaning of life?" His replies come out slowly, thoughtfully, and sometimes haltingly as he searches for just the right words. Here are some of the answers she has recorded:

- It's important to find a good mate. I've been so lucky. Fannie brought me Candy, and I told her, "You sure brought me a pretty one."
- When something is hard or sad that you're going through, think *This will be over.* It won't last forever, and when you stick it out and look back, it will give you a good feeling that you didn't give up.

- Always remember you have a Master, and He's real.
- Don't make any enemies. I think I did pretty good with that. I don't think I have one.
- Don't drink too much. Don't smoke.
- Dismiss things you can't change and move on, or it will bug you. Just let it go and work through it.
- Take care of your family. Raise your kids the best you can. Be nice to people. Help the poor.
- Don't get drunk.
- Don't let people pick on you, and don't pick on people.
- Don't do anything that would hurt somebody. Always take the easy way with people.
- Try to help when you can, and don't let the Boogey Man get you.

September 14, 2017

I spoke at a senior center last month. Overall, it was a good experience, but I'm still licking my wounds over the reaction of one woman with a walker. She came in late and missed my introduction, where I talked about struggling with how much of the intimate details to release to the public and concluded that the raw truth would be more beneficial to caregivers than a sanitized version. In my speech, I told the funny scene that happened in Bermuda when Drew insisted on wearing his underwear to the beach. Everybody in the room laughed. Except for this one lady with the walker who scowled the whole time.

After the others bought books and said glowing things, she came up to my table. "You're not going to like what I have to say." She paused and blurted out, "I do not like your book" (which, of course, she hadn't read). "Your story offended me. You don't make fun of people who have an illness. And you never laugh at them. What's worse, you tried to get us to laugh. Ha! You call your book, *I've Never Loved Him More*? You know *nothing* about love."

Her words stung. "Thank you for letting me know how you feel," I said and managed to smile.

I couldn't get her insult out of my head. The soul searching began immediately and lingered for days.

First came the love issue. Should I have left out the Bermuda story? Does it embarrass Drew? *I'm following Jesus and doing my best to keep in step with the Spirit. I know God is love; therefore, I know love.*

A friend suggested that I focus on the many times people have told me how much the book has helped them, especially the "funny parts." I did a mental exchange (a positive to replace the negative) when God reminded me of the seven-year-old girl who was drawn to my book by the cover and title. Her Aunt Susan (a neighbor who cares for her) told me that she has anxiety issues and doesn't understand a lot of the book but "feels the love," and it calms her down. The other night when she suffered a major disappointment, she comforted herself by reading the "funny parts" at bedtime. Isn't that just like God to choose a child to take away the sting of the hurtful words of an older woman?

Next, I wondered if the woman with the walker was a bitter, frustrated, resentful person who may have even had a touch of dementia. Regardless, if there was even the slightest nugget of truth to her admonition, I wanted to learn from it and adapt my remarks in the future. From now on when I'm invited to speak, I'll mention to the event planner that my audience is caregivers and family members, not the elderly (although most seem to enjoy it).

Finally (which I should have done in the first place), I sat with the Lord. Instantly, He brought Philippians 4:8 to mind:

> *Finally, brothers and sisters,*
> *whatever is true, whatever is noble,*
> *whatever is right, whatever is pure,*
> *whatever is lovely, whatever is admirable—*
> *if anything is excellent or praiseworthy—*
> *think about such things.*

When I think of the woman now, I thank God for her willingness to say aloud what she could have easily kept to herself. And I pray for her.

September 16, 2017

Just when I needed affirmation the most, I received an unexpected call from a reader named Anna Wallace. She had weathered the Alzheimer's journey with her husband, who recently passed away, and wanted to tell me how much my book meant to her.

"I could have substituted my husband's name for Drew's in so many places," she said. "You have told my story."

She has been through the difficult final stages that I have yet ahead of me. We had a very meaningful and enlightening conversation, and then she read a poem to me over the phone that she had clipped from *Gaither's Homecoming Magazine*. Since Drew can still communicate, I'm not yet in the place this poem describes, but it sets the tone in preparing me for the day when he can no longer respond. It also helps me appreciate how much of him I still have. I asked her to mail it to me so I could share it with others. Here it is:

Soul Mates
by Carolyn G. Beverly

When we first met so long ago,
our hearts were young and gay.
My eyes caught a glimpse of a nice young man
the Lord had sent my way.

To hear your voice on the telephone,
it gave my heart a thrill.
Had I found my soul mate at last?
Could this love be *really* real?

The years that we shared together
made our life complete
until one day a stranger came—
one which I could not defeat.

Why did dementia rob us?
The answer, I'll never know.
I love you now as in the beginning.
I am here! But where did you go?

Sometimes you hear, but you don't answer.
Your thoughts, I can't understand.
Your loss of time and days remembered . . .
with no response when I hold your hand.

I guess that's why there are "soul mates,"
because love goes beyond words and deeds.
When times of understanding surpass us,
we're overwhelmed with each other's needs.

I'll do my best to care for you.
I hope that you will always know
I love you now as in the beginning.
I am here! But where did you go?

September 18, 2017

To speak or not to speak. That is the question.

In preparation for tonight's speaking engagement at the Lewes-Rehoboth Rotary, I arranged for Tom Beach, a volunteer from Hospice, to stay with Drew. I had everything planned, and he was scheduled to arrive at 4:00. At 2:45, while getting dressed, I had a pang of conscience and thought it would be good to give Drew a little notice.

"I can't believe this! You lined up a *babysitter* for me?" Drew was furious with me. "You think I need a stranger to entertain me while you're gone?"

Next time, I'll keep my pang of conscience to myself. On and on, he raved and got himself all agitated, almost to the point of hyperventilating. He quizzed me on "why," and I explained that, in the evenings, he doesn't know where he is and thinks he needs to go home. He said that I was the one who needed help, not him.

"I won't be here when the guy comes," he said, and I could tell from the look in his eyes that he meant it.

"Would it help if I called him and told him not to come?"

"You could do that?"

"Yes. I can, and I will."

I was able to reach Tom before he left to come to Georgetown. He was very understanding and assured me he'd be available on other occasions when the time came. As soon as I had that resolved, I called Dana. Fortunately, she was available and agreed to come by to visit with her dad.

After I got all that squared away, I went to see what kind of emotional state Drew was in. Would he still be puffed up and preoccupied about needing to get away from the stranger? No, he was perfectly calm and sitting in his recliner. So, very matter-of-factly, I told him I was going to dash out and pick up a cheeseburger for him. When I got home with it and announced I had a dinner meeting in Lewes, he thanked me for the cheeseburger and said, "Have a good time."

I didn't mention that Dana would be coming. *He'll find out when she gets here.*

September 22, 2017

It was a rough night. We went to bed at midnight, and at 12:45, Drew asked, "Are you awake?" I was because he kept asking me questions. So, I turned on the TV and channel surfed between Daystar and Trinity Broadcasting Network until two a.m. when I finally hit the off button.

Drew continued to be restless throughout the night and kept getting up to go to the bathroom. Each time, he would wake me to ask, "Where is this place?" and then roam around the house, trying to find something that looked familiar. I kept going back to sleep each time, until he said, "Why are you sleeping with me? Why are you in my bed?"

That made me sit up and have an actual conversation with him instead of just mumbling the bare minimum and rolling over. I keep our marriage certificate on the desk in the bedroom for handy reference, and he looks at it now and then. This time, he wanted to "study it," so I turned on the lights, and we sat at the kitchen table. It took about forty-five minutes for me to convince him that we were married, but eventually, he "got it."

After that, I was unable to get back to sleep, so when I heard him snoring peacefully at four a.m., I got up and went to my office to work undisturbed.

He slept soundly until noon and awoke with some congestion. During breakfast, his nose began to drip, so I handed him a napkin. When I suggested he blow his nose, he gave me a blank stare.

Doesn't he know how to blow his nose?

"Here you go, hon." I held the napkin up to his nostrils and told him to blow. Again, he gave me a blank stare, so I demonstrated by blowing through my nose. It was like teaching a child, and he responded well. Whoever suspected my beloved would need to be coached on something so basic?

So, this is what the late moderate phase looks like. It's exhausting. Hopefully, I can grab a nap this afternoon.

October 20, 2017

My friend, Hope Flinchbaugh, emailed three questions to me today: "May I ask how I can pray for you? What is your lifestyle right now? What are Drew's needs?"

These specific questions caused me to stop and think. I've been so busy trying to keep on top of things and intentionally "making time for myself," that I haven't taken inventory of what a "normal day" looks like. Here's what I wrote back to Hope:

> What I need prayer for most is more quality TIME at the keyboard without distractions. At this moment, our cat is blocking the monitor with her tail and nudging my fingers with her nose (which makes for interesting typos) while Buttercup is panting for attention in the background. This means I will need to get up and walk to the kitchen to give them an evening snack or let them outside (or both). I slept wrong last night, and my right hip hurts when I try to walk, so I've been hobbling from place to place, feeling like Peg Leg Pete. Drew is sitting in a chair in the corner happily singing, "I was strolling down the street one day," and announcing, "quarter to nine." I took time out to have lunch with friends from twelve-thirty to two, which felt good at the time, but now I have to play catch-up. A publishing client stopped by unannounced this morning, and someone else came to buy two books this afternoon, not counting three phone calls from prospective clients, and suddenly, it was four o'clock and time to go to dinner. I want to sit here and work! But I can feel my attention span withering by the second. After I feed the pets, I think I need to take a shower and try to settle into bed as neither of us slept very well last night. So much for getting any work done today or tonight.
>
> Drew is content but confused most of the time as he doesn't know where he is or who I am. It takes a lot of explanation for him to comprehend that this is his home in Georgetown, and I live here, too.

Hope's questions slowed me down and helped me look at the broader picture. It appears I've fallen into the habit of doing whatever is required of me without thinking things through. For example, scheduling a once-a-week lunch with friends to be sure I have "me time" is a double-edged sword. They desire to help me relax, and I do relax when I'm with them, but it heaps more stress on me because every hour away from my desk puts me farther behind in my work.

What to do? Hmmm. Maybe instead of lunch at a restaurant, we could have a "working lunch" in my office where I can have them help me with filing, prioritizing, or brainstorming ways to streamline things. Nah. That would defeat the purpose of "me time."

I already have Elizabeth Boerner coming in once a week, and she's coaching me to be a better delegator. If I could share a load of mundane, time-consuming tasks with her, too, that would take the pressure off.

The problem is that when people say, "I'm here for you. Just let me know what you need," I tell them I'm grateful and will let them know. But I haven't figured out how to identify specifics that they can do. The root of the problem is that I must retrain myself from a lifelong tendency of feeling like I should do everything on my own.

In 1973, shortly after I began working at Delaware Tech, I remember the Dean of Instruction's secretary, Anne Pennington, saying, "Candy, you know what's wrong with you? You don't let anybody help you out." That stung, but she was so right. For some reason—maybe perfectionism, control, a desire to prove myself, or fear that others will not meet my standard of excellence—I cling to tasks that others could do.

And I'm still doing that. My business is growing and flourishing, but it will wither if I don't allow others to pitch in and help. It's time to pry my fingers loose and learn to behave more like an administrator and less like a secretary.

And thus began my conversation with God:

"But, Lord, I *love* the role of secretary. During my entire career, I have been used to having my boss tell me what to do and when to do it. I get great pleasure from the hands-on activity of typing and all the other responsibilities of clerical work."

"**Rather than looking for direction from an earthly boss, look to Me. There is a time to type and a time to oversee. You have not noticed, but I gave you a promotion long ago. In truth, you are My cleric, My servant leader. For decades now, I have ministered through your clerical gifts and talents. During this time, I have also trained you in an administrative capacity to lead by example.**"

"Lord, I get the play on words, cleric and clerical. And I've known since 1983 that You've chosen me for grassroots ministry. But why would You promote me to greater responsibility now when Drew is declining from Alzheimer's and needs me most?"

"**Did you not tell someone the other day, 'I always thought I trusted the Lord completely, but I see now that I hadn't scratched the surface of what it means to trust Him'? Because of your circumstances, you now *trust the Lord your God with all your heart and with all your soul and with all your mind and with all your strength* (Mark 12:13). This is how you love Me, by trusting Me, by keeping in step with the Holy Spirit's halts and nudges. You have been faithful in the little things, My daughter. I am entrusting you with much. 'With the measure you use, it will be measured to you—and even more' (Mark 4:24).**"

"But, Lord, I am content with little."

"**This is a flawed perception. You feel fulfilled because you have been obedient to Me, but you have reached the maximum capacity of your efforts. True contentment comes from being right with Me at any given moment. I desire to stretch you further, beyond your ability to personally handle every detail of your business and your life. You can choose to shrink back, but I will not be pleased, and you will quickly find your contentment turning to frustration. Will you continue where I lead?**"

"Yes, of course, Lord. I never want to disappoint You and know You only want the best for me. I trust You to bring the right people across my path and teach me how to explain to them what needs to be done. Help me, Lord. I don't know how to do this."

"I know what you need and who you need. But remember, *My thoughts are not your thoughts, neither are your ways my ways* (Isaiah 55:8). Even mistakes and missteps have a purpose, so fear not. Pay close attention to the checks and promptings in your spirit. If you are discerning, you will move forward with confidence. I am with you always, especially during this period of transition."

So the big takeaway from my journal entry is threefold:

1. True contentment is being right with the Lord at any given moment.
2. I am committed to following Him wherever He leads.
3. He will choose people along the way to help me.

I think I'm working too hard at this.

October 28, 2017

As we were driving to Salisbury, Drew said, "I don't remember where you said we were going."

"We're going to the movies," I said. "It's a Christian movie—*Let There Be Light*."

I could hear the enthusiasm in his voice. "Sex every night?"

Ha! His poor hearing makes for interesting conversation.

"The secret of life isn't what happens to you
but what you do with what happens to you."

— *Norman Vincent Peale*

CHAPTER FIVE

The Search Is On

November 3, 2017

Dana discovered something the other day that I learned some time ago but never thought to mention: *Don't ask in advance. Just matter-of-factly tell him at the time.*

She came to stay with Drew while I was at a book signing. For more than a week, she had looked forward to taking him to Harbeson (where his mother was raised) to search the graveyard for Jarvis family headstones. Her plan included a trip to Rehoboth for lunch at Cracker Barrel. Not knowing better, she asked him if he wanted to do these things, and he said, "No, I don't want to do that."

With as much enthusiasm as she could muster, she tried to coax him. "Come on, Dad. It'll be fun."

"NO! I want to stay here."

So, Dana got him a quarter pounder from McDonald's, and they ate at the kitchen table. But, I have to say, even in her disappointment, she told me they had a great visit. "If I'd had my wits about me," she said, "I could have handed him his coat and told him it's time to go."

That's the best way to handle the bathing issue, too. If Drew had his way, like many dementia patients, he would skip bathing altogether and just put the same clothes on every day—or never take them off.

After several tries at asking, "Are you ready for your shower?" or "Do you want to take a shower?" I've learned to say, "Your water is nice and warm, just the way you like it. Let me help you get those clothes off."

I stand outside the shower and peep in every few minutes, handing him the soap and a washcloth and shampoo as he's ready. Sometimes he asks, "What do I do with that?" but he's still able to clean himself with a little direction. I can see the time may soon come when I'll need to ask a professional for some guidance on how to bathe him.

November 15, 2017

I attended the Delaware Dementia Conference and learned to identify triggers that prompt internal anxiety. I also learned that Alzheimer's patients yearn for security. So I'm on the right track when I tell Drew, "All you need to know is that you're in a safe place with someone who loves you."

November 19, 2017

Things are happy around here with the holidays approaching and the Lord being so very present. I'm feeling more than fulfilled with Drew's company and my publishing and writing. As I sat at my desk this afternoon, joy bubbled up within me for no particular reason—so much so, I didn't know if I could contain it and was surprised that I didn't laugh aloud. I can't recall such spontaneous joy without a catalyst of some sort. It caught me by surprise, and I sat there basking in it. It was as if the Lord hugged me and invited Mom, Dad, my grandparents, aunts and uncles, Malorie Derby, Angela Sayin, and every other deceased saint I had ever known to hug me at the same time. Love throbbed within me as though it were tangible.

Thoughts of *It's a Wonderful Life* floated through my memory. I'm not in nearly as much trouble as George Bailey was, and Clarence Odbody hasn't made a personal appearance to me, but a lot of people have assured me that they're keeping me (and Drew) in their prayers.

Maybe this is what it feels like when prayers hit the mark in heaven and are then poured out on the recipient.

After the feeling subsided and slipped gently away, I had a smile on my face and a knowing in my heart that God is pleased with me. *It is well with my soul.* Whatever triggered this holy, joyful moment gave me pause to reflect on how much I have to be truly thankful for.

Drew sat in the corner of my office, reading a book he picked up from my collection in a pile near the chair.

"Listen to this," he said and began reading the introduction of *Power in Praise* by Merlin R. Carothers.

"That's a great book," I said. "Keep reading."

"You've read it?"

"Read it? That book changed my life. God used it to bring the two of us together."

I had his full attention, so I took him back to the time when I was a single mom, divorced and miserable from dating anyone who asked me out. I was desperate for a husband. One night, I propped myself up in bed in my apartment in Milford and picked up Merlin Carothers' book.

Here are some passages that grabbed me:

As long as we praise God with an eye secretly looking for the expected results, we're only kidding ourselves, and we can be certain that nothing will happen to change us or our situation.

Praise is based on a total and joyful acceptance of the present as part of God's loving, perfect will for us. Praise is not based on what we think or hope will happen in the future. This is an absolute 'law,' clearly observable in the practice of praise.

We praise God, not for what we expect will happen in or around us, but we praise Him for what He is and where and how we are right now.

Praise is not a bargaining position. We don't say, "I'll praise you so that you can bless me, Lord."

To praise God is to delight ourselves in Him. The psalmist

wrote, *"Be delighted with the Lord. Then He will give you all your heart's desires"* (Psalm 37:4).

Notice the order of importance here. We don't make a list of our heart's desires and then delight ourselves in the Lord to get them. We're first to be delighted, and once we've experienced being delighted with God, we'll discover that everything else becomes secondary. Still, God does indeed want to give us all our heart's desires. Nothing short of that is His wish and plan for us.

I told Drew that I prayed, "Lord, if You want me to be married, You can look down from Your heavenly throne across the face of the earth and see every eligible bachelor. You know me and what I need in a husband. And if You want me to be single, help me to like it."

I awoke the next morning, *thrilled* to be single! I danced around the kitchen thinking, *I don't have to share a closet with anybody. Things stay where I put them. I don't have to answer to anybody if I want to get up in the middle of the night and clean out a closet or read a book. I have Kim to love and enjoy and share my affection.*

That night, I wrote a long list of pros and cons for what I wanted in a husband and put it in my Bible.

Within a few days, Mom and Dad came back from Panama for a visit. I told Mom about my prayer and showed her my list. She read it and said, "Honey, I don't think there's a man on the face of the earth who could live up to the things on your list."

"Maybe so," I told her, "but if not, that's okay. I'm happy, and it's going to take someone very special to make me give this up. I'm not settling for anything less."

Drew was hanging on every word as I continued.

"Mom and Dad left to visit relatives in North Carolina. While they were gone, Fannie marched me across the street, through your back door, and into your kitchen. You were eating dinner at the bar with Dana and Troy.

"Fannie said, 'I brought you somebody,' like I was a present or something. And you said . . ."

Drew beamed as he recalled the day that changed both our lives. "Sure brought me a pretty one."

"You had me right there," I said as we both laughed. "Fannie told me later that after I drove off, you danced in the street. You called me that night, and we met for a long lunch the next day at the Blue-Gold Inn. Over our glasses of wine and beer, we told each other our sad divorce stories. When I finished mine, you looked deep into my eyes and said, 'You look like a woman who needs to be appreciated.' It could have been just a line, but you meant it."

"Yes, I did," he said.

"And you've been appreciating me every day since."

Back to our story. "And then you said, 'I need your advice.' You asked what I thought you should do about Dana, who was fifteen and wanted to go out with her friends who could drive.

"'Tell me about Dana,' I said. 'Does she get good grades? Is she a good girl or a troublemaker? Are her friends partiers or level-headed?' You gave me all the right answers, so I said, 'You might want to let her go but make it conditional, so you could pull in the reins if she messes up.'

"From then on, we couldn't stand to be apart and talked for hours on the phone every night. A week and a half later, Mom and Dad got back from North Carolina. They had no sooner walked through the door when I grabbed Mom's hands and said, 'I met the man!'

"She and Dad exchanged sad, pitiful looks, but I forged on. 'He's everything on my list!'

"'You just *met* the guy,' Dad said. 'You can't possibly know that much about him.'

"'Oh, but I do!' I said. 'He's kind and gentle, a good father, goes to church, loves pets—he has a Collie named Ginger and a cat named

Bullet—he's got a great sense of humor, a good job, a great reputation. People keep telling me "That Drew Abbott, he's a nice boy." Everyone says he's the real deal, just unlucky at love. He asks for my opinion, and he listens to me, really listens.'

"'We just don't want you to get hurt,' Mom said."

I held up Merlin Carothers book. "And this is why I said this book changed my life. Remember my prayer? For a year and a half, I'd been driving past your house twice a day, five days a week, taking Kim to and from Fannie's to babysit. All that time, she could have introduced us, but she didn't until a few days after I prayed. I think the Lord was waiting until I learned to praise Him and trust God."

Over these many years, praise has become a habit that has served me well. Who knows? Maybe today's wave of unexpected joy came as a bonus for a lifetime of taking 1 Thessalonians 5:16-18 (NIV) seriously:

> *Rejoice always, pray continually,*
> *give thanks in all circumstances;*
> *for this is God's will for you*
> *in Christ Jesus.*

November 23, 2017

Drew has been singing, "It's beginning to look a lot like Christmas," since June, and now it truly is beginning to look a lot like Christmas. He's been asking what kind of present he should get me. I told him that I'd order a couple of tunics and a KardiaMobile to monitor my atrial fibrillation (A-fib) and help him wrap them for me. Between now and Christmas, I'll forget about them and be surprised. The real surprise will be if he hides the boxes where neither of us can find them.

I usually get him gift cards for restaurants, but this year I doubt if I would appreciate their value. When I ask what he wants for Christmas, he says, "Why don't we let Santa decide?" Which reminds me of the four stages of life:

1. *You believe in Santa Claus.*
2. *You don't believe in Santa Claus.*
3. *You are Santa Claus.*
4. *You look like Santa Claus.*

I guess I'm in transition from stages three and four since I have a broad face and a round little belly that shakes when I laugh like a bowl full of jelly. I'm chubby and plump, a right jolly old elf—okay, okay, enough of myself!

I need to put on my Santa thinking cap and come up with something Drew will enjoy. He doesn't like board games, just got a new pair of shoes, has more than enough shirts, sweaters, and other practical stuff. What could I give him that would make him feel the kind of joy a child experiences on Christmas morning?

About half an hour later, he was roaming through the house, trying to find anything in his surroundings that looked familiar and came across a cherry-red vintage model car on a shelf. Two years ago, it caught his eye while we were shopping for our nephews in the drug store, and I bought it for him on a whim. As far as I know, he hasn't looked at it since, until now.

He carried it to me with outstretched arms. "Who does this belong to?"

"It's yours, hon."

"Mine?" Except for the wrinkles, his smile belonged to a six-year-old.

"Santa gave it to you," I fibbed. "Maybe he'll bring another one this year. Would you like that?"

He nodded. "I used to play with metal trucks," he added with a wistful look. "I don't know whatever happened to them."

I had my answer: Classic Tonka trucks! Away to the computer, I flew like a flash, tore open the browser, to Amazon I dashed. And what to my wondering eyes should appear? *Click here, buy now!* Oh, will *he* be surprised! While I was searching, so lively and quick, I thought of toy soldiers he played with while sick. With a click of my mouse and a twist of my head, Christmas this year would be nothing to dread.

November 27, 2017

We were having dinner at Bob Evans in Rehoboth, and I said, "This salmon is excellent."

"Huh?"

"This salmon is excellent," I repeated, with the same response. After the third, "huh?" I pointed my fork at the salmon and said, "Fish. Good."

"Fish, good?" he echoed.

"Yeah," I smiled. "I thought short words would be easier for you to understand than, 'This salmon is excellent.'"

Whether the culprit was his hearing, his Alzheimer's, or both, he got it, and we shared a hearty laugh.

December 5, 2017

Drew and I stopped by to see Kim and our grandkids tonight. We relaxed on their couch in front of the crackling fireplace, admiring their Christmas tree. Drew sat quietly beside me, sipping his Coke, petting Rosco, and glancing at the television. He only mentioned how pretty the tree was three times.

While he studied the tree and interacted with Kade and Saige, Kim whispered to me, "Wow! What a drastic difference from two nights ago when Troy and I stayed with him."

She leaned closer to me, and we carried on a conversation that Drew couldn't hear because of the background noise and his hearing loss.

"He's so content tonight," she said, "so comfortable with you sitting next to him. On Sunday, he was unsettled—asking every minute where you were, when you were coming home, what time you would be back—over and over." Her eyes watered, and she choked up. "It's so emotional for me—the contrast."

She wiped her eyes. "At one point on Sunday when Troy couldn't stand the repetition, he said, 'Dad, your girlfriend always leaves you a love note. Let me get it for you.' He handed him the marker board I had prepared and told him to read it aloud. Dad read every word and, no sooner had he finished than he asked, 'When will Candy be home?'"

I told Kim that Drew could read and comprehend, but only for a few seconds. "By the time he finished reading, he'd forgotten what it said."

Kim nodded. "Yeah, that's what happened, so Troy said, "Read the note. What does it say?'

"'It says she'll be back by 5:30.'

"'What time is it now?'

"Dad looked at his watch. 'Four forty-five.'"

Kim told me she was impressed that Drew could still tell time. But she was *most* impressed by the change in his demeanor when my car pulled into the driveway.

"Your sweetheart's home!" she told him. His face lit up, his posture straightened, and his shoulders relaxed as he moved back from the edge of his seat and settled into the cushion on the couch.

Another wave of emotion washed over her, and her voice caught in her throat. "I wish I could have videotaped him so you could see the contrast of how agitated he is when you're gone compared to how content he is when you're with him. It's as though he doesn't know how to function when you're apart." She paused. "But you can't see that because he's always content when you're together."

I glanced at Drew and smiled at him. He smiled back, and I squeezed his hand. Then I turned back to Kim and spoke softly. "This must be what the Bible means by, 'the two shall become one.'"

"I'll tell you this," she said. "Watching the difference in him is what love looks like."

December 10, 2017

We had our first big, beautiful snow of the winter this weekend. Anticipating a lazy day, I was still in my pajamas in the afternoon, watching a Hallmark movie when the phone rang. I hadn't talked with my friend Pat Atkins in quite a while, and we had a lot of catching up to do. I'd been on the phone with her for about ten minutes when Drew asked me where to find the broom. I motioned to the closet and watched him locate the broom and go out the front door to sweep the porch.

I continued to chat, carrying the handset from one end of the house to the other as the conversation took me from the kitchen to my keyboard. I vaguely remember nodding to Drew when he poked his head into my office to say, "I swept the snow off the car . . ."

"Do you have any problem with Drew wandering?" Pat asked.

"Oh, no," I said. "He's too safety conscious to stray far from home. But at this point, he doesn't know where home is. When we come back from dinner or Walmart, he always says, 'This is a nice house. Who lives here?' so it's a good thing he doesn't drive anymore."

I told her how Troy filed the key to the GMC truck down so it still fits into the ignition but doesn't turn on, and how I let Drew keep his keys in his pocket because it's a comfort to him.

"Even the key to the Cadillac?" she asked.

"Yep." I told her how I thought about taking the Cadillac key fob off his key ring a year ago but hadn't gotten around to it because it didn't seem to be a problem. He was content for me to drive him around.

As Pat and I were bringing our conversation to a close, I realized I hadn't seen Drew in a while. When I glanced out the front door and didn't see him in the yard, I walked through the house as we talked, expecting to see him in each room—no Drew.

That's when I noticed the car wasn't in the driveway.

"This has been a great conversation," I said, purposely avoiding any mention of the anxiety building inside my chest because I didn't want her to feel guilty for distracting me. "Thanks so much for calling."

I raced to the bathroom to throw on some clothes and heard the sliding glass door open.

"Drew?"

It was Troy, who had come to shave his dad and was surprised to see me, thinking I had gone somewhere in the car.

As soon as I told him about the missing Cadillac and father, he said, "I'll go look for him," and raced out the door.

At one-fifty, I called Wyatt, my state trooper son-in-law, to ask his advice. He gave me the non-emergency number for the police. Just as I was about to dial, Dana called to say that Troy had let her know about Drew and the car. I could hear the restrained panic in her voice as she suggested I call the police about issuing a Gold Alert.

"Gold Alert?" I asked.

"Yes, like an Amber Alert but for missing disabled or elderly people," she said.

I told her we were on the same wavelength and that Wyatt had given me the non-911 number. We cut our call short so I could call that number.

While I was on the phone with the police, Wyatt's number popped up on Caller ID, and I asked if I could put the officer on hold. It was Kim calling to say that Wyatt wanted to remind me that we had OnStar and they could locate the car. I conveyed this to the police, and they assured me that an officer would be coming to the house in a few minutes to coordinate everything and for me to go ahead and call OnStar.

Troy came back after talking with Dana to be sure we were all in sync instead of continuing his search. What a comfort to have him with me as I sorted through the information overload and stifled my mounting anxiety.

I flew to my computer and opened my browser. *OnStar.* I typed the word and hit enter.

OnStar: Home popped up. (click)

https://onstar.com (click)

https://www.onstar.com/us/en/home.html

My brain felt like it was swimming in molasses. *User name? Password? Think. Is this what it's like for Drew every day? Focus, Candy, focus. OnStar login.*

I sat there, staring at the monitor and wanted to shake it. Suddenly, I remembered! My fingers flew over the keys, and another page opened to my account. *Where's their contact information? Where's their number?* I scrolled down, then up, then down again. *Focus, Candy, focus.*

At last, my eyes found the Contact Us link at the bottom of the page. I dialed 1.888.466.7827 and pressed 1 for stolen vehicle/missing person and 3 to report a stolen vehicle or missing person. *Why can't these automated recordings talk faster?* The associate came on the line, located my account, and said I would need to file a missing person report with the police.

"I've already spoken with the police, and an officer should be here at any minute."

She placed me on hold to look something up.

Just then, the officer from the Georgetown Police Department arrived at our door. Troy invited him in, and we introduced ourselves while I held the phone to my ear. As soon as the OnStar lady came back on the line, I handed the phone to Officer Calloway. Within minutes, OnStar began tracking the car, and he was on his way to find Drew, promising to call me as soon as he knew the location.

In no time, Officer Calloway called. "We've located him in Millsboro, and the car is still moving, so that's a good sign."

I breathed a sigh of relief. *He's not in a ditch or worse.*

I called Kim to let Wyatt know, and she said he was scheduled to report for duty soon, so he threw on his uniform and was already out looking for him. I mentioned that we would need someone to drive Drew home and someone else to drive the Cadillac. She said that Kade and Saige were home and she and they would take care of it.

She didn't get an answer when she called Wyatt because he was busy following the clues he heard on his radio: first on Morris Street near the Millsboro Fire Station, then on Washington Street, and that the Georgetown Police had spotted him at PNC Bank.

They didn't have to pull Drew over because he pulled in of his own accord. When Wyatt arrived, he found the Cadillac parked and centered perfectly in the drive-through ATM lane. Why he wound up there is anybody's guess as we have never used that particular bank, and it was a Sunday. Wyatt, a Delaware State Trooper, Chad Morris with the Millsboro Police, Officer Calloway with the Georgetown Police, and possibly others showed up at the scene.

Wyatt took the lead and explained the situation. "This is Kim's dad, and he's harmless. He has Alzheimer's, so don't approach him like he's done something wrong. He just took off with the car and doesn't know where he is. Talk to him like he's a friend. Whatever you do, don't startle him."

He approached Drew. "Hey, this is a surprise seeing you here. What are you up to today?"

Drew looked relieved. "I was on my way to Milford, and well, I guess I got lost."

"It looks that way. You ended up in Millsboro. Why don't you get out and stand over here with me? One of these nice officers will move your car off to the side while we figure out how to get you home."

About that time, Kim arrived with Kade and Saige. "I always thought of Dad as a big man," she told me later. "I guess it's because when you're a kid, that perspective sort of stays with you. But he looked so small with the officers standing around him."

Kade drove the Cadillac home with Saige in the passenger seat, and Wyatt gently persuaded Drew to ride with Kim. On the way home, Drew offered to give our daughter twenty dollars for being so kind and coming to his rescue.

"No thanks, Dad. You've always been generous. I'm glad to help."

"Come on, take it," he coaxed. "I'm sure you can put it to good use." Then, he noticed the car in front of them. "That tag looks familiar. Isn't that my car?"

Kim assured him that it was his car and noted what a good job Kade was doing driving it home for him. He agreed, and they had a nice chat the rest of the way back to Georgetown.

There's no doubt in my mind that God watched over him during the whole ordeal, and he was oblivious that he was in danger.

When they arrived home, Troy and I were standing in the snowy front yard to greet them before they had a chance to get out of the vehicles. Drew looked relaxed and cheerful. I hugged him long and hard and said, "So, I understand you had a bit of an adventure!"

He tilted his head. "I got lost and didn't know where I was, but then a whole lot of nice people showed up to help me out. I've never had so much attention." Then a broad grin spread across his face. "I'll have to do this again soon. It was great!"

As we made our way into the house, Kade handed me Drew's keys, and I handed them back and whispered, "Please take this off (the Cadillac key fob); I need to hide it." After he did, I handed Drew his key ring and dashed into the kitchen to hide the key fob in the back of the silverware drawer.

My knees were weak and buckled from relief. We sat together in the living room, where Drew was calm and entertaining. "I've never had so much attention. Maybe I can pull it off again on Wednesday."

Why Wednesday? There is no rhyme or reason to why he says or does anything, and I knew he had no idea what day of the week it was, but Wednesday must have sounded specific enough to make his joke sound real.

I asked him where he was going, and he said, "You know . . . to Milford to turn in my papers for the . . . you know . . . the class."

No, I didn't know anything about any papers or a class, and Milford is in the opposite direction from Millsboro. So, I smiled sincerely and mumbled something about how responsible a person he is.

None of us had eaten lunch, so I heated the soup I had made the day before, and the five of us enjoyed it together. When Kim and the kids were ready to leave, she said, "Mom, do you realize what time it is? Two-fifty."

I didn't understand why that would be significant and gave her a puzzled look.

"It was 1:50 when you first called for Wyatt—exactly one hour ago."

From my panicky beginning until everything was fully resolved and normal again was a mere hour? I could have sworn at least twenty-four hours had passed.

Thank goodness for OnStar, for compassionate and efficient law enforcement, for a tight-knit family, and for a merciful God who looks out for lost Alzheimer's husbands.

December 21, 2017

Okay. I'm officially on "tilt." I just took Buttercup to the vet for her annual shots at 10:00, only to be told that her appointment was at 11:00. This wouldn't be noteworthy except the vet staff also told me I was a *week* early.

Too much on my mind lately. Christmas is four days away, and there is so much that isn't done yet. I bought gifts early, and they're still not wrapped. I think I'll wrap the presents for other family members and dispense with wrapping the gifts I got for Drew to give me and the toys and pajamas I bought for him. The freedom of *not wrapping* is the gift I will appreciate the most. He won't know the difference, and it will take the pressure off since I won't have wrapping paper to cut, fold, and tape or paper to crumple up and toss in the trash. Some part of my obligations and responsibilities has to go, and right now, that part is wrapping gifts for the two of us.

I feel better already.

"You gain strength, courage, and confidence
by every experience
in which you really stop to look fear in the face.
You must do the things which you think you cannot do."

— *Eleanor Roosevelt*

CHAPTER SIX

New Year, New Challenges

January 1, 2018

We watched the ball drop in New York City at midnight, which is our typical bedtime these days. When we were working, our pattern used to be to get in bed around 9:00 to watch TV or read and then be asleep by 10:00, but at this stage of our lives, we've turned into night owls.

I'm getting used to Drew sleeping twelve hours, usually waking up around noon. And I'm accustomed to his questions of *Who are you? Do you have a car? Where do you live? When are we going home?* But I wasn't prepared for his first question of the year:

"Who am I?"

"Who are you?" I mustered up my most enthusiastic voice and said, "You are Drew Abbott!"

He gave me a confused stare. "What does that mean?"

What does that mean? It meant he didn't know who he was? I tried not to let him see the confusion I felt. Instead, I forced a smile as if I meant it. "What that means is, I'm the luckiest girl in the world! Why? Because I'm married to you—Drew Abbott!"

"I'm Drew Abbott? And we're married?"

I knew his next question would be "how long," so I launched into my typical spiel, and 2018 was off to an off-balance but familiar start.

January 3, 2018

On Christmas Day, after our annual family brunch, we had gathered in the living room to exchange gifts. When Drew got up from his usual seat on the couch for a moment, Natalie slid into his spot so she could talk with Trevor and Jill. When Drew got back, Natalie was deep into conversation, so he took the vacant chair she had previously occupied near the front door and beside the tree. He became instantly confused about where he was.

Kim teaches fifth grade and shared with me that today's English lesson was about point of view, and she used Drew's situation as a real-life example. It was powerful for her students. Here's what she told me:

> After experiencing Dad's perspective on Christmas from the chair by the door versus his normal spot on the couch (opposite wall), I chose to share the story with my students for a quick activator for our English Language Arts, Unit 4, on Point of View. I explained how he kept repeating himself, wondering whose house he was in. After helping him see that he was in a new seat and that it all looked different to him than normal, he calmed down.
>
> I asked my students to select a new seat for our read aloud and be prepared to tell me how the room seemed different when they looked at it from a different perspective. They were amazed at how everything looked smaller (if in the back versus the front of the room), bigger if they had moved to the front (near the board), or how it was harder to concentrate on the reading because they were too busy looking around the room or through a door they had never noticed before from their original seat. It's funny how such a little change can make such a huge impact on how we see things.

An exercise for caregivers of people with dementia is to smear Vaseline on the lenses of their glasses. This allows us to see how distorted things look through the eyes of someone with Alzheimer's. But, warning: It's hard to get the smeary petroleum jelly off. I used Dawn, hot water, and then a mixture of equal parts of water and vinegar to remove any leftover traces of Vaseline or detergent.

January 5, 2018

Drew usually wears sweatpants and a sweatshirt to bed, but I gave him red and black plaid pajamas for Christmas. He put the bottoms on for the first time tonight, paired with his red cable knit sweater. What a fabulous look! When he came into my office wearing his new outfit, I said, "Wow! You look great!"

"When I look down," he said, "I think, whose legs are these?" We laughed. It was funny the first time, but he kept saying it over and over, and I got tired of pretend-laughing.

"Come on," I said. "I'll fix us a nice cup of hot tea." He followed me into the kitchen. When the steaming cups were ready, I put some music on, and we sat at the kitchen table.

Earlier in the day, I had enjoyed the adult coloring book that Betty Kasperski, my friend and fellow author, gave me for Christmas. So far, this is one of the few ways I've found to truly relax. Other "stillness" exercises like reading usually put me to sleep, but coloring allows my hands to be productive while my mind is free for the creative juices to flow. I ordered a second coloring book for variety and hoped I could entice Drew to try it. I opened my coloring book and picked up where I had left off.

After a while, Drew said, "That looks like fun."

"It is!" I said. "And guess what? I got one for you so we can play together." I put the other coloring book in front of him. "Here you go Find a page that appeals to you, and I'll help you get started." He chose a design with a series of spokes with tiny circles.

I picked up an orange gel pen, reached over, and colored in the five circles of the first spoke while he watched carefully. "Your turn," I said, and handed the pen to him. To my amazement and joy, he continued to the next spoke, and the next, and completed the entire outer ring.

The Pandora oldies station played happy tunes while we sipped our tea and chatted over our coloring. He stayed focused and seemed content, with no evidence of his nightly confusion. We worked on our coloring books for a full hour, and *not once* did he ask any of his usual repetitive questions.

Discoveries as a caregiver arrive in snippets, little at a time. "Busy hands are happy hands" comes to mind. It takes effort to find activities that Drew can do, and what works one day may not interest him on another. But this was a good day. He and I "worked" side-by-side like we had so many times before in our "real" life. Today may have been coloring books and gel pens, but it was as satisfying as when I used to help him compile residential appraisals at the keyboard.

January 6, 2018

While Storm Brody swirled around outside, I enjoyed a typical day inside at the keyboard with Drew behind me in his usual chair.

Above the clackety-clack of the keys, I heard him say, "Have I told you lately how much I love you?"

I swiveled around in my chair to face him, and he continued: "If someone offered me $10,000 for you, I'd say no. If they offered $100,000, I'd say no. There's no amount of money I'd sell you for."

Awww, so sweet—I think. Sell me? Let's not get hung up on that part. Although his compliment may have missed the mark, I know he's trying to tell me in *every* way he can how much he appreciates me. This carries me through times when we have other conversations like this one that took place between four and five a.m.:

[*I was standing in the dark when Drew got up to go to the bathroom.*] "I couldn't find you! What are you doing?" *Waiting for Buttercup to come back in.* "Who's Buttercup?" *Our dog.* "We have a dog?" *Yes, a Cocker Spaniel.* "How long?" *Almost eight years.* "Are you sure? I don't remember a dog." *You'll know her when you see her. Here she comes now.* "Buttercup! Where have you been?!"

[*Back in bed*] "Who are you to me?" *Your wife.* "You mean we're married?" *Yes.* "But we've never even lived together." *We've lived* together every day and every night for forty-two years. "So, you're taking care of me?" *Always.*

"Where am I supposed to be?" *Right here, right where you belong.* "Are we going home today?" *We are home.* "How did we get here?" *We live here.* "In Georgetown?" *Yes.* "Where is everybody?" *The kids grew up, moved out, and have homes of their own.* "But where's Howard?"

Howard is Drew's older brother. A lightbulb came on for me. Did he see things through the eyes of a teenager still living at home with his parents and three brothers? When he asked where everybody was, I answered from my perspective, not his. And if he thinks of me as his mother, no wonder he has difficulty understanding that we're married.

He kept peppering me with questions that jolted me every time I dozed off. Finally, I mumbled, "I'll answer all your questions in the morning." And, still, the questions continued, so I threatened, "If you don't stop talking, I'm going to have to move to the couch." Even so, I knew he was capable of following me to the couch where the interrogation would continue. But it worked. At last, we slept.

January 8, 2018

Drew came out of the bathroom, chuckling. When I asked why, he just laughed harder.

"Come on," I said. "What's so funny?"

"I just thought up a good bumper sticker." He laughed some more and finally got the words out: "Everybody Farts."

A picture flashed through my mind of the two of us merrily riding along in our shiny red Cadillac SRX with that sticker on our back bumper, leaving a trail of drivers laughing in our wake. Ha! Nothing like a little senior citizen potty humor to brighten your day.

Who knew farting could be so much fun? We're getting pretty creative when it comes to flatulence quips. For example, he broke wind when he stood up to pivot to sit in the transport chair, and I said. "Ah, jet-propelled!" as I pushed him forward.

Another time, I had my hand on his butt, trying to get him moved up in the bed when he farted on my fingers. I yanked them away. "Eww, gross!" He grinned and said in his best James Cagney voice, "Sweetheart, I blew you away!"

Once, when he farted long and low at the dinner table, he gave me a sheepish look and said, "Air freshener."

My standard reply is, "Quit farting around."

January 10, 2018

I went to Smyrna today to embark on a fitness program with Body Wisdom Wellness DNA. After attending a presentation by Ladonna Graham about the value of cleansing the gut, I told her I wanted to sign up for everything she had to offer: Weight Loss, Diabetes Management, etc. Today was the day!

We began with an hour-long colon cleanse treatment, getting the junk out of my intestines that had been there for who-knows-how-long. I spent most of the day with her going over my medications and health history, asking questions, getting an overview of what to expect, and learning of miraculous testimonies. Ladonna is a scientist and customizes treatment based on each person's needs and DNA. She took measurements and "before" pictures—typical stuff—but unlike other weight-loss programs, she sent me home with bottled water she had infused with nutrients my body needed.

I came home feeling energized and more optimistic about my health and well-being than ever before.

When I prayed, "Why did it take so long, and why did I have to get this fat?" the Lord revealed that I used to subconsciously look down my nose at people who were obese and wonder why they didn't do something about it. Now, I *am* one of those obese people and have gained newfound empathy for them.

January 11, 2018

I leave in the morning for my annual writing retreat with The Crue, an escape I've been looking forward to for months. The thing about caregiving is that you can't just pick up and go whenever you like. You have to plan ahead. Here are the instructions I'm leaving with our three adult children who have eagerly agreed to provide coverage:

FRIDAY

I'm leaving around 2:00. Troy will check on Drew off and on throughout the afternoon. Troy will take all three trash bins to the curb after 6 PM.

Kim or Wyatt will come around 4:00 or 5ish to take Drew out for dinner and stay with him until about 8:00.

Troy will stay with Drew until Dana arrives in the evening.

Dana should be able to be here around 9:30 to stay overnight. Drew's bedtime medication is in the cabinet above the silverware drawer; use the PM compartments. His toothbrush is the navy blue one, and he'll need you to put the toothpaste on it but can brush his teeth himself. If you give him a washcloth and soap, he can wash up in the sink. (I'll see that he showers again on Monday.) He sleeps in the red sweatshirt and plaid pajama bottoms (on the chair by the sewing machine). He likes to get in bed and watch (or listen to) TV and has been staying up until ten or midnight. When you're ready to go to sleep, he should be compliant but may ask questions in the night. Expect him to get up and go to the bathroom a couple of times in the night. I hope you're comfortable sleeping in the recliner.

SATURDAY

Drew usually sleeps most of the morning and wakes up around noon. Troy will help him get dressed (if Drew hasn't already). His morning medication is in the cupboard above the silverware drawer (see AM compartments). Can you take care of getting him a bowl of cereal or lunch (maybe McDonald's)?

Dana will take Drew to dinner and stay overnight. Troy, check with her to see what time she'll be coming.

SUNDAY

Troy will check on Drew around noon to see if he's up and get him dressed, give him his morning meds, and a bowl of cereal or lunch.

Kim will come as soon as she has Saige situated with her sports commitment (maybe noon) and stay until I get home around 4ish.

I added sections about Buttercup and Midnight and taped a copy to the corner of my desk for handy reference. "Call me at any time for any reason," I said—the same conversation you would have with any babysitter.

January 15, 2018

My weekend writing retreat was the most relaxing, refreshing, renewing time I can remember since The Crue began meeting fifteen years ago. We laughed like crazy, gained tremendous insight from our workshops, enjoyed food and fellowship, and recaptured zeal for our writing. Most of all, I felt the Lord's presence and savored the word He gave me for 2018: *Restoration*. Following our final devotional, after each of us had prayed, I broke the silence by saying, "This is the first time I have felt this peaceful in three years."

All reports from the kids about Drew over the weekend were positive, so I felt relieved. I thought he handled the weekend without me very well, but I was premature in my evaluation. Little did I know there would be serious whiplash.

My first night home, Drew peppered me with questions throughout the night—all night long. He wanted to go home and asked where to find his shoes. I tried to get away with saying, "I'll get them for you in the morning," but he insisted. Finally, I mumbled, "By your chair."

January 16, 2018

The last time I looked at the clock was 6:00 a.m., and I vaguely remember hearing him say, "I hope you're having fun bullshitting me about where my shoes are."

A phone call woke me up at 8:10 a.m. I reached for the phone, but it stopped ringing. Then I heard Drew talking on the kitchen phone. I laid there listening and could tell he didn't know who he was talking to. Rubbing my eyes and fluffing my hair, I shuffled into the kitchen just as he hung up and turned quickly toward the living room. He was wearing his pants, shoes, and coat.

"You're up and dressed already? Where are you going?" I asked.

He whipped around and gasped. His eyes were wide. "Where'd you come from? I was going out to find you!"

All along, I'd been *right there in our bed*, but he had gotten used to Dana sleeping in the recliner for the past two nights and was so disoriented, he didn't see me. After fixing breakfast, I got him calmed down and thought things were returning to normal.

And then the next night came and catapulted us into a whole new realm.

Again, the questions were constant and went on for hours. I'd barely get back to sleep when he'd lean over me and ask where his shoes were so he could "go home." I stalled him time after time and said to get back in bed, but he kept appearing beside me. Somehow, during the badgering, I fell asleep—most likely from sheer exhaustion.

Around 1:30 in the morning, I awoke to Troy's voice. "Come quick! Dad's been outside." While I was sleeping, Drew had gone out in his pajamas and socks with no coat in twenty-nine-degree weather.

I raced to the living room and sank into the love seat next to Drew, where Troy had put him. I wrapped the fringed burgundy throw and my arms tightly around him and rubbed his icy hands. Troy took off his socks, went to get clean ones, and Drew's story poured out of him.

"I didn't know where you were," he said, "so I went looking for you. I tried to get in the car, but it was locked, and I couldn't find the key. *(Praise the Lord!)* I got turned around and didn't know where I was. Then I fell. I got up and fell again. I don't know how many times I fell. No one was there to help me. I didn't know where I was. I knocked on someone's door, and I could tell they were in there, but they wouldn't come."

I hugged him, rubbed his frozen fingers, and kissed his cheek.

He looked at me as though seeing me for the first time. "And here you are! It's a miracle! I went looking for you, and here you are! What are the odds that I would find you? Right here! So close."

So close, all right. I had been sleeping in the same bed with Drew when he got up and went outdoors to find me.

While putting clean, dry socks on Drew's feet, Troy said, "And then you came to my house, Dad. You knocked on my door, and I brought you home to Candy."

Afterward, Troy told me he hesitated to answer the door at that hour, but *something told him* it might be his dad. Thank the Lord that Drew managed to find Troy's house, and Troy answered the door! What his dad said to him is heartbreaking: "Please, sir, can you help me? I'm stuck in a bad dream and can't wake up. I hate to bother you, but is there any way you can help me find my way home?"

The trauma of this experience would be tempting to retell a hundred times, and in the retelling, I would relive the agony of it. So, I'll focus on my word for the year, *Restoration,* and trust that the Lord will guide us moment by moment and restore my peace.

Oh, and we'll be putting additional locks on the doors.

January 19, 2018

Drew kept a running barrage of questions going all night and kept getting up to walk around the house looking for something familiar. He finally fell asleep around 5:15 in the morning, and I did, too.

I tried to nap in the afternoon, but Drew kept the questions coming—questions on steroids—rapid-fire, constant repetition. I gave up on the nap and suggested we go out for an early dinner. In the restaurant, Drew picked at his salad and salmon. He looked pale and fragile, and I urged him to eat, but he said he wasn't hungry.

We went to Walmart afterward, and he said he didn't feel well. I took one look at him and rushed him to the men's room, where he got sick twice. I left the full cart in a corner and brought him home immediately. Troy came over to stay with him while I went back to retrieve the groceries. It's a good thing we're only six minutes away. He seemed fine when I got home and now has resumed his battery of questions. I hope we can sleep tonight.

He didn't get sick again. It happened once before, the same way—he looked queasy during dinner and ate very little, then vomited about a half-hour later. In both cases, we had eaten the same food, and I didn't get sick. I don't know whether to be relieved that this isn't a virus or concerned that it keeps recurring for no evident reason.

January 22, 2018

Last night we went to bed at 10:00 and Drew slept until 1:30 a.m. when he got up to go to the bathroom. He didn't know where it was, so I pointed him in the right direction and waited a few minutes. When I didn't hear anything, I got up and found him sitting on the toilet, which I thought was just fine. Until he asked me if it was okay to "go" there. He had found his way to the toilet, but his brain wouldn't tell his bladder that it was okay to pee.

"How do I do it?" he asked.

"Just relax and let the pee come out," was the best instruction I could come up with. After a few minutes, I turned the faucet on, thinking the sound of running water might prompt him. Nothing. He sat. I stood nearby. We waited. Still nothing.

And then, just as I was about to give up, the slightest trickle came out. Slowly, but surely, success.

When he finished, I took him by the elbow, walked him back to the bed, and tucked him in. He settled down nicely and slept soundly until morning.

I stared into the darkness for a long while feeling helpless and wondering what other parts of his body would forget how to function. How does that old gospel chorus go?

One day at a time, sweet Jesus,
That's all I'm askin' of You.
Just give me the strength
To do every day what I have to do.
Yesterday's gone, sweet Jesus.
And tomorrow may never be mine.
Lord, help me today, show me the way
One day at a time.

February 5, 2018

Today was just an ordinary day, but it included a happy incident that I will savor for the rest of my life. I was bent over the dishwasher, putting silverware in the drawer, when Drew quietly came and stood beside me. I noticed his legs and feet but didn't give his presence any real thought.

As I reached for a couple of spoons, he said in the sincerest voice, "You are the most precious thing I have in my life."

Never have I heard more beautiful words or seen such a loving look in his eyes. I straightened up, hugged him, and told him so. Then I grabbed a pen and notepad and wrote the exact words down so I would always remember.

The special moment was just that—a moment. A gem frozen in the memory of my life and one he wouldn't be able to retain. He meandered off to the bedroom to watch TV. I left the notepad on the bar in the kitchen, finished unloading the dishwasher, and went to my office.

About five minutes later, he interrupted my typing. "Did you write this?" he asked. "It says, 'You are the most precious thing I have in my life.'"

Before I swiveled around in my chair, I knew he was holding the notepad, and my heart gave a joyful lurch. "Yes, hon, I sure did write that. And every word of it is true." I took a breath. "And, you know what else? You said those very words to me not long ago."

"I did?"

"You did. And those words touched me as deeply as they touched you."

He folded the note and tucked it into his wallet.

March 6, 2018

While I was getting dressed for bed at 8:30 the night before last, Drew decided he needed to check the car to be sure it was locked. A few minutes later, he came wobbling into the bedroom, saying, "I fell—hard," and later, I found his smashed watch on the floor. I can't imagine him falling so hard he knocked the watch right off his arm. He has some bruises, but no other trauma that I could see.

I've been putting the Door Guardian on at bedtime (extra lock from Alzstore.org), but now I'll need to train myself to do it as soon as we come in from dinner. Tonight, I realized for the first time that his appetite is slipping. We ordered Chicken Marsala at Bella Capri, and the waitress brought the main dish while he was eating his salad.

"Another meal?" he asked. Then he refused to eat the meal claiming he was full.

I put one piece of chicken on his salad plate and cut it up, so at least he ate that much protein. An hour after we got home, I fixed a smoothie with spinach and banana for a snack, and he only drank a few sips. His clothes are beginning to look baggy. I'm going to stock up on Boost and get him to drink that instead of Coke.

March 14, 2018

We've had an upheaval. On Friday night, the 9th, I called for an ambulance at 2:00 a.m. because Drew's legs were almost useless, and he fell in the bathroom getting up from the toilet. When I got to Beebe Hospital around 2:30, the emergency room doctor had already lined up a battery of tests.

They needed a urine sample to test for a UTI, but he refused to use the urinal, so they inserted a Foley catheter. He hates those things! *(Who doesn't?)* Still feeling like he had to go, he kept trying to get up and I suddenly had a full-time job coaxing him to stay on the hospital bed. All the tests came back clear and negative, so they did a CT scan and found a small bleed in his brain.

A brain bleed?! Outwardly, I know I appeared calm as the doctor announced they would need to transfer Drew to Christiana Care Hospital by ambulance. Inwardly, I was green Jell-O.

Drew is a world-class worrier even on a good day. I knew he couldn't hear what the doctor and nurses were saying or comprehend the diagnosis, but it was clear to him that something was dreadfully wrong. His eyes were wild with panic as the EMTs wheeled him down the hallway.

I jogged alongside the stretcher saying soothing words and assuring him I'd be there as soon as I could. They loaded him into the ambulance, and I stood alone watching them drive off.

Shuffling my way to the car, the only sound I was aware of was my shoes scuffing the pavement. My thoughts reeled as I tried to digest what was happening. Cars passed me going home, and each time one breezed by, another question taunted me. *Who should I call first? What should I pack? What loose ends do I need to tie up? What's happening with Drew? Would he remember what I told him? Can Troy take care of Buttercup?* Too much to think about. Everything felt like it was in slow motion. I decided to give in to it and take my time. I couldn't wrap my head around what was happening.

Dana arrived at Christiana Care about fifteen minutes before I did, and Drew was in restraints when I walked in. The nurses said he kept asking for Candy and fighting to get out of bed, and they had to call security to wrestle him into submission. I caught a glimpse of him looking wild-eyed until he recognized me, and then he calmed down immediately.

"His arms and hands are strong," one nurse said. "He kept gripping our arms and throwing punches. I call him Steel Man."

Drew didn't appreciate the compliment. I guess it was a compliment.

Pam Halter lives about thirty-five minutes from the hospital and brought me peeled and cleaned shrimp, fresh pineapple chunks, and mandarin oranges, which I ate while she and I sat on a bench in the hallway. I didn't realize how much I needed her presence, her hugs, her lively conversation, and her food. What a godsend!

It was a rough few days. Saturday evening, as I was beginning to say my goodbyes and find a hotel, the second-shift nurse fairly begged me to stay overnight.

"If you're not here," she said, "it will be hard on all of us."

So, I slept two nights in a very uncomfortable recliner. Their attempts to soothe me with warm blankets and pillows didn't do much to prevent me from developing kinks in my back, neck, and hips. But the experience sure did give me a fresh appreciation for my own bed. Drew and I had both been awake from 1:30 a.m. on Saturday until midnight. What is that, twenty-two and a half hours? But we slept until around 7:00 a.m. on Sunday. The second night, we developed stuffy noses, finally got to sleep around 2:00 a.m., and the nurse woke us up at 5:00 to take his vitals. From then on, there was a steady stream of activity, so we had a total of three hours' sleep the entire weekend.

March 15, 2018

A physical therapy nurse came in and had me walk Drew down the hallway with a walker, up some "practice" stairs, and back to his room. He passed and qualified for discharge.

The hospital sent us home with a brand-new walker (covered by Medicare) that afternoon. I had no difficulty driving home, but within two hours of settling in, Drew fell again—softly, but enough to set off my alarm bells about what life will be like from now on. I was functioning on fumes for lack of sleep and was in no shape to face important decisions when we got home. I forced myself to focus.

The hospital sent a visiting nurse who met with me for three hours the day before in the hospital doing paperwork, and she'll come back again on Friday with another nurse who will check Drew out. Fortunately, I have a regularly scheduled appointment with Dr. Palekar, our primary care physician, later this week and can fill him in on everything.

Mary Jo from Delaware Hospice came tonight to sign Drew up for their Palliative Care program, which will allow a seamless transition into their lovely facility in Milford when the need eventually arises.

Doris, my dear friend, had planned to go to our Alzheimer's support group with me later tonight, but I was too exhausted to consider going and needed to be home to meet the Hospice nurse, so I asked Doris to come anyway and visit. She brought a new box of checkers for Drew and played a few rounds with him at the kitchen table while Dana and I talked in the dining room with Nurse Debra.

Debra asked me to have Dr. Palekar prescribe Palliative Care, and I'm planning to do that. I told her that Drew is wearing Depends briefs now because of his urgency to urinate. We're dealing with incontinence for the first time, and I bought flushable wet wipes for good measure.

Doctors say that the bleeding has already begun to absorb into his brain and should be completed in two to three weeks. They expect him to be able to regain some strength in his legs, but another fall and hitting his head could send him back to the hospital.

"You won again," I overheard Doris saying. What a comfort to have her entertaining him.

Our routine of eating out every night has taken a hit, but that's not a bad thing as I can control what we eat better than restaurant food with who-knows-what's in it. Hey, I'm pleased to report that I hit the 20-lb. weight-loss mark and am doing well with my eating plan.

Drew and I both developed runny noses and sneezing on Sunday night, and now we have full-blown colds on top of everything else.

The kids have been great filling the gaps, especially Troy (praise the Lord!), and I have friends pitching in with meals and Drew-sitting. I'll even be able to attend our writer's group on Saturday and go to lunch with them as usual because Dana insists.

My biggest fear is that Drew will get up in the night while I'm sleeping, so I ordered a bed alarm (a pressurized pad with a WiFi device). Hope it works.

In spite of all this, Drew's sweet disposition and sense of humor remain intact. And here's the silver lining: His repetitive questions have almost totally ceased. I don't have a clue how that happened or how long it will last, but it's giving me a wonderful reprieve.

"Circumstances
make a person neither strong nor weak—
they only show which he is."

— *Anonymous*

CHAPTER SEVEN

Caregiver Information Overload

March 15, 2018

The past few days, I've been living with *Caretaker Information Overload*, a phrase I just made up. I'll explain. Ready? Here we go:

On Tuesday, Debra, from Christiana Care Visiting Nurse Association, came to do the intake paperwork, which took a few hours.

Another visiting nurse, Susan, will be here tomorrow, and I'm supposed to mention to her that I'm interested in having someone help with Drew's care (bathing, dressing, toenails, etc.). Since this is a medical referral, I'm hoping that Medicare will cover this.

Kim Watkins, our social worker, came today to fill out paperwork and go over the services we were eligible for. It turns out that we have too much monthly income to qualify for most things, but I told her I'm interested in Meals on Wheels since our normal routine of going out to dinner every night has come to an abrupt halt. I plan on cooking, but it sure would be nice to have a meal delivered now and then that I didn't have to labor over. Besides, it does my heart good to see as many friendly faces as possible.

Kim gave me the number for a company that can install a railing for Drew's side of the bed as well as the contact information for the Delaware Dementia Respite Care program, which I hadn't considered before. This reminds me that I should probably step up my requests for Hospice volunteers and contact some of the friends on the list I've been building who've said, "Call me when you're ready for help."

I left Drew at the kitchen table just long enough to walk the social worker to the door, and when I got back, I found him on the floor. I asked if he hit his head, and he said no. Just as I pushed the chair out of the way and tried to figure out how to get him up, the doorbell rang.

"Oh, good," I said. "Stay put. Don't move. Whoever it is can help."

Kim had forgotten something (thank goodness), so I ushered her in, and in no time, we had Drew upright in the chair. Confirmation that I need help.

This afternoon, Lorna, the physical therapist, came to evaluate Drew. He was feisty with her, saying, "I can run faster than you, and I can fight better, too." She took it in stride while I sat there wondering where *that* came from. Lorna feels confident that PT will strengthen his legs so he'll be able to walk independently (without the walker). She'll work with him tomorrow to establish his exercise routine and come twice a week for four weeks.

He's been eating less and is losing weight, so the nurse suggested I give him small meals six times a day instead of three square meals. That's do-able.

Drew has been having difficulty swallowing his pills lately, so tonight I'll begin putting them in applesauce.

Speaking of applesauce, Doris and her husband, Donald, prepared a wonderfully healthy home-cooked chicken dinner and delivered it to us, artfully arranged. Doris knew what I'm eating these days and nailed it (no tempting grains, sugars, or dairy). She even includedg cloth napkins and a jar of *applesauce*. I was as excited about the applesauce as the rest of the meal.

"I haven't even had time to put it on my grocery list, and here it is!" I grinned. "He'll have no trouble taking his pills tonight."

Okay, back to the recommendations that Debra, Kim, and Lorna gave me:

- I picked up all the throw rugs that could present a hazard, but I need to be alert to other things like dog toys that may be in Drew's path.

- We already have a "right height" toilet in the master bathroom but may consider getting an elevated toilet seat with handles for the guest bath by my office. Drew sits with me while I'm working and will want to use that one.

- We have grab bars in our shower stall, but Lorna said I need to get a shower chair that has a backrest. This is the kind of thing that Social Services would have covered if our income was twenty-five hundred dollars a month or less. But Amazon Prime's 1-Click order button works for me.

- The hospital gave us a transfer gait belt, but it's woven and has a complicated fastener. The nurse suggested I look on Amazon for a quick-clean one with an easy buckle, and I found a red one that should work well.

- The wireless bed alarm and bed pad arrived today, so now I need Troy to help me figure out how to hook it up and where to position it under the fitted sheet.

- Another common-sense thing is lighting. There's no sense in stumbling around in the dark when I can flip a switch to see where we're going. I'm embarrassed to admit that these past few nights, I've been guiding him to and from the bathroom with his walker by only the glow of nightlights.

A week ago, I had no idea I'd be dealing with all of this, but I've known for some time that a fall can propel things to a whole new level in a hurry. My friend Hope reminded me of Isaiah 11:2 that refers to the Spirit of the Lord as *the Spirit of counsel and might,* and said, "May you know Him today by that name."

My head is spinning with all the new appointments and details I have to sort through on top of my already full responsibilities with household finances and my publishing business. But it is well with my soul because I know Who is in charge.

March 16, 2018

Drew is still stuffed up from his cold and can't learn how to blow his nose. He only knows how to sniff in. And he constantly has his finger up his nostril. Yuck. I rolled my eyes about that for a while, but when he kept digging, I got a flashlight and looked. It seems to me that he has a growth, so I asked Sharon, the visiting nurse, what she thought.

"Yes," she said, "that looks like a polyp to me. I'll need to follow up with an ENT doctor when Drew is strong enough to be out and about.

The ailments just keep coming. When I was a child and thought about what I wanted to be when I grew up, I had three standard answers: a ballerina, a teacher, and a nurse. Maybe this is as close as I get—dancing gracefully around Alzheimer's challenges as they pop up, giving lessons on how to solve unsolvable puzzles, and getting on-the-job training on front-line nursing. I changed my mind. I don't want to be a nurse. Too late. I am one.

March 19, 2018

The physical therapy is strengthening Drew's legs, and I no longer panic when I find he's walked halfway to the bathroom without his walker.

But the reprieve from his repetitive questioning appears to be short-lived because his previous pattern is back. I'm not sure if the brief period of mock-normalcy was helpful or not. His relapse into rapid-fire questioning hit me harder than when I was accustomed to it. *It is what it is*, I remind myself as I try to recapture the ease I felt before when I gave my autopilot answers.

Tonight, when I said, "The water's ready, let's get your shower," he balked.

"I'm fine. I don't need a shower."

Hmmm. Let's see. He got home from the hospital on the 10th, didn't bathe while he was there, and today's the 19th. "You're not fine," I said in my sweetest voice. "It's been more than a week, and sponge baths can only do so much."

"You go ahead. I'll get a shower tomorrow."

No. He wouldn't. I realize that some people with dementia get to the point of being stubborn about their hygiene, but for some reason, I didn't expect Drew to be one of them. Sure, I've had difficulty sneaking his favorite clothes away from him long enough to get them washed and back in time to help him get dressed. But now, here he is with his face set like flint telling me, "No shower!" My coaxing went unheeded except to make him more agitated with *every* approach I tried.

"Fine," I said in defeat and turned my back to him to make an ugly face. Before I could stop myself, I added, "Have it your way. But I'm not talking to you again until you get a shower." Did I really spit those words out at him? Oh, well, maybe *that* would work. At least it would give me an excuse not to answer his questions.

He slumped into his recliner, and I checked the temperature of the water that was still running in the shower. Then I remembered the last time I took a shower, I came out to find him looking all over the house for me. So, I went into the kitchen and wrote on the marker board, "I'm in the shower in the bathroom," and left it on the counter where he'd be sure to see it.

As the warm water streamed over my head and ran down my stiff neck, I let it soothe my raw emotions and pictured the stress floating down the drain with the soap suds. Just as I was beginning to feel truly relaxed, a hand yanked the shower curtain back and scared the bejeebers out of me!

"Oh, there you are!" Drew said.

In a flash of genius that countered my fright, I said, "Come on in, big boy; the water's fine." And, don't you know, he did! Drew doesn't respond well to being told what to do, but he's pretty cooperative when playfully asked to get naked together in the shower.

March 20, 2018

This is Drew's eighty-second birthday. Trevor, Jill, and Brooklynn came on Sunday with a cake and we sang Happy Birthday. I kept things quiet for him today with a home-cooked meal because he can't handle commotion and isn't strong enough yet to go to a restaurant.

What did I give him for his birthday? A baby monitor! With the tiny screen, I can see him from my office when he's in his recliner or the bed at the other end of the house.

With each card he opened, he'd ask whose birthday it was. "My birthday?" Followed by, "How old am I?"

"Eighty-two."

"Eighty-two? But I feel like a kid."

And every time I'd smile and say, "There's a lot of little boy in this man."

March 21, 2018

A couple of weeks ago, when Drew could barely stand up without keeling over, I told the social worker I would be interested in having a nurse's aide. Since then, he's been getting steadily stronger from physical therapy. I didn't realize that Christiana Care had arranged for a nurse's aide until a bright-eyed gal appeared on our doorstep at 11:30 a.m. and introduced herself. Drew had been sleeping but came into the kitchen when he heard the doorbell and our conversation.

"Oh," she said. "You must be Mr. Abbott. I'm Sharon, and I'm here to give you a bath!"

"No," he said. The look on his face was priceless. "I don't think so." He turned and hot-footed it back to the bedroom as fast as his wobbly legs would carry him.

And, in disbelief, I watched her follow him, and I trailed along behind her.

"No, you can't go back to bed," she said as he reached for the covers. "It's time for your bath."

"I can't?" he said. "Watch me."

As much as her boldness shocked me (especially having been through our shower episode two nights ago), I could only imagine how Drew felt. Here was a total stranger not only interrupting his sleepy morning routine but demanding that he allow her access to his naked body. Didn't she think about getting acquainted first and maybe take a tour of the bathroom?

"Um, excuse me, Sharon," I said when I managed to find my voice. "We need to have a little talk."

By the time I ushered her into the dining room, she had started to figure things out. "You weren't expecting me, were you?" she said.

"No, actually, I wasn't—and, as you can see, we're not quite ready for your help. I must have gotten the appointments confused because our visiting nurse is also named Sharon." I explained that I might have needed help in the beginning, but we were managing fine now that Drew's legs were stronger.

We agreed that one visit was sufficient, so Sharon made a note on her chart and told me she would cancel the other authorized visits. I thanked her, and she breezed out the door as cheerfully as she had come in. The whole thing took place in less than seven minutes.

Drew won't remember this when he wakes up, but I'll be snickering about it for a while. And when it comes time for a "stranger" to offer help with his hygiene, I'll be sure to request that we approach it with the tenderest of care.

March 31, 2018

Michele Fletcher is an angel. She came to the house today to cut Drew's hair instead of having him come to the salon. How many beauticians (barbers) make house calls these days?

April 2, 2018

Lorna came today for Drew's PT. While she filled out information on her computer, the three of us sat at the kitchen table, and Drew made faces at me, trying to get me to laugh. He would stick out his tongue, roll his eyes, scrunch up his mouth, and exaggerate a smile. I would look away each time, and when I turned my head in his direction, he would make another silly face. He has done this before, usually at Michele's salon when she has him in the chair, and he can see me from across the room. If she ever saw him do it, she never mentioned it. This time, Lorna caught him.

"Are you okay?" she asked.

Aha! The jig is up!

Drew blushed with an expression that looked exactly like a little boy caught with his hand in the cookie jar.

The laughter burst out of me like water breaking through a dam.

April 5, 2018

Well, Visiting Nurse Sharon's last day was Wednesday, and I'll miss her. In these few short weeks, we've become close friends.

Today, Lorna filled out her Christiana Care physical therapy discharge paperwork. Drew has shown amazing improvement, and it's going to be my responsibility from now on to do PT with him so we can guard against his risk of falling. The exercises are not hard, and I certainly need physical activity, too. I figure every other day should be just about right. After all, we bought a brand-new set of two-pound ankle weights and didn't want them to go to waste.

May 4, 2018

Buttercup is having some health problems, and it's up to me to figure out what to do. About a month ago, she ruptured a tendon in her hind leg. I knew surgery was out of the question because of the expense and the strain on an overweight dog, so I've been giving her Cosequin DS, and she seems to be improving.

Last night, I awoke to the sound of heavy, raspy breathing and a desperate-sounding moaning. She was lying in her bed, foaming at the mouth, twitching, drooling, and paddling all four legs. I approached her from behind and touched her back. She reared her head up and looked at me with panic in her eyes and bared teeth. For the first time, I was afraid of my sweet dog. It was over in about a minute.

When the seizure passed, I noticed she had urinated on her bed. She was disoriented and wobbly when she got up but followed me to the door to go out and wiggled her stub of a tail. Ah, my Buttercup is going to be okay. After getting some fresh air, we came in, and I filled her water bowl. She lapped it up and stretched out at my feet. When I moved to the bed, she moved to hers, which I had lined with bath towels. I'll do a deep cleaning tomorrow.

Settling into bed, with Buttercup on my left and Drew on my right, I was acutely aware of the absence of my husband's compassion, advice, and helping hands. During daylight hours, I have easy access to loving family, friends, and volunteers. But in the middle of the night, it's just God and me. But God is enough.

May 10, 2018

Drew and I ate on the deck tonight with perfect temperatures and a gentle breeze. I fixed leftover salmon from the Georgetown Family Restaurant, fresh broccoli/cauliflower in one of those microwavable steam bags, and a salad (which took the most time to chop everything up).

I'm enjoying cooking and controlling what goes into my mouth. I'm up to twenty minutes at a time on the elliptical machine and am feeling stronger and better able to help Drew because I'm "taking care of myself."

I'm trying to feed Drew six times a day because he only nibbles and is losing weight. Loss of appetite seems to be one of the steps that take place with dementia. I had to buy him new pants that are two inches smaller, and he wears medium shirts instead of large. He looks very handsome!

His legs are getting weaker again despite the physical therapy we're doing three days a week, but he can still get around if I hold onto him and keep him from moving too fast.

Last night I accompanied him to the bathroom at 2:00 a.m. because he didn't know where it was. When he got through the doorway, he didn't know which way to turn and then pointed to the shower and asked, "Do I go here?" This is a new turn of events and probably an inkling of things to come. He needs help getting dressed now but can still button his shirt after I get it on him. Did I mention that he wears Depends all the time now?

June 22, 2018

I've been out of commission for two weeks. On June 6th, I had a dental implant, and on the 8th began experiencing achiness from head to toe. I called the oral surgeon and asked the receptionist to relay my symptoms to the doctor and have him call me. She said what I described couldn't possibly be related to the dental work, and I took her word for it.

Over the weekend, my aching morphed into excruciating, shooting pain in my head like someone stabbing my ears with an ice pick with ten seconds of relief between spasms. I am too tough for my own good and didn't seek help until Monday when I went to the clinic. They sent me by ambulance to the ER, where they did a CT scan that showed a tiny meningioma (benign tumor, like the one that triggered Drew's Alzheimer's). They did an MRI to be sure and told me it wasn't the cause of my pain and is so minuscule it should never be a problem. I had total support all day. Dana followed the ambulance, Kim and Wyatt came to the ER around 3:00, while Troy and Doris stayed with Drew.

The PA at the hospital diagnosed me as having a migraine and sent me home with a prescription for an injection they promised would give me immediate relief. Kim helped me figure out the syringe, and I took the shot at nine. By 12:30, I felt *worse* and wished someone would go ahead and cut off my head, which was jerking violently from right to left and then from left to right. Although I was so weak I could hardly put one foot in front of the other, I lugged Drew's shower chair from the far end of the house and put it in our shower where I let the hot water run over me until it ran cold. I felt a little relief by then and took two Tylenol, two Excedrin Migraine, and the ibuprofen that the dentist had given me. Tossing and turning with exhaustion, I managed to get a little sleep.

I don't remember how I got through Sunday, because I was still hurting like crazy, and that's the day Drew decided he didn't know me or where he was. He needed to "go home." While I was trying to nap on the couch, he went outside and attempted to get into the car but couldn't. Our neighbors watched him for a while and then brought him inside the house. It didn't take long before he started the same running monologue.

Around 10:30, I decided to take him for a ride so he could see he was in Georgetown and give me turn-by-turn directions to "his house." He was in his pajamas but insisted on taking his wallet with him, and I didn't have the strength to argue with him. We drove to The Circle downtown, which he recognized, and he directed me back to our driveway, thanked me politely, and let himself into the house. I sat in the car for a few minutes savoring the solitude. When I opened the door, he was sitting in the living room. "Hi, hon," I said. "I'm here to fix your breakfast." He nodded and waved me in. I took a big breath, trying not to let him see me grimace from the pain.

By nightfall, he reached into his back pocket and asked, "Where's my money?" I waved to the desk in the bedroom, and he said, "It's not there."

So, I dragged myself out of the recliner and got up to find it in one of the usual places he would have put his wallet. It had vanished. For four days, I heard the same questions about his missing money, and I gave him my stock answer, "You lost it on Sunday." I was beginning to think I needed to apply for a new Medicare card, etc., but on Thursday night, as I was getting ready to wash my face, I saw a brown lump on top of the bars of soap in the linen closet. *Could it be? YES! It was his wallet! Ahh, one less thing to worry about.*

For some mindless activity when I couldn't think, I binged on TV movies. In one of them, *Bridge of Spies*, an international prisoner (Mark Rylance) who was being exchanged for another spy maintained a deadpan but pleasant expression no matter the circumstances. About four or five times when things looked like all hope would be dashed, his lawyer (Tom Hanks) asked, "Aren't you worried?" Every time, the prisoner would appear unruffled and say, "Would it help?"

Those three words, *Would it help?* were fresh in my mind on Monday morning, when Kim picked me up for my appointment with Dr. Palekar.

On top of the debilitating pain, he discovered I was in full-blown A-fib. My pulse was 120/140, so he called my cardiologist who took me off one medicine, doubled another, and added Digoxin. I was in too much discomfort to talk, so Kim explained all I had been through and mentioned the dental implant. She asked if the tooth could have been the culprit.

"Absolutely," he said. "No wonder the migraine medicine didn't work." Dr. Palekar added another medicine to help me relax and said to schedule an appointment with the cardiologist and a neurologist (to have six-month MRIs to monitor the meningioma.)

When I had my follow-up appointment with the oral surgeon,

I told him the whole story, and he said it was definitely the tooth ("mandible something-or-other") and apologized profusely for his receptionist who was in training (the part about "never giving any medical advice" must not have registered). Next time, I will insist on talking with the doctor!

I saw the cardiologist today, and my heart is in PERFECT RHYTHM! Praise God! He ordered an ECHO for follow-up. If the A-Fib shows up again, we can either change medication or consider a cardiac ablation like I had in 2015.

I still have to make an appointment with the neurologist, but Dr. Palekar said he could guarantee 110% that my meningioma is slow-growing, and I won't live long enough for it to need attention.

Now that I'm feeling better, I have two weeks of emails to wade through and backlogged work, bills, and sundry stuff yelling at me for attention. I will pace myself and stop when I'm tired. And, as I promised our kids, I will follow up with Delaware Hospice and their Transitions and Palliative Care services as soon as I can.

July 8, 2018

For a month, I haven't been able to do much except the bare necessities. My energy is just now coming back, and I'm overwhelmed by all the things that are jumping off my desk, shouting, "DO ME!" It's taking all the self-control I can muster to focus on one thing at a time.

Drew's preoccupation with "going home" is wearing thin. Today, when he replayed the same mantra, a voice came out of me that sounded like Alice Kramden from *The Honeymooners*, "Awww, cut it out!" which shocked both of us. Drew was genuinely puzzled, and I couldn't believe I had said out loud what my inner self thought.

Unable to explain what "cut it out" meant, I told him the truth instead of nursing his denial and giving him my usual spiel.

"You have a disease called Alzheimer's," I said very matter-of-factly, "and it steals your memory. Every day you want to 'go home' because you don't recognize *this* is your home. You were awake from twelve-thirty until six-thirty this morning, insisting that we had to 'go home' because you thought this was a house you were appraising, and the owners would come home and find us in their bed." Visions of Goldilocks danced in my head. That explanation registered, and we had a good heart-to-heart talk. But that only lasted five minutes before he said, "So are you ready to go home now?"

July 9, 2018

Dana came to stay with her dad tonight while I went to the support group, and she said he was talkative and entertaining. As they sat together looking out the back door, Drew said, "If you walk outside, there's chicken pops, and they go boom, boom, boom."

Then they moved onto the deck and sat in the rocking chairs. "If you're walking down the road and four men are walking toward you, just smile and be nice because they might want to give you some food."

"Life is hard, Dad."

"Yeah," he agreed. "But it can be fun, too."

He chuckled.

What's so funny?" she asked.

"Pickle snickle," he said, and laughed harder.

Later, after they moved to the living room, Drew became agitated and began voicing his usual concern about going home. He informed her that he had to leave, and Dana countered it perfectly. "You can't leave, Dad, because I promised Candy you'd be right here when she got back."

"Oh," he said. "You promised? And Candy's going to look for us right here?"

"Yes. This is where she'll be looking for you. And if you're not here, she won't know where to find you."

"Okay, then, if you promised. I'd better not go anywhere!" From that moment on, he was content.

Oh, I don't want to forget to share a helpful acrostic (Q-TIP), I learned tonight from the group leader that I'm sure will come in handy:

Quit
Taking
It
Personally

"To ignore an insult
is the true test
of moral courage."

— *Author Unknown*

CHAPTER EIGHT

Adapting to the New Drew

July 10, 2018

Lots of things have changed in the past four or five or six months, and I've been remiss in recording them, so I'll try to catch up with a bulleted list:

- I filled out an application for a handicap permit to hang from my rear-view mirror, had Drew's neurologist authorize it, and finally got to the Division of Motor Vehicles to pick it up. The first time I used it, Drew went with me to BJs, and his legs got so weak as we were walking in those aisles, he could barely put one foot in front of the other. I told him to wait outside by the shopping carts while I dashed to the car a few yards away. As I was backing out of the parking space, I noticed a "helpful lady" taking Drew by the arm and trying to get him to take a few steps. I caught her eye as Drew pointed to me, and I could tell she realized she had made a mistake, so she patted him on the shoulder and disappeared into the store. Previously, I would leave Drew alone in the car with the heater or air conditioning on while I ran into Walmart to pick up a few things, but I read that you should *never* leave an Alzheimer's patient alone in a running car. I think my best bet is to leave him home.

- He still wants to help but is too unsteady for me to let him. When I got home from the grocery store last time, he came to the car to help unload the trunk, and I told him, "Your job is to hold the door open for me." That worked for a while. But I put the bags on the love seat in the living room to get more, and when I came back, Drew wasn't at the door. Instead, he was trying to carry bags to the kitchen. Fortunately, I got there in time to catch him as he fell into the love seat with both bags. "Oops," I said as I helped him up. "It looks like you need to get back to your post on door duty!"

- I ordered an identification bracelet for Drew engraved with his name, our phone number, and "memory impaired." I hope we don't have any more issues with his wandering off, but at least this will give him some way to find his way back to me if it does. He wore it without complaint for the first few days and then took it off during the night (which is when he might wander). Since then, he has refused to wear it. Oh me, oh my. I waited an hour and slipped it back on his wrist, and—so far—it's still there.

- Drew is increasingly bothered by the slightest breeze, and I have a ceiling fan in my office that keeps me comfortable while I work. He sits with me and fusses about "the wind." Instead of turning it off (not everything is about *him*), I said, "How about if I get you a blanket?" He shook his head. "A sweater?" Nope. "Earmuffs?" He laughed and didn't whine again about the fan.

- Troy is so faithful about shaving Drew every other day. After he left yesterday, Drew asked, "Why does that man like to do that?" I smiled, and a wave of sadness washed over me. "That man is your son. He does it because he loves you."

- It's not uncommon for Drew to say, "My dad is still living, right?" or "I haven't seen my mom lately." His dad died in 1968 and his mom in 1985. He handles this news well when I break it to him, but I understand it's better not to confront dementia patients with the truth because some grieve as if it just happened.

- At first, Drew's Depends were dry most of the time, but his incontinence is becoming more of an issue now as I have to offer "fresh underwear" at least twice during the day. Sometimes he takes off his pajama bottoms and briefs during the night because I'll find them hidden under the bed. So far, he still handles bowel movements on his own, so I'm thankful for that, but he rarely remembers to flush the toilet. I guess that puts me on round-the-clock yellow water lookout duty.

- He can no longer dress himself. A few months ago, I could lay his clothes on the bed and come back to find him dressed. He still fastens buttons and ties his shoes, but he needs help figuring out that the pants go on his legs and the sleeves of his shirt are for his arms.

- He can still brush his teeth, but I must put the toothpaste on the brush and hand it to him. He doesn't know what to do with it when he's finished brushing, so I make sure I hang around long enough to put it in the toothbrush holder.

- He doesn't want to do his physical therapy exercises anymore, and I don't have the energy to insist, so his legs are getting weaker. I've learned to instruct him every time we approach steps to put both feet on each step before going to the next. I wrap my arm in his to steady him while he goes to the car and say something like, "I just love being close to you like this."

- Six months ago, he only needed my help cutting steak or other meat. Now, I routinely cut up even soft food like his egg on half a slice of toast.

- He continues to lose weight because he'll eat a few bites and say he's full.

- One morning, he awoke distressed, mumbling about "parking cockeyed," and I told him it was just a dream. That was before

I found the chair by the desk on his side of the bed turned completely around. He must have grabbed the back of the chair and tried to "steer" it into place. I can only imagine how much he struggled with that while I was sleeping.

- After months of having to retrieve the daily paper from the front yard without having him even glance at it, I canceled our subscription. And don't you know, one day out of the blue, he remembered his former routine and went outside to "see if the paper is here." Of course, it wasn't, but by the time he came back in, he didn't remember why he went outside.

- He doesn't know the difference between the phone and the remote or how to use either one. To him, the television is a radio.

- For a while, I was able to give Drew his pills with applesauce, but he tired of that and balked. At this point, he opens his mouth like a baby bird, and I place a few pills at a time on his tongue and put a glass of water in his hand. If I don't do that, he will try to chew the pills. Yuck!

- TV no longer holds his interest, but the westerns channel (*Bonanza, Gunsmoke, Little House on the Prairie*) and some lighthearted sitcoms like *Everybody Loves Raymond* and *Golden Girls* have sparked a laugh or two. Many times, Drew will nap with the TV on and is content to sit in a room with no entertainment. I grapple with the need to expose him to more stimulation and activity, but he is unsteady on his feet, so even a slow walk is dangerous. He used to enjoy checkers but isn't interested now. Besides, planning activities seems like one more chore than I can handle. I console myself that he's content. The best I can do is take him for a drive each day, which gets him out of the house and provides a change of scenery.

- One thing that hasn't changed is Drew's gratitude. He still says, "thank you" for the small things, like when I give him a cup of coffee, water, or a sandwich.

- I'm grateful he's still here at home so I can wrap my arms around his shoulders and give him spontaneous hugs whenever I like. Those tender touches help him maintain a sense of security and belonging as well as provide a cheerful, loving atmosphere. This much I know: each hug helps *ME!* I'm glad he still responds well to my show of affection, and his kisses are just as sweet as ever. Almost always, he'll ask for more because he doesn't remember the first one. Fine with me!

- The other day, Pandora radio played a slow song that reminded me of when we first met, so I started swaying back and forth in the kitchen with my arms around an invisible person. I motioned for him to join me, and he stood up and wobbled his way toward me. For about ninety seconds, we held one another and danced just like old times; suddenly he'd had enough, but it was nice while it lasted.

- Over the past six months, the desire for sex has diminished in both of us. This came about without any discussion. It's as though we're tuned into the rhythm of one another's bodies and instinctively "know" these things. He's still playful, though, and pinches my butt when I walk by. "Naughty boy," I wink and say as I keep moving toward the other room. We may not be having intercourse, but our intimacy for one another hasn't diminished one iota.

July 17, 2018

I finally got beyond my procrastination and called Delaware Hospice. The time had come for me to avail myself of its many services. And how responsive they were!

On Monday, Karen came to process the intake papers. She assessed Drew's condition, went over the details of how things work, and got approval from the Hospice doctor to include Drew in the full program. Because of our involvement with their Transitions program, I already had a good idea of what Delaware Hospice offers. The overview assured me that all would be well at each stage.

Before Karen left, she put in motion a lot of follow-ups.

On Tuesday, we had a get-acquainted visit from Marjorie, the Hospice chaplain. She'll be coming to us once a month or as needed. As she was about to leave, Fed Ex delivered Drew's "Comfort Pak," and she reiterated that I should keep it refrigerated. This is a kit primarily for emergencies or end-of-life issues, which fast-forwarded me into thinking of things that lie ahead. *Scarlett O'Hara, anyone?* "I can't think about that right now. I'll think about that tomorrow." For now, the box is safely stored in the refrigerator.

On Thursday, Drew's new Certified Nursing Assistant (CNA), Ella, came in the morning. She serves as the Hospice aide to ease the pressure for both of us, and she'll be here every Tuesday and Thursday.

Tom Beach, the Hospice volunteer, stayed with Drew this afternoon while I went to my pulmonary appointment. He has a wonderful, outgoing personality, and things got off to a good start as long as I was present to answer questions when Drew hesitated. Tom asked what his favorite music was, and Drew said, "As long as it's pretty." When I announced it was time for me to leave for my appointment, I thought they were getting along famously.

But when I got home, both Drew and Tom were strangely silent, and their body language was tense. Tom told me that, in his attempt to get acquainted, he asked questions that Drew couldn't answer.

Drew had some questions for *him*: "Why do you want to know?" "Why are you prying?" and "Why are you here?" Tom responded that he wanted to be his friend. Drew said he didn't need any friends, and it went downhill from there.

But, good sport that he is, Tom agreed to try again next week when I have another appointment. Fingers crossed.

Tomorrow, nurse Candace will stop by, and I was told to expect weekly nursing visits after that. This is a big step for Drew to have so many "strangers" in the house, but at least they don't come all at once, so there is very little commotion.

I thought it would be hard for me to keep track of all the people coming and going, but Hospice made it easy. Each one has been gentle and caring, and they approach their work with such grace that there are no hard edges. I will read the Delaware Hospice handbook that explains all the details about who does what.

July 18, 2018

Last November, the cardiologist reviewed Drew's lab work, and everything was normal. We talked about the heart valve he had replaced eight years ago with a life expectancy of about ten years, so they recommended a nuclear stress test. I scheduled the appointment but had an uneasy feeling.

What if the stress of the test triggered the very catastrophic event it was designed to prevent? What if the test showed he *needed* a new aortic valve? Would I subject him to invasive surgery when I know that the trauma of it (and anesthesia alone) could cause a person with dementia to spiral downward? Would he come out of surgery combative? I always said the only reason I would put him in a nursing home is if he became a threat to me, to himself, or others. Would he even survive the surgery?

I talked it over with the kids, and it was unanimous that Drew's comfort and quality of life was our top priority. I canceled the nuclear stress test and may do the same with some of his other doctors' appointments as it is getting more and more difficult to get him out and about. Did we make the "right decision"? I don't know, but we talked it through, and all four of us agreed with no reservations.

So, when I was asked if we wanted "DNR" status (Do Not Resuscitate), which means no CPR would be administered in the event of heart failure, I was prepared. Still, I had to steel myself against the normal reaction to do everything possible to prolong life. In our case, medical intervention could prove to be unkind to us all, especially Drew.

The greatest takeaway I got from my meetings with those who came was to "call Delaware Hospice first," not 911.

July 19, 2018

Now, about Ella and Drew's first experience with a stranger in the bathroom while he's buck naked—or is it "butt naked"? According to Google, both are correct. Either way, this is about as vulnerable as a person can get, and I wondered if he would be able to turn the other cheek *(tee-hee)*.

Unlike the enthusiastic aide in March who burst in and announced, "I'm here to give you a bath," Ella eased into the topic after giving Drew time to become familiar with her. She is not only a beautiful woman but has such a kind servant's heart.

Of course, Drew was resistant to the idea.

We talked while he slowly finished his breakfast, and she acknowledged his hesitation, not pressuring him in the least. I realized that if today came and went without Drew bathing, it would be up to me to handle it alone again. So, I eased out of the kitchen chair and slipped into the bathroom, where I turned on the shower.

"It'll take a minute for the water to get hot," I matter-of-factly announced when I came back to the table.

Drew finished his breakfast, and I cleared the table while Ella and Drew continued to chat. And then came the moment of truth. I checked the water. Perfect temperature. Could we do this?

I guided Drew to the bathroom, and he followed my lead without complaint. "Here," I said. "Touch the water to be sure it's not too hot or too cold."

He did. It was just right. And then, without coaching, he began disrobing while Ella stood by the door. He expressed concern about a stranger watching him, so she stepped back until he got into the shower. After Drew was standing beneath the running water, she returned to stand quietly in the wings. I didn't think Drew knew she was there until I handed the soap to him, and he said, "Are there any other people out there you want to invite in for the show?"

Ella and I laughed, not only at the humor but from relief that he was doing this!

Drew was on a roll. "Maybe you want to go out front and see how many neighbors you can round up. Maybe you want to charge admission."

Suddenly, his humor broke through into clarity and transformed his brain fog and my trepidation into laughter.

Drew allowed Ella to dry him off and get him dressed from that point on. Because of the slow and gentle introduction and Ella's explanation that "we don't want you to fall," it was a positive experience, and I'm hoping he will begin to look forward to the care she provides for him. I know *I'm* already looking forward to the relief she provides for me.

July 23, 2018

Tom is coming at 10:15 this morning to stay with Drew while I go for an ECHO test. I'll leave while Drew is sleeping, but he's bound to wake up before I get back and will no doubt be alarmed to find a man in the house! What to do? Trust Tom to explain? Write a note? What would I write?

I sat quietly and presented the dilemma and my many questions to the Holy Spirit. Within seconds, the solution flashed in my mind. Drew is accustomed to having my publishing clients come to see me. Tom can be one of them. In my mind's eye, words for the note came, as surely as if I had already written them. I jumped up, hurried to the kitchen to get the marker board, and wrote: "Drew, I asked Tom to wait here until I get back. Please make him feel at home."

I thought about explaining the publishing part in the note but felt the Lord had given me those specific words, so I explained my plan to Tom and let him elaborate to Drew.

The Outcome: I arrived home at noon to find Tom and Drew in the living room in the same seats as last time, but the mood was much brighter. Tom said he'd had a chance to do some reading and thought "the publishing arrangement" would work out well. We chatted about how heavy traffic is in Sussex County this time of year, which led to stories about speeding tickets and kind police officers who issued warnings. Drew didn't say much but seemed engaged. After about fifteen minutes, Tom and I compared notes about our next appointment, and he left.

Before Drew could pepper me with questions about our visitor, I said, "Okay, let's move to the kitchen, and I'll get our breakfast. How about some nice eggs and toast?" And that was that.

July 26, 2018

On Tuesday, when Ella came, I waited until she was almost at the door before I told Drew. As I moved toward the living room with him following behind me, I said, "Your nurse's aide will be here any minute to help you get your shower. Oh, look! She's here now!"

This time, he was fully receptive. When she said, "I'm here to get you ready for the day," *he took her hand* and let her lead him to the bathroom. I paced around as I gathered his clothes, expecting to be needed, but there were zero awkward moments. This seems like a miracle to me.

Today, I was hoping for something similar. Instead, Drew greeted her with distrust when he heard the word "shower." Although he complied with all her instructions, he was reluctant and kept saying that this would be the "last time." She just kept doing the next step, talking in soothing tones as she dressed him, helped him brush his teeth, and guided him to the living room where he sat on the couch. Before leaving, she leaned toward him and said, "Mr. Abbott, you know what? I enjoyed it," and he responded, "I did, too."

August 2, 2018

During most of our marriage, Drew and I have had stimulating conversations, and he has always had words of wisdom for any situation, even if he could only conclude that a problem was "an unsolvable puzzle." But it's difficult now to find anything meaningful or satisfying to talk about over dinner. Instead of fulfillment, frustration builds in me from the repetition until I want to scream and run from the table. Mostly, we sit in silence while we eat.

Tonight, an idea flashed through my mind. Instead of asking him questions about things he wouldn't be able to answer, I presented hypothetical questions to see what would happen. Winner! He thought long and hard about each one and stayed fully engaged. Here's how it went:

"If you could have any job in the world, what would it be?"

"To go out in the yard and collect hundred-dollar bills. My day's work would be over when I had all I could carry. And then I'd have to do it again the next day."

"If you had all the money you needed and could travel anywhere in the world, where would you go?"

"That's a hard one. What are my options?"

"You could go to a tropical island, to Europe, to Canada, or anywhere in the United States—California, Florida, New England, the Midwest— anywhere."

"Somewhere in the United States," he said. "I would be content going to the beach. We could get in the car and ride down to Selbyville."

I laughed. There is no beach in Selbyville, but it's a short drive to Fenwick Island and Ocean City, and both are familiar to him.

I was on a roll, so I asked another question: "If Jesus sat down and joined us here for dinner, what do you think He would talk about?"

"First of all," Drew said, "I want to say how much I appreciate you as a couple." *Was he speaking as Jesus?* "You treat each other the way it should be." *He was!* "And for people who don't, they should try to get that way."

Now, that gave me holy goosebumps and a glimpse into the appreciation he feels for what we have.

August 4, 2018

I've been reading a lot lately—novels, caregiver non-fiction, devotionals, and end-time prophecy books. This morning, I read an overview of how this generation is witnessing a convergence of all the global symptoms that the Bible predicts will happen before Jesus returns.

Last month, when Marge visited, she asked us if we had any spiritual goals, and my immediate reaction was, "To be raptured!" Drew said, "To know Jesus is with me all the time."

So, in light of nuclear saber-rattling, cataclysmic events, civil unrest, government corruption, and threats of terrorism worldwide, I am comforted by the fact that the Lord is close to us, and we are safe in Him, regardless of the chaos around us. In our little world in Georgetown, despite Drew's advancing Alzheimer's symptoms and the increasing demands on me, I can still choose to fill our surroundings with peace.

I closed the book, connected our Bluetooth speaker to my Kindle, and played the Andrea Bocelli station on Pandora radio. Then I joined Drew at the kitchen table where we lingered over freshly brewed coffee. I grappled with whether to share with him the state of the world and decided I would because this moment of tranquility provided a remarkable contrast. He comprehended it, and our appreciation for the oasis we shared was all the sweeter. I basked in his clarity of mind and ability to recognize how blessed we are. For the next hour, he didn't ask, "Who are you?" "Where are we?" or pester me to pack because we needed to "go home."

August 14, 2018

At last night's support group, I was reminded of a fabulous resource: Teepa Snow and her instructional videos on YouTube.com for caregivers of people with dementia. The tutorials helped me immensely when Drew was in the beginning stages of Alzheimer's, but I hadn't thought of them in a while. Drew and I are both in a different state of mind now that the disease has progressed, and Teepa has clips that provide different techniques that I can apply right away.

Her video "Living at Home with Mid- to Late-Stage Dementia" demonstrates how to turn making peanut butter and jelly sandwiches into an activity I can share with Drew so he feels involved, giving him a sense of satisfaction.

"Calming and Comforting a Person Living with Dementia" is a short, powerful role-play video that shows how to console someone who becomes agitated and is in distress.

For more extreme cases, "Ten Ways to De-escalate a Crisis" through effective communication provides valuable instruction of what to do when a patient is anxious and gets out of control (screaming, hitting, scratching, throwing things, terrified, etc.). I haven't experienced this yet (and hopefully never will) but watching this video has prepared me in advance to handle this sort of behavior effectively. Telling the panicked person to calm down (our natural tendency) doesn't register with a person who has Alzheimer's and may feel threatened. Instead, Teepa shows how to:

Remove the threat	Breathe in sync
Create space	Calm the voice
Be on his/her side	Relax the body
Get at or below eye level	Attend to needs
Use hand under hand	Be willing to go where s/he is

August 21, 2018

Every morning, Drew comments on what a nice backyard we have, and the conversation usually results in my having to get the deed to prove we own the house and yard. Today, it took a different twist.

DREW:	That's a nice backyard. Who owns it?
CANDY:	We do.
DREW:	We do?
CANDY:	We *do*. You've owned it for sixty-three years.
DREW:	Who owned it before?
CANDY:	I don't know.
DREW:	So, you don't know who owned it?
CANDY:	That's right. I have no idea.
DREW:	Who is that?
CANDY:	I have no idea.
DREW:	I know.
CANDY:	Well, if you know, why don't you tell me?
DREW:	I don't know.

Ha! He didn't get it when I switched gears, but I had fun with our version of Abbott and Costello's "Who's on First? (What's on Second, I Don't Know Who's on Third)."

For some time now, I've been aware that it's not *the quality* of what Drew does that matters but that he's involved in *the doing*. If he is content, engaged, and willing to do what I encourage him to do, I consider that a success. It gives me pleasure to see him make an effort, and the words, "Good job!" often pop out of me. At this point, we're moving into more passive activities like listening to music together or taking a drive.

He can still move the wet clothes from the washer into the dryer and take the dry ones out but needs guidance with every step. I've stopped asking him to push the buttons because explaining got to be tedious for me. But we still do the laundry together. Being his ornery self, it's not uncommon for Drew to pull my underpants from the dryer, toss them on his head, and ask with a silly grin, "Is this where I'm supposed to put these?"

I say, "Of course," and we laugh. His playfulness is as important to our day as getting the laundry where it belongs.

Every day, if things are silent for too long, Drew will fill the void by singing—usually, a few lines of "I'm Gonna Sit Right Down and Write Myself a Letter," "Only You," or "Happy Trails." And I know that before I close the blinds at night, he will chant at least four or five times, "Eenie Meenie Miney Mo, catch a bullfrog by the toe; if he hollers, let him go." He always recites the whole thing.

It dawned on me that I'm more relaxed now than a year or two ago when I was preoccupied with fitting all his jobs and mine into my schedule. Somehow, there *are* enough hours in a day, after all. It's funny how tasks move along more quickly when I'm intentional about giving up the things that cause me stress and frustration. I've learned to be quick about saying no to things that I used to try to say yes to because I felt I *should*. "Shoulds," "musts," "have to's," and "oughts" don't fit in with my plans to take care of myself. Besides, God's got this.

September 19, 2018

I ran some errands while Drew was sleeping and left him alone for ten to fifteen minutes. Just in case he got up before I got back, I filled his cereal bowl with Raisin Bran, sprinkled it with sugar, and put his pills and a glass of water on the table. I suspected he might pour the water on his cereal, so I put a note under his spoon, "Your milk is in the refrigerator." Feeling pleased that I'm learning to anticipate things that can go wrong, I strolled out the door and to the bank and post office.

By the time I got home, Drew was sitting at the kitchen table eating his cereal. Before I got close enough to look inside his bowl, I noticed an empty Coke bottle in front of him. Sure enough, he had poured soda over his cereal and was happily munching away on the last few bites. Hmm. Either his taste buds have changed so he doesn't know the difference between Coke and milk, or he's testing a new flavor sensation to see if it'll take off.

The thing the devil thought
would break you
is the thing God knew
would make you.

— *Facebook*

CHAPTER NINE

Big, Big Trouble

October 5, 2018

It's 10:15, and I'm sitting alone in a booth at the Georgetown Family Restaurant, having scrambled eggs, crispy bacon, coffee, and water. Tom volunteered to come to stay with Drew for a few hours every Friday morning. That way, I could have some consistent, predictable "Candy time."

I haven't been able to write for a while, so I brought my laptop with me to catch up a bit. Several things have transpired that warrant recording:

Sleepless Nights/Rehoboth

Drew went through a spell with insomnia and motor-mouth. It was like he became a wind-up toy with no off button. I tried everything to get him to settle down, including begging him to be quiet so we could get some sleep.

"Okay," he agreed. "I'll be quiet." And two seconds later, "Just one more question," which led to another and another. He had forgotten his promise to be quiet. After two nights of perpetual questions and no daytime naps, he gave me a clue as to what the root problem may be.

"I've worked hard all day," he said, "and I need to get out of here."

"Where would you like to go?" I asked.

He answered right away, "Rehoboth."

Aha! He needs a change of scenery! With Drew's legs getting weaker and being more unsteady on his feet, we've been eating at home more often and going out for dinner only one or two nights a week, so he's been cooped up in the house.

I picked up my purse. "Okay, let's go!"

"Where are we going?"

"To Rehoboth."

"What a great idea!" He beamed. "You won't believe this, but I was just thinking about Rehoboth."

I smiled and allowed myself to take the credit. "Imagine that. What a coincidence."

He hasn't been using his walker. (He likes to "park" it). On a whim, I put it in the back seat of the car, then went back to guide him by the arm to the passenger seat. After helping him lift his legs to get in and reminding him to scoot his bottom over to get centered, I reached over him to put his seat belt on, and off we went to Rehoboth Beach.

As we approached the Avenue, he kept saying, "I haven't been here in years. Everything looks so much better than I remember."

I parked in front of Nicola's and helped Drew into the restaurant. I've learned to choose a table near the door so he won't have to walk too far, and we got a window seat. As he gazed at the cars driving by, he was alert and bright-eyed. His conversation was the usual repetition but more energized.

The weather was ideal with a balmy breeze and sunny skies. After dinner, I didn't want our outing to end, so I drove between the Boardwalk Plaza and Atlantic Sands. I put the walker by his car door when he got out, and he grabbed the handles without complaint. It was a short, downhill walk to the boardwalk, and he navigated just fine. Since it was after the season, there were very few people around, so we had the beach all to ourselves. We sat on a bench for a while and enjoyed each other. He filled my soul with sweet words of appreciation, and I knew they were genuine, that he was lucid. For this moment, I had my Drew back. I basked in it and tried to commit it to memory.

"This is the best day of my life," he said, echoing my thoughts. I put my head on his shoulder, and we savored each other's presence.

Wet Rot

Two years ago, I knew the joists under our house were wet-rotted, and the foundation needed attention. After agonizing and considering the extensive disruption of our household the repairs would cause, I concluded that the house was still standing, and Drew's emotional state was too delicate to handle the chaos. So, I turned a blind eye to the problem and fixed my attention on other pressing matters.

Meanwhile, the house has continued to sink, and a black/brown fungus keeps creeping up around the base of the toilet in the guest bathroom. I had to remove the welcome mat from the front porch because the door scraped, preventing it from opening. While Drew blithely peppers me with questions throughout the day about who and where he is, other questions swirl around in my head:

Who should I call to get an estimate of the scope of the work that needs to be done?

Will the house need to be raised?

Would we need to tackle it from the top down and tear out the floors?

How expensive will it be?

Where will I get the money?

Will we have to move while the work is being done?

Where would we go?

Could Drew even handle the disruption?

How much mental and emotional damage would Drew suffer from the catastrophic impact of all these changes?

Brandon, who cleans for me once a month, lined up a plumber to address the toilet situation, so at least that's resolved, which motivated me to contact a company that specializes in mold and crawl spaces. I got up the nerve to call for an appointment, and the guy came to look. When he pulled the board away from the cinder blocks, he said the crawl space was only eighteen inches high, and he only works with foundations that are three cinder blocks tall. The insulation is hanging down on sagging chicken wire, and the beams have pretty much disintegrated. Plus, *there are bees in there!* I gazed into the pitch-black opening from a safe distance and felt like I was looking into hell itself.

"It's worse than I thought," I gasped, surprised at how weak my voice sounded.

He shook his head. "I'm so sorry. I won't be able to help you. My guys are all bigger than I am, and they wouldn't even be able to get under there."

He left, and I trudged into the house to share my devastation with Alice. She comes twice a week to help in my office and is a ready sounding board. We're on the same spiritual wavelength.

I poured out my guts to her, wringing my hands and punctuating my distress with hopeful phrases like, "God is in control," and "This is another lesson in trusting Him to work everything out." When I ran out of words, the compassion in her eyes soothed my soul.

"While you were talking," she said, "the Lord reminded me of a story I heard a long time ago in a sermon.

Pearls

A ten-year-old girl dreamed of owning a strand of pearls and pestered her parents for them. They listened attentively and explained that they couldn't afford it but would remember that this was her heart's desire.

The little girl decided to save her allowance so she could buy the necklace herself. Week after week, month after month, the little girl squirreled away her nickels, dimes, and quarters. She visited the Five and Dime store often, admiring the imitation pearls in the glass case and checking the price. At last, the day came when she had just enough money, and the owner of the store called the clerks to gather around. With great ceremony, he honored the little girl by placing the strand of plastic pearls around her neck.

When she came home, her mother shared her joy as they stood before the mirror together, admiring the necklace. That night, when her father came home from work, the little girl ran up to him, expecting an equally enthusiastic response. "Look, Daddy! Look at my pearls!"

Instead, he wore a sad smile. "They're beautiful, and I'm very proud of you." And then he uttered unbearable words. "Honey, this is going to be difficult, but I want you to give me your pearls."

"Daddy, no! I can't give you my pearls. They're mine. I bought them with my own money, and I've waited so long."

"Please, he said, "will you give me your pearls?"

"Why, Daddy? Why do you want my pearls?"

"I can't tell you," he said. "Do you trust me?"

"Yes, Daddy. I trust you, but I can't give you my pearls. I just can't. I've only had them a little while and can't bear to part with them."

Every night, the little girl's father would tuck her into bed and ask the same question with a hopeful expression, and every night, she gave him the same answer. Each time she told him no, his hopeful expression turned sad, and his shoulders slumped as he left the room. The little girl felt worse and worse about disappointing him. He was a good father and always wanted the best for her. Before she fell asleep on the third night, she decided that as important as her pearls were to her, they must be important to her dad, too, and she made up her mind to give them to him the next day.

As soon as he came through the door after work, she stood there waiting. "Daddy, I don't want you to be sad." She lifted the necklace over her head and held out her pearls. With a sob in her throat, she said, "Here. You can have my pearls."

He beamed, and the joy on her father's face took some of the sting out of her sacrifice. "Don't move," he said. "I'll be right back." With that, he turned and left the room with her pearls in his hand.

The little girl cocked her head and gazed up at her mother, who patted her shoulder. They stood there, waiting in silence. The only sound was the ticking of the clock in the hallway. At last, the little girl heard her daddy's footsteps.

He hurried toward her, got down on one knee, and handed her a blue velvet box. "This is for you, sweetheart."

The little girl ran her fingers over the box and caressed it. She never knew a box could be so beautiful.

"Go ahead," her father urged. "Open it."

Inside, on a bed of ivory satin, lay a radiant strand of cultured freshwater pearls.

"Now you know why I wanted you to give me your imitation pearls," he said. "You were holding onto what you thought you wanted when I had something better for you."

Alice reached for my hand. "God knows what you need, where you need to be, and how to get you there." Her eyes searched mine. "This situation with your house has not caught Him by surprise. Who knows? He may be using it for a purpose you can't even imagine."

She is so right. I don't know what will happen with the foundation problem, but I do know that God is a good Father and wants the best for His children. After all, He knew long before I did that Drew Abbott and I should be together. The Lord used the discomfort of my divorce and unemployment in the 1970s to uproot me from the comfortable place I thought I wanted in Dover to an hour commute to Georgetown, where God had something better in mind. Something I never anticipated. Someone who told me on our first date, "You look like a woman who needs to be appreciated," and who has been appreciating me ever since.

October 11, 2018

I noticed a definite decline in Drew this past week with more difficulty walking and increased confusion. His legs are so weak he needs help getting to his feet after sitting and then is unstable. Jenna Caraway, a friend of mine, loaned us her transport chair, and now I use it around the house to get Drew from room to room.

Most of the time, he doesn't know me and asks if I work here. I tell him yes, that my job is to keep him happy. He used to laugh when I said that, and now he simply nods and says, "That's nice." He's beyond the denial stage and wants to know what's wrong with him, so I'm straightforward in telling him that he has Alzheimer's (which he can't comprehend). "It steals your memory," I say.

He responds by giving me a fearful, trusting look and says, "I don't know what I'd do without you."

He's right, of course. And it's uplifting to be needed and appreciated. I'm aware that the appreciation factor may well drop off at some point, so I'm banking these affirmations to draw on later.

He has trouble finding the bathroom in the night. I ordered a bedside commode to have it ready for him when he can no longer navigate with my help.

October 26, 2018

Drew didn't feel well. Loose bowels—all over the bathroom, leaving a trail from the doorway to the toilet. I was in the other room when it happened.

He had another blowout later. This time, I saw how it happened. He started pulling his pants down as soon as he felt the need to go, and said, "Shit, shit, shit," all the way to the toilet. Yep, that's what he did, *shit, shit, shit,* all the way there. Reminded me of a nightmarish version of *This Little Piggy* went to market going wee, wee, wee, all the way home.

"Wait until you get to the toilet," I said, trying to hike up his Depends, but he just swatted my hand away and told me to stop pulling him down.

After another round of clean-up, I called Hospice to ask for a nurse, and the switchboard operator said one would call me back. When she did, I was standing in the doorway of the bathroom, talking with her when Drew came up beside me. I had the phone in my right hand explaining the situation and reached for Drew with my left hand to steady him. Suddenly, his eyes rolled back in his head, and his body jerked. His left arm flailed out and knocked books off the bookcase. Then his whole body stiffened. I wrapped my left arm around him and said soothing words to assure myself as much as him.

"It's okay. It's okay. I've got you," I said as I lowered him to the floor. In the next breath, I spoke into the phone, "He's having a seizure."

"I'll be right there," the nurse assured me. "I'm about fifteen minutes away." What a comfort to have her on the line when this happened. I wasn't alone. Help was on the way.

Drew's lips were taut, his face was sheet-white, and I wasn't sure he was breathing. *Is he dead?* ran through my mind.

I put the phone down and turned my full attention to Drew. Color had already returned to his cheeks. He asked what happened, and I told him he fainted. I couldn't bring myself to tell him he'd had a seizure and to stay still, that a nurse was on her way.

She arrived shortly afterward, and I reported that he had some blood in his stools. She asked if I had saved it, but I told her all I could think of was cleaning it up. She wanted to know what color it was—bright red, black? No, it was pink. Just a hint. She said if it became bright red, it could be an internal hemorrhoid, and black meant it would be digested blood. Her advice to me was, "Keep an eye on it," and to save it for her to see next time.

Gross.

We slept for about an hour. At 11:30, I used the transport chair to get Drew to the bathroom again, but afterward, his legs were too weak to stand and pivot back into the chair. So, I held him while he sank to the floor, put a pillow under his head, and covered him with a blanket. Now what? I called Hospice for advice, and they said to call 911 and tell them it was a non-emergency, that I just needed someone to help me get him back to bed. I did, and they said they would come right away.

Drew kept trying to get up, but I told him to stay put, that an EMT would be there soon. He kept saying, "They're not taking me to the hospital, right?" and calmed down each time I assured him "no hospital," that they would just be helping him get from the floor to the bed.

The paramedics were very efficient, kind, and gentle. They got him settled, and right after they left, Drew tried to get out of bed. Somehow, I managed to deter him enough that he stayed put and went to sleep. I didn't.

October 27, 2018

I called Delaware Hospice in the morning because Drew had a huge amount of red blood this time (which I didn't flush in case the nurse needed to see it). She took one look and said, "That's not a hemorrhoid; it's a G.I. bleed, and you're going to need help." She asked if I would be interested in a bed at the Hospice Center if one became available, and I said yes. She checked, and there was a waiting list with three ahead of us but said they usually had a quick turnover.

I called a meeting of the three kids. While we waited for Kim to arrive, I helped Drew get comfortable on the love seat in the living room.

Speaking in low tones, Troy did his best to convince Dana to trust my decision about Hospice. "I shave Dad every other day," he said, "and I've watched him—I study him and I've seen his decline."

Dana's voice was emotional but restrained. "I'm here as often as I can be and see his decline, too," she said. "But this is an emergency. We have to try everything to stop the bleeding. I talked with people in the medical field before I got here. One told me there was a medicine that could perhaps stop the bleeding to save Dad's life."

"But we're on Hospice," I said, "and if there's medication that can stop a G.I. bleed, we can ask them about it."

Her voice became unsteady. "Hospice should be a last resort. We need to get him to a hospital. I'm not going to let my dad bleed to death without knowing we tried everything."

"Let's go to the kitchen," I suggested as emotions escalated. We moved to the kitchen, leaving Drew alone on the love seat.

I felt my heart begin to thump and race, so I hid in the bathroom until I could collect myself. *My heart, my heart. I have to protect my heart.*

I called Kim from my cell phone to see how far away she was. Kim said she was praying for the Lord to give us all the right words and help us see things through His eyes. That calmed me down.

Sitting there on the toilet lid with my head in my hands, my thoughts swirled. *What's happening? Am I losing Drew faster than I ever imagined? Please, Lord Jesus. Help me through this. Help all of us.*

Coming to grips with the possibility that this might be the end of life as we knew it, my heartbeat slowed to almost normal. I wiped my eyes, inhaled a deep breath of strength that came from someplace other than myself, and stood up. Before I could leave the bathroom, I heard Troy shout a curse word and slam the sliding glass door. He never swears.

I stepped into the kitchen, and he was gone.

No explanation from Dana. The minute she saw me, she jumped back into the same points she had made before.

"No, no, no," I said and held my palm out as a stop signal. "I'm not going to talk about this right now. Wait until Kim gets here." I moved past her to join Drew on the love seat.

"What's going on?" he asked as I plopped down beside him.

"We're having a little family meeting," I said. "Troy will be right back *(I hope)*, and Kim is on her way."

Kim came in the front door just as Troy came in the back, and the five of us gathered in the living room. I gave a carefully worded overview since Drew was sitting right next to me.

"I trust Candy's decision," Troy said, and Kim agreed.

Dana gave her "Yes, but" speech, which had grown louder as though she felt her points were not being heard about what we needed to do to prolong her dad's life. "I'm not saying we need to jump into surgery, but if there's a medicine that can stop the bleeding, we need it."

I knew she believed she was doing the right thing—she was passionate to defend him—but I also knew with all my wildly beating heart that she wasn't right.

"Dana," Kim said, "let's calm down and take a step back to look at the big picture. We have to be honest about this. Dad's not going to get better. Mom's the one who's here with him every minute of every day, and she knows better than anyone what's best."

Kim's comments struck me as the voice of reason. God gave her good words.

Troy and Kim had faced reality, but Dana was resistant to the idea that this was different from all the other health crises, and her dad couldn't be "fixed." Dana just wasn't able to back down and see things from our perspective.

Drew and I sat side-by-side on the love seat while the kids' conversation intensified with tears and even shouting, which is rare at our house. A couple of times, Drew asked, "What are they talking about?" and I replied that they were working through some things.

Before Dana came, she had sought counsel from two people in the medical field and asked them to tell her what they would say to anybody who experienced this kind of bleeding. They both told her it required immediate attention. One of them even said, "If I were you, I'd have him in the car right now and be on my way to the emergency room."

It struck me that my relationship with Dana could be at risk. Our opposing views of what was best for Drew seemed irreconcilable. We both wanted to do the right thing. I was convinced that Hospice, not the hospital, was what he needed.

Unable to comprehend the heated conversation, Drew retreated to a safe place and started singing, *Only You*. Envying his peaceful oasis, I sang with him: "Only you . . . can make me feel this way; only you . . . and you alone."

Drew's steady voice and calm demeanor served as a stabilizing force for me. I allowed myself to be swept into his world as we sang to one another, which provided a much-needed escape for me. We smiled and gazed into each other's eyes as though oblivious to the mounting tension.

Dana seemed in a distant world, too, steeling herself to be the same fierce advocate she had always been for her dad during his pre-Alzheimer's days. "In my heart of hearts, if we don't do everything possible, I don't think I could live with myself. I could never get over it."

"Dana," Kim said, pointing her hand toward us. "Look at them. They're sitting there holding hands and *singing* to each other. They're so beautiful together. See how content they are? Isn't that what we want for them?"

Dana nodded. "Of course, but . . ." and then she fought even harder for what her father would want.

By then, our duet was over, and I rejoined the conversation, speaking calmly. "In order for Medicare to pay for hospitalization, we'd have to have Hospice release him from their program," I said. "And I count on their services."

"This is not about money! This is about my dad!" Dana's voice broke. "If we don't get him to the hospital, he could die!"

"Let's say we do sign out of Hospice so Medicare would cover treatment. Say we take him to the hospital for the medicine, if there is such a thing," I reasoned. "Just going there would be traumatic for him. They would put him through tests, poke and prod, and what if they recommended surgery? Would you want to put him through that? Alzheimer's patients don't do well with anesthesia. Their brains can't handle it. Most times, they spiral down and end up in worse shape than they went in; sometimes, they go into a coma. Most likely, he would come out of the anesthesia combative, and I'd be the one to have to handle that."

"This is not about you."

Her words cut like a knife.

"This is my dad!"

Yes, and he's my husband. I've been taking care of him 24/7 and know his every heartbeat. I envisioned the panic in his eyes as nurses wheeled him down the hallway to the operating room where I couldn't go. The confusion alone could cause a catastrophic event, not counting the anesthesia, and in his weakened condition, he may not even survive the surgery. *How will Dana live with herself if he dies on the operating table?*

"Are you going to take over for me?" I asked Dana, challenging her, and instantly regretted it because I had no intention of relinquishing my role.

Kim leaned toward Dana. "Not to be ignorant," she said, "but you and I both work full-time, so unless you plan on retiring or quitting your job and helping mom out full time—which I know I can't because I have two kids about to go to college—then we need to trust Mom."

Dana hung her head while she regrouped and then returned to the suggestions her nurse friends had made.

Kim and Troy changed the subject, recalling Drew's colon surgery eight or nine years ago and how he had ICU Psychosis the night they put him in the step-down unit.

"Boy, does that bring back painful memories," I said. "I had no sooner gotten home from my day-and-night vigil and put my head on the pillow when the phone rang. It was Drew talking gibberish. I had to rush back to the hospital after midnight because he had ripped off his gown, thought the nurses were trying to poison him, and insisted he needed his wallet to pay for the room. He was swinging at everybody who came near and had to be restrained."

Kim chimed in. "And he didn't have Alzheimer's then."

The phone rang. It was the nurse calling to say a bed could be available in Milford as soon as tonight or tomorrow, and they were expecting me to stay there with Drew. I relayed this news to the kids.

"No. He needs to go to the hospital at least for testing," Dana insisted.

"I hear you, Dana, but your dad is going to the Hospice Center. That's settled. It's the right thing to do." I wasn't budging, knowing in my heart and soul that I was doing the right thing and would just have to risk alienating, and possibly even losing, my stepdaughter.

"No, it's not," Dana sobbed in defeat. The conversation became sprinkled with apologies that we wish it didn't have to be this way, and we ended in a group hug as Drew looked on.

Kim stuck around for some mother/daughter quiet talk and helped me write up a list of things to pack.

After she left and I was alone with Drew, I realized that tonight's confrontation was harder on me than any other part of the whole Alzheimer's ordeal. I rely on the full support and harmony of every member of my family more than I realized.

After I changed Drew and got him settled in for the night, I faced the real culprit.

"Devil," I said under my breath, "you get your hands off this family. It is written in James 4:7, '*Submit yourselves to God. Resist the devil, and he will flee from you.*' Right this minute, I'm submitting myself, Drew, Dana, Troy, and Kim to God Almighty and telling you Begone, Begone, Begone! You have no place in our lives."

And then I thanked the Lord for protecting Drew and for restoring our family unity, trusting Him to work everything out.

October 28, 2018

Delaware Hospice Center sent an ambulance for Drew, and I was impressed with the quality of their hydraulic lift and padded stretcher. He went without complaint, and I drove ahead to be in Milford to greet them when they arrived.

The facility was exquisite, so inviting, and peace filled. As soon as Drew was settled into his suite (complete with outdoor patio), I was escorted on a tour and found everything tastefully, elegantly appointed. They have a fully equipped family kitchen with fresh coffee, tea, even packaged oatmeal; visitors' restrooms and a spa with a shower; family sitting rooms, a reflection room (chapel), family support room, formal living room, children's playroom with toys, and personal laundry services. The most impressive thing is the kindness and friendliness that permeates every inch of the place.

Drew's blood pressure is so low from the bleeding that he is only vaguely aware of what's going on around him. But he's restless and keeps saying he has to go to the bathroom. His brain is not communicating with the rest of his body, so he has difficulty standing or getting his feet to move, not even to take baby steps. When we do manage to help him shuffle to the bathroom, he doesn't know how to position his behind where it needs to be, even when I press against his hip to guide him. It's like his body has the brakes on.

I learned helpful tips from watching the nurses, like pulling up on the back of his waistband to help lift, steady, and guide him to sit down.

He was "out of it," barely able to communicate.

One time I pressed the call button and, instead of waiting until somebody came, I automatically began supporting Drew under his armpits and helping him stand. The nurse came in and took over, giving me a most compassionate look. "You've been doing this all by yourself at home?" That was a reality-check-moment for me. *I need more help! For real. And soon.*

October 29, 2018

I prayed HARD. *Lord, this is happening too fast. Dana and Troy aren't ready to lose their dad. I'm not ready. Give us strength. It's a lot to ask, but please stop the bleeding. Give us more time.* And He *DID!* The bleeding stopped pouring out and reduced to a trickle. By evening, there was no sign of blood! One of the nurses said the words that were on the tip of my tongue, "It's a miracle."

We were able to come home from the Hospice Center a day and a half after we got there.

The Lord not only healed Drew's G.I. bleed, but Dana had a conversation with Barb, her RN friend and, they talked about end-of-life issues. Dana had a paradigm shift.

"I'm so sorry," my stepdaughter said as we walked down the hall together at the Center. "It was like I was trapped in a nightmare and nobody would help me, but now I see I was wrong." She stopped walking and we faced each other. "Candy, you made the right decision, and I'm so grateful. Dad's the most important thing in my life, but you're important, too. In fact, Barb says you're even *more* important, because without you, everything would fall apart."

All is well in the relationship department.

Hospice arranged for a hospital bed to be delivered to our house around 12:30 p.m. and said Drew could go home between five and six. Troy took care of relocating stuff in the bedroom to make room for the hospital bed.

I stayed with Drew, waiting for time to pass. Instead of turning on the TV, I set up my Bluetooth speaker and played Pandora. Drew picked up my Kindle and became fascinated with the pictures he found there. The hours passed gently with soothing visits from not one but two chaplains. We sipped hot tea and enjoyed one another as though we were on vacation.

When the EMS guys came into Drew's room with the stretcher and told him they had come to take him home, he looked surprised and offended.

"Home? I *am* home."

"No," they said, "you're not home. We're taking you home to Georgetown."

He turned to me to back him up, but I agreed with them, not him. "You're crazy," he said to me. "This is Georgetown, and this is my home."

I smiled. "No, hon. This is not Georgetown. We're in Milford at the Delaware Hospice Center."

"We're not in Georgetown?" he asked.

The three of us told him we were in Milford, and instead of acquiescing, he only steeled himself more.

"But I own this place," he said as if that would settle everything.

The guys and I exchanged amused glances, and I marveled at their patience while Drew continued his monologue ending with, "If this is not my home, then who owns this house?"

"This is not a house. It's a facility," I said. "And it's owned by a private organization—Delaware Hospice. It's like a hospital that feels like a five-star hotel. There are sixteen rooms here, just like this one."

He seemed to comprehend that and tried another approach. "Well then, I paid for this room."

"No, you didn't, honey. It's free. They haven't charged us a cent."

"Ha! No way!"

I reached for his hand. "It's true."

The EMS guys backed me up. "Delaware Hospice doesn't charge for the room, the food, or anything here. It's a rare and wonderful thing they do."

Drew looked at me. "How'd you find out about this place?"

"I did my research. Pretty clever of me, huh?"

"I'll say." He shook his head and looked happily defeated. "Either you're all lying, or I'm the dumbest person on the face of the earth." And he allowed the guys to help him onto the stretcher.

The ambulance crew delivered Drew to our house and got him settled in. Dana came shortly afterward and brought us dinner, so she was here while the nurse conducted an exit interview and demonstrated how the hospital bed worked. Dana listened attentively while the nurse told me to let Drew determine how much or how little he eats or drinks and that comfort, safety, and dignity are what matters most at this point. That sounded like the kind of thing people say when the end is near. *Please, Lord, a little more time with him?*

And then she told me I couldn't leave him alone for even five minutes from this point forward.

Ouch! 'Bye, bye, freedom.

God is good,
a hiding place in tough times.
He recognizes and welcomes
anyone looking for help,
No matter how desperate the trouble.

— Nahum 1:7 (MSG)

CHAPTER TEN

Reach Out, I'll Be There

October 30, 2018

Drew didn't fuss about getting into the hospital bed last night, probably because he was exhausted from the last few days. His only comment was, "I guess I don't have a choice." The hospital bed has a pressure relief mattress, which we put on the lowest setting. It gives a soothing sort of hum, and he didn't complain a bit. I slept on his side of our king bed so I could be right next to him. That way, I could tell if he tried to get up. He slept soundly and comfortably for the most part with four incidents of squirming that I was aware of. I rearranged his covers, and we both slept fairly well.

Then, this morning, he woke up fully alert to his surroundings. "Why am I in this 'baby bed?' I want to get in the 'big bed.'"

So, I helped him climb up into our king-sized bed, where he slept for another two hours. I guess this is going to be like transitioning a child from the crib to a big bed a little at a time, only in reverse.

The nurse who came to the house last night told me that a time would come when Drew would be bed-bound. I already knew that, but I didn't realize we were getting so close until the hospital bed was right there in our bedroom.

Drew was straining to stand, so I pulled him up by the back of his waistband and supported his arm. He shook his head. "I don't think I'm being very fair to you."

"You're the fairest person I know," I said and thought *I need to get some help.*

Early this morning, I sent an email to my "inner circle" to identify ways they can help me ask for help. In my message, I told them that Drew is losing the use of his legs, and I can no longer leave him unattended for even five minutes or lift him when he falls. The good news is I've had many people offer to help. The bad news is I haven't figured out how to ask for it. I proposed making a checklist of areas where people would feel comfortable pitching in and making a schedule that wouldn't be too overwhelming for anybody.

Our planning meeting will be Tuesday, November 6th (Election Day), and I'm giddy with anticipation!

October 31, 2018

At 3:30 a.m., I helped Drew get to and from the bathroom. Now he's settled into bed and sleeping peacefully, but I'm wide awake. *Ahh, the perfect time for a cup of Sleepy Time hot tea and quality time with the Lord.* I sensed the angels surrounding me as I opened my Bible and felt the Holy Spirit's presence as He whispered calming messages to my spirit from Jeremiah 17:7-8 (AMP), which I had circled years before.

"Blessed [with spiritual security] is the man who believes and trusts
in and relies on the Lord
And whose hope and confident expectation is the Lord.
"For he will be [nourished] like a tree planted by the waters,
That spreads out its roots by the river;
And will not fear the heat when it comes;
But its leaves will be green and moist.
And it will not be anxious and concerned in a year of drought
Nor stop bearing fruit.

"How do you do it?" people ask. *This is how I do it.* This is how I guard my peace and fill up when my mind, body, and emotions are spent—the sustaining power of God and the ready avenue of prayer. I immerse myself in it and am learning to not do it "my way."

Thank You, Lord, for healing Drew's bleeding so quickly and thoroughly. Thank You for helping Dana and keeping our relationship intact.

November 1, 2018

Ella got Drew showered and dressed, and the weather was spring-like. It seemed only right to take Drew for an outing since I had errands to run. He sat in the car while I went to the bank, the post office, and the pharmacy. On the way home, I realized we hadn't eaten lunch, so we stopped by the Georgetown Family Restaurant. I helped him hobble in, and we sat in the nearest booth.

While we waited for our soup, Drew asked, "What do I do?"

A sense of purpose is important to a man—to anybody. But I didn't think about that when I answered, "You're retired. You don't do anything."

Immediately, his shoulders slumped, and the light went out of his eyes.

I saw my error and tried to erase the hurt. "No. That's not right. I'll tell you what you do: You take care of me, that's what. You make sure I feel appreciated. You keep me happy. You provide a nice home, clothes, food—everything I need. And I'm grateful."

He perked up, and I wanted to keep the momentum going. "Now, let's talk about what you did before you retired." I told him about his career with Bedford Motors and his appraisal business. He sat taller. That he was well respected, always treated people fairly, and had served twenty-two years as a town councilman. By the time our waitress cleared the dishes away, I had figured out the answer I should have given him in the first place. "You asked what you do. In a nutshell, you only do what you want to do and nothing else. You used to define success as being master of your own time, and that's what you are."

I noticed he held his head a little higher as I helped him hobble out of the restaurant.

Tonight, Dana brought us a salad from Subway and chicken from Royal Farms, and we had an impromptu dinner with Troy around the kitchen table like old times. The only person missing from our original family of five was Kim.

The phone rang, and suddenly, there she was! I told Kim that Dana had had a breakthrough and said she was sorry for the things she said Saturday night, that she felt like a caged animal who was helpless and panicky. Kim said to tell her she's been praying for her, and I said, "You know, what? She's right here. Why don't you tell her yourself?" While Troy, Drew, and I ate, Dana and Kim had a good conversation that erased any hurt feelings.

After dinner, Dana shared with me that she had cried out to the Lord about how she would cope with her dad's passing. "I don't think I'll be able to handle this when the time comes," and she felt a strong impression to look up John 16:33 in the Amplified Bible:

"I have told you these things, so that in Me you may have [perfect] peace and confidence. In the world you have tribulation and trials and distress and frustration; but be of good cheer [take courage; be confident, certain, undaunted]! For I have overcome the world. [I have deprived it of power to harm you and have conquered it for you.]"

She told me the words, *I have overcome the world,* jumped out at her, and she realized she had been grasping for worldly solutions instead of trusting the Lord. As if to drive the point home, another unprompted and very strong thought penetrated her mind, "Read chapter eight." She recognized the voice of the Holy Spirit and knew right away which book that meant: a devotional by David Jeremiah she had recently brought into the house after driving around for weeks with it in the back seat of her car. She said a strange, tingly sensation surged through her as she opened the book. Sure enough, chapter eight featured the very same passage, John 16:33 (NKJV):

"These things I have spoken to you,
that in Me you may have peace.
In the world you will have tribulation;
but be of good cheer, I have overcome the world."

She beamed as she told me this was "life-changing" for her. We basked in the awareness of how God reveals His active presence to those who have ears to hear and eyes to see.

"It may seem like you'll never forget the experience," I said, "but you're going to want to write it down so you'll have it to refer to when the time comes."

Drew stayed alert during dinner but then spiraled into a nosedive after Dana and Troy left. Confusion and weakness overpowered him as though he had spent every ounce of cognition and energy he could muster.

As I helped him get ready for bed, he peppered me with one question after another:

"How do I put an end to this? How do I stop it? Is there a switch you can flip to turn this off? Am I always going to be this way?"

I didn't attempt to answer. After I tucked him in, I sat next to him on the edge of the bed. He grabbed my hand with an exceptionally strong grip and locked eyes with me. "Please be honest with me. What's going on? Will I ever be normal again?"

I recognized it as a moment of clarity for both of us, the husband-wife bond of sharing the sacred trust our marriage was built on. "You have Alzheimer's disease," I said slowly. "First, it stole your memory, and now it is robbing you of the strength in your legs."

He nodded that he understood, so I continued.

"Your brain is unable to send the right signals to your legs to make them do what you want them to. And you're getting weaker, so it's difficult to stand. There is no cure for this disease; it will get worse, and it leads to death." Then I added quickly, "We all die. But you're in a safe place, and I'll be right here with you until the very end."

"I hope it comes quickly," he said.

We kissed fervently like old times, and he fell asleep.

I paced around the house for a while, letting the reality of our conversation sink in.

November 2, 2018

Drew slept all night and all day, except when he had a bowel movement that he managed to smear all over his behind and the toilet seat. He can barely walk, but I managed to get him cleaned up enough to get him back into the bed. Flushable wipes for his bottom and Clorox wipes for the toilet and floor did the trick. The transport chair is a lifesaver because he doesn't have enough strength to stand for very long, and I can wheel him around. The hardest part is getting him turned around to get in and out of it.

After getting him situated in the hospital bed, I hunted around and found a basin. This was my first attempt at giving him a bed-bath. I could use some instruction on how to do it right, but at least he's clean. In no time, he was asleep again.

When he finally woke up at 6 p.m., he ate half a sandwich. He's confused, of course, but alert and aware when I nudge him. I'm at peace and keep reminding myself that God is present in this household.

November 6, 2018

What a relief to be surrounded by my inner circle of caring friends and family tonight. Our conversation flowed gently, and I learned some things about myself I wouldn't have discovered without them. We listed areas where I could ask for help:

Groceries. As we talked about having someone shop for me and bring groceries, I realized I savor my outings to Walmart, where I can pick out my fruit and leisurely browse the aisles. I was surprised to conclude that I would prefer to have someone stay with Drew so I can get out and have a brief change of scenery.

Laundry. I could bag up our dirty clothes and linens and have someone pick up and then return them clean and folded. But as kind as this would be, I felt a sinking feeling. Until now, I hadn't realized how much I like doing laundry. It's mindless, productive, satisfying work, with Drew nearby, which makes us both content. Okay, scratch laundry from the helpers' list.

Clean out and organize (closets, drawers, cupboards). Now, there's an area I would appreciate help with! With forty-plus years of accumulation, every space in the house is crammed full. Yep. This I could eagerly ask for help with again and again.

Declutter (especially books). Yes, please! Send in the volunteers.

Cleaning. Definitely. Especially spider webs and raking leaves.

Errands (make bank deposits, check the box at the post office, pick up prescriptions). Oh, yes. I could part with these responsibilities. The key to asking for help is to be specific, and I'm beginning to get a feel for how this looks.

Meals. Mmm, how wonderful to have meals (homemade or from a menu) delivered a couple of times a week. I would love to have whoever brings the meal stay and share it with us or, better yet, cook it here so the aroma fills the house.

Transportation. Offers to drive me places so I can sit back and relax.

Keep Drew company while I spend time at the keyboard in my office to get some work done.

My circumstances hadn't changed during our meeting, but my perspective flipped one hundred and eighty degrees. Mentally and emotionally, I made the leap when this resonated within me: I not only *COULD ask for help* but *SHOULD ask for help* and *WOULD ask for help*.

After everyone left, I felt light and free. Nothing had actually changed, but I no longer felt overwhelmed by day-to-day responsibilities and the compulsion to handle everything myself. *We have a plan.* And I won't have to execute the plan alone. We may not have even begun to tame the chaos, but little by little, we will, and I already have a sense of order. These eager helpers are sensitive to my needs and wishes and are committed to following through. When I have trouble articulating my need, they make timely observations. Oh, yes. This is love in action. How blessed am I!

November 8, 2018

Bonnie Kay, Kim's mother-in-law and my dear friend, showed up at my door and asked if there were any errands she could run for me. Since it was Return Day in Georgetown with streets blocked off for the parade, I asked her to come back the next day to make a deposit at the bank and check the PO box for mail. In the meantime, she noticed leaves piled up on our front porch and swept them off. Until then, I hadn't even noticed. What a difference it made to my mental state to have them gone.

By the time Bonnie Kay left, Ella, who had come a half-hour earlier, finished giving Drew his shower and dressing him for the day. She had no sooner seated him on the couch in the living room when Drew commented on the activity outside our window as people flocked to the center of town. As if on cue, Betty, her two grandchildren, Alice Nagle, and Jenna Caraway, popped in for a brief hello before leaving for the parade.

Return Day, a Georgetown tradition held two days after each election, has always been an important event for Drew since he served as councilman for twenty-two years and was actively involved in it. Today, he didn't know what Return Day was, but he understood the excitement generated by it. There he sat, all clean and dressed, giving me a wistful look. It was a mild, sunny day, and I thought about how good the fresh air and stimulation would be for him. But how to get him there—ah, Jenna's transport chair!

"Do you want to go to the parade?"

"What do you want to do?" he asked.

In no time, I had him bundled up. I carried the chair down the front steps and opened it up, then went back and helped Drew shuffle from the living room, through the front door, and down the three brick steps. He could barely stand but asked why we didn't just "walk uptown" to watch the parade. It took a while, but I got him turned around and into the chair, and off we went, rolling smoothly along the side of the road and up the sidewalk until we reached the crowd and the sound of marching bands. People parted, and I wheeled Drew to the curb where he had a front row seat.

It was exhilarating, and I could tell Drew was enjoying himself. After about twenty minutes, he'd had enough, and we rolled back home.

It was a full day. A good day. And we took naps.

November 9, 2018

True to her word, Bonnie Kay came this afternoon and took care of the errands, which gave me a sense of accomplishment. I felt relieved not having to go out.

Drew's right leg is weaker than his left, and I coached him in getting it to move where he wanted it to be. With hands-on assistance, I gave him step-by-step instructions on how to position himself in front of the toilet or into bed. This afternoon, I was in the kitchen and could hear a small voice calling from the bedroom but couldn't tell what he was saying. When I got closer, he was calling, "Teacher, teacher." Mixed thoughts and conflicting emotions ran through me. Sadness that he didn't know who I was, but pleasure because he always respected and trusted his teachers and esteemed me by acknowledging a role I didn't even realize I was playing.

November 15, 2018

Music is good for both of us, setting a soothing tone or perking us up. I had an Oldies station on Pandora, and when *Reach Out I'll Be There* by the Four Tops played, the old lyrics carried new meaning. Years ago, it would have been Drew singing the words to me when I was struggling with something. Today, since the Holy Spirit is my Comforter, I picture the Lord assuring me that I can reach out and He'll be there. Or, it could also reflect Drew's need and my dependability—that all he has to do is reach out and I'll be there:

"Reach Out I'll Be There"

Now if you feel that you can't go on
Because all of your hope is gone
And your life is filled with much confusion
Until happiness is just an illusion
And your world around is crumbling down, darlin'

(Reach out) Come on, girl, reach on out for me
(Reach out) Reach out for me
Hah, I'll be there with a love that will shelter you
I'll be there with a love that will see you through

When you feel lost and about to give up
'Cause your best just ain't good enough
And you feel the world has grown cold
And your drifting out all on your own
And you need a hand to hold, darlin'

(Reach out) Come on girl, reach out for me
(Reach out) Reach out for me
Hah, I'll be there to love and comfort you
And I'll be there to cherish and care for you

(I'll be there to always see you through)
(I'll be there to love and comfort you)

November 18, 2018

Drew not only can't follow a TV program enough to understand it but is agitated by the "noise" of voices and sound effects. Comcast's Easy Listening channel seems to be the solution, and he often comments, "pretty music." My main goal is his comfort.

Drew is sleeping more and is awake less. We had three good nights in a row without wakefulness or incessant questions, and I was happy about that until I realized he was sleeping throughout the day, too. When I calculated how much time he was awake, it was only three out of forty-eight hours. And his appetite has dwindled to a few bites a day and a few sips of water or Boost. He is no longer interested in Coke. I've been coming to grips with his decline over the past few weeks.

Troy came over to shave Drew in bed, and his dad was able to comply when asked to lift his chin and turn his head but kept his eyes closed the whole time the electric razor trimmed his whiskers. Afterward, Troy and I talked at length about how the body shuts down, and I reminded him that the nurse said I should let Drew determine how much food or drink he wanted and not to force him. We rejoiced that Drew is at peace, has no pain, and is lucid for the most part. We're especially grateful that his personality is intact even though he may not know who we are. Since we can't estimate how many days or weeks we may have with him, we're fully appreciating the time we do have.

Dana sent me a text about coming over tomorrow at lunchtime, and I replied, "I think you should come today." Immediately, the phone rang. "What's wrong?"

I filled her in on the turn of events, and she came right over. Both she and Troy are coming to the point of acceptance, which is a tremendous comfort to me. While Dana and Troy sat by their dad's bedside and chatted with him and each other, I went grocery shopping.

I saw Ruth Baxter at the store, a friend who was recently widowed, and asked her how she's handling her grief.

"I guess I haven't let go yet," she said. "I still feel like Jim is in the other room." I could see myself adopting the same approach and realized that I'm being conditioned, a little at a time, for the inevitable.

Hospice typically comes in during the last six months to help terminally ill patients deal with the dying process. Out of curiosity, I opened my Delaware Hospice folder to see when I signed Drew's official paperwork, and it was July 20th, just four months ago.

Kim called. "Mom," she said, "I had a God moment a little while ago."

I said, "Then, I'll need to know all about it."

She told me that while cooking dinner, a strong thought came that she should write her eulogy for Drew, so she grabbed a paper and pen and started writing. "I don't know if I'll be able to read it at the funeral when the time comes, but I'll read it to you now so you can tell me if anything should be worded better." The words flowed from her heart onto the page and through the phone into my ear, touching my heart at a depth I could not anticipate. I would not change one word.

When the time comes, her eulogy is bound to evoke happy tears.

November 20, 2018

Drew ate better today than yesterday and has been awake for six hours at a time instead of three. The nurse mentioned the possibility of a "slide board" so I can get him from the bed to the transfer chair when he can no longer stand and pivot, but it sounds cumbersome.

I've been unsettled and irritable all day. All my best mental strategies have failed to calm me. It's as though a slow rage is boiling beneath the surface, and I have to catch myself so I don't lash out at whoever I'm near.

Now that I think about it, this didn't start today. I first noticed it on Saturday at the writers' group when I decided to indulge in sweets that are not on my "acceptable food" list: donuts, coffee cake, and coconut custard pie. When I brought my plate to the table, outspoken Ben blurted out, "Hey, Candy, you planning to share that?" I spit out my reply, "Nope, I'm going to eat this all myself. I haven't had sugar since January, and today's the day!" And promptly began shoveling it into my mouth. To make matters worse, I brought leftovers home and continued to load up with calories, guilt, and disdain until I said out loud, "Candy, what are you doing?!"

What happened to the self-control I've been exercising since January? I've worked hard to lose fifty pounds. Do I want to blow it now? No! So, why am I stuffing myself with food that I know is harmful to my body and can sabotage what I've worked so hard to accomplish?

Because I'm *angry*. I'm downright *mad*. The truth is, I'm mad at myself for being out of control, for giving in to my cravings and justifying that "I deserve it" to soothe myself.

I'm infuriated about what Alzheimer's is doing to my Drew and to the life we once had.

I'm enraged that our security is threatened, that I have to be on alert every minute of every day, that even when I have time to myself, it's "planned."

I'm aggravated to have lost the freedom to come and go as I please and to work without interruption.

I'm upset when Internet connections are slow, when links don't work like they're supposed to, and people don't do what they promised.

I'm livid that I'm forced to think about what life will be like without Drew and frustrated that I have to console his children when I need consolation myself.

I realized in March of 2017 that I haven't cried in a long time. I still haven't. Dozens upon dozens of people have assured me they're praying for Drew and me, and maybe my lack of tears is because their prayers and God's grace are insulating my emotions. It's as though my tear ducts are taped shut. Maybe I'm in denial. Maybe I'm afraid to cry for fear of not being able to stop. Maybe my "on duty" button doesn't have an off switch. Maybe the Holy Spirit has placed a bubble around my heart to cushion me.

In writing this, it dawned on me that by deliberately disrupting my healthy eating habits on Saturday and introducing massive amounts of sugar, I poked a hole in the bubble of my safe place. And a little at a time since then, my peace has been leaking out and is being replaced by the raw feelings I've been suppressing for months—even years.

My new intern Jodie came today, and I vented to her about my incessant irritability. Having to interrupt her intern training and our publishing project to check on Drew multiple times didn't help, no matter how much I sweet-talked him to fake my mood. I finally wheeled him into my office, where he sat and dozed while we worked. By the time Jodie and I finished our publishing tasks, and she was ready to leave, Drew had been sitting in the corner of my office for a while. As we joined hands for a parting prayer, she turned to him. "Mr. Drew, is it okay if we pray?"

"What?" he asked drowsily.

"Is it okay if we pray?" she repeated.

He frowned. "Is it okay to pray? I always pray—all the time. Yes, it's okay. You *should* pray!"

By the time Jodie finished her prayer, my feelings had settled down for the first time in days, and I felt more like my soft, pliable self. The prickly part had departed. In my quiver of tools, when I was scrambling to get my peace back and regain control, why didn't I think to *pray?* Even Drew knew to do that! Regardless of how out-of-control I feel at any given time, I can center myself in the knowledge that God is concerned about all the things that concern me, and He not only hears me when I cry out to Him but is the only One with the true solutions. *Forgive me, Lord, for my flimsy efforts to fix myself.*

I had no sooner recorded my deep soul searching when Kim called, and I told her about it. "Mom," she said, "it's a full moon." Then she went on with a litany of crazy things she experienced in her fifth-grade classroom in Millsboro that morning:

She couldn't log into her computer to record attendance. After multiple tries, she found someone had changed her password.

Once she got in, the computer pen wouldn't allow her to write assignments on the smartboard, so she got even more riled up—all in forty-five minutes before the students arrived.

Then, a mysterious brown liquid appeared all over the floor that hadn't been there moments before. Kim and her students scrambled around, trying to figure out what it was and where it came from. Soda! From an open can in a girl's backpack where she had hidden it.

"And Wyatt can top that," Kim said. She went on to tell me that our son-in-law, a State Police SRO (school resource officer) in Seaford, had an equally bizarre day:

A six-year-old exposed himself in the cafeteria, of all places, waving his wee-wee at everybody.

Then, not one but two students hit teachers. One of the kids had autism, which might have been understandable, but—get this—the teacher wanted him arrested!

Since the full moon affects tides, and human beings are made up of 60 percent water, I guess that can throw us all off balance and make us a little loony. Comparing my situation to Kim and Wyatt's, I realized that my day in the house with soft music playing felt better than chaos in the workplace. The "hitting" incidents reminded me how blessed I am that Drew is not combative as some Alzheimer's patients can be. For this, and many other things, I am thankful.

November 21, 2018

I had the brilliant idea to put a little brass bell next to the chair where Drew sits in the bedroom. I showed him how to use it, asked him to ring it constantly while I scooted down the hallway to the other end of the house to test if I could hear it from my office. Bingo!

"Perfect, hon. I can hear it just fine. I'm going to work for a little while, and if you need me, all you have to do is ring the bell, and I'll come running."

Silly me. I should have known better. No sooner had I sat in my office chair than I heard the bell. When I raced in to report for duty, there he was with an ornery grin plastered on his face.

"You need something?" I asked.

"Yes. I wanted to see how fast you would get here."

Okay, then. I told him that his experiment seemed to work just fine. After the third time, I took the bell away and brought him with me to the office.

November 22, 2018

Thanksgiving Day. Normally, we would go to Dana's for her customary feast, and then to Kim's in-laws for dessert, but this year, it seemed wise to stay home since Drew is so weak, and Dana's husband John has a cold. The last thing we need is germs. I bought a turkey to make the house smell good and have leftovers, and Dana suggested we have a quiet Thanksgiving here on Friday, and she would bring side dishes. Great idea!

I put A Christmas Carol in the DVD player to set the tone and possibly evoke some memories for Drew. Midway through the movie, he said, "Have you ever seen anything worse?" Ebenezer Scrooge and his negativity and the ghosts of Jacob Marley and Christmas Past didn't sit well with Mr. I-Want-Everything-Happy.

Kim, Wyatt, Kade, and Saige brought heaping plates to us before the movie was over, so we didn't get to see Scrooge's transformation into a caring, kindly person through the visitations of the other two ghosts. We ate at the kitchen table, and Kim said grace. She got choked up in the middle of it, telling me later that waves of memories of Thanksgivings-past threaded through her mind along with the possibility that this would be our last Thanksgiving with Drew.

November 23, 2018

Troy couldn't make it to Dana's yesterday, so I invited him to join us for dinner. Just as everything was coming together, our grandson Trevor and great-granddaughter Brooklynn popped in for a spur-of-the-moment visit, so we had a full table, great conversation, and gentle stimulation for Drew.

After everyone but Dana had left, she and I said it reminded us of the monthly family dinners I used to host after Drew's heart surgery in 2008, a pattern which had fizzled out long ago.

"Let's reinstate our family dinners," I said. "Once a month worked well before."

Dana said softly, "Don't you think weekly would be better?"

Ouch! Reality check. And role reversal. *Definitely weekly!*

December 2, 2018

Myrna, my sister-in-law, gave me a big bag of incontinence products that a friend had left over after her husband died, and that's how I discovered Abena Abri-Flex Premium L3 overnight protective underwear. ' They're wonderfully absorbent briefs. Although more expensive than Depends, these pull-ups are worth the money because I don't have to change them as often. Convenient, too, because Amazon delivers them to my doorstep.

"You treat a disease,
you win, you lose.
You treat a person,
I guarantee you win,
no matter the outcome."

— *Patch Adams*

CHAPTER ELEVEN

Family Dinners & Failing Legs

December 6, 2018

We had our second weekly family dinner tonight. Thursday evenings suit everyone, and the togetherness is doing us all good. Dana brings the main course (crockpot or something she can pick up after work), Kim provides the vegetable and maybe dessert, I make a salad and bread or dessert, and Troy fills the dishwasher, so it isn't too much trouble for anybody. I'm enjoying the excuse to use our best china and glassware, cloth napkins, and candles. Drew seems to enjoy the conversation and laughter but isn't overwhelmed because there are just enough of us to fit around the dining room table. I want these to be memorable times as we relax. *(Can you hear the soft music playing in the background?)* Already, this is proving to be a time of bonding and encouragement and keeps us all in tune with how Drew is doing.

I asked Drew to say grace. He didn't hesitate, and it was precious: "Dear Lord, our heavenly Father, *(pause)* I say grace tonight *(pause)* to You *(pause)* and all Your friends. Amen."

December 7, 2018

I have grown to look forward to my Friday three-hour alone time with no musts, shoulds, or oughts tugging at me. My weekly time of refreshment with no advance plans (other than to get into the car and see where it takes me) serves as a time of clarity and perhaps preparation for widowhood, which is silently inching closer. Where I once shared Drew's lively conversation and laughter, now I willingly embrace the solitude of dining alone with the companionship of my Kindle or laptop. I am learning to savor my own company. And I know that Drew will be there when I get home. He may not know me, but he needs me. I can't imagine coming home to an empty house. But one day, I will. Looking ahead at the inevitable helps to condition me for the future and increases my appreciation of the present.

Where to go today? Someplace cozy and off the beaten path. The car headed east on Route 9 toward Rehoboth Beach, but the light was green as I approached the five-points intersection, so I went straight through it and into Lewes. Where can I get a nice breakfast? Ah! Maybe Nectar is open. A parking space awaited me, and the warm atmosphere of the eclectic place welcomed me.

The hostess seated me at a small wooden table by the wall beside a massive fireplace that blazed gaily. I chose the chair that put my back toward the door and sat facing a floor-to-ceiling bookcase with artfully arranged volumes that could have easily come from the Abbott library: Agatha Christie, Alfred Hitchcock, Norman Rockwell, Webster's Dictionary, Holy Bible.

I ordered Apple Cinnamon Oatmeal (lightly seasoned oats cooked in almond milk and topped with sautéed apples, pecans, raisins, and flax seeds) and a Lean Green Machine smoothie (green apple, cucumber, basil, spinach, lime, and jalapeno). Torie, my waitress, kept me supplied with fresh coffee and water as the muted conversation of others floated around me. It was heavenly.

December 13, 2018

Wayne Clark forwarded an article to me from the National Institute of Health on Aging, "5 Holiday Tips for Alzheimer's Caregivers" (see Appendix II) and his email said, "I know you are already doing all of these tips." His thoughtful confirmation that I'm on the right track did absolute wonders for my morale.

In a separate email, the Upper Room staff posed the question, "Are you feeling overwhelmed by stress this Christmas season?" And then suggested that we get a cup of tea, sit down, and follow seven tried-and-true techniques for restoring calm (see Appendix III). The best part of this list is that you don't have to do many of these activities before you feel better.

December 15, 2018

So many little things can catch me off guard.

Drew is sleeping more now, eighteen out of twenty-four hours, and his inactivity is making his bowel movements sluggish. The nurse recommends apple juice, more water, and prunes to alleviate constipation. I hope my home remedy doesn't result in diarrhea because he can't make it to the bathroom in a hurry.

Just when I think I'm going to be getting him from one room to the other in the transport chair, he surprises me and walks on his own. Yesterday, he went to the bathroom without me and *locked the door!* Fortunately, he came out of the bathroom before I slipped into full panic mode.

Solution: I asked Troy to come right over and turn the knob around, so the lock is on my side of the door.

I've learned the value of a very important word: TOMORROW. Since Drew can't remember anything from one moment to the next, if I answer his questions with the magic word *tomorrow*, he almost always drops the issue and is content to wait. For example, when he says, "Let's go home," I tell him, "We're staying here just for tonight. We'll go home tomorrow." His shoulders visibly relax. He's satisfied. It puts his concern at bay and makes it manageable for him—and me. *Tomorrow* has become my favorite word.

Yesterday, Ella came later than usual to get Drew showered and dressed, and he was sitting comfortably in the recliner.

"No!" He would have none of it!

We left the room and came back to try again, and he was still adamant. Since it's more important to keep him calm than get him dressed, I told Ella to forget it today, and I would see her tomorrow. Caregiving isn't about efficiency; it's about caring.

Tomorrow became today. This time when Ella came, Drew was finishing up his breakfast, which is our normal routine. He seemed delighted to see her and uttered no complaint as she wheeled him to the bathroom in the transport chair.

December 19, 2018

Half asleep around 12:30 a.m., I heard Drew get up to go to the bathroom and said, "You need help, hon?"

"No," he said. And promptly fell. Thankfully, he didn't hurt himself.

I, on the other hand, strained my back struggling to get him from the floor to the recliner. Try as he might to help me help him, his legs had zero strength and were as useless to us as rubber bands. Somehow—huffing and puffing, grunting and groaning, muttering and sputtering, pulling and tugging—I managed to get him from the recliner into the transport chair.

There was no way, with my now-aching back, that I could or would attempt to get him back into our king-sized bed.

Who should I call? Dana said she and John could "come right over at any hour," but she looked exhausted at dinner, and I knew she had a stressful day ahead of her. Our pastor, Mike Williams, repeatedly told me to call whenever I needed help, so this time I did, and he answered right away. But it turns out he was recovering from hernia surgery and couldn't lift anything heavy.

Next step: Call 911 non-emergency to request the EMTs. I had barely hung up the phone when Pastor Mike appeared at the front door.

"I can't lift him," he said, "but I figured I could be here for moral support."

We chatted for quite a while and figured the ambulance must be on another call. Mike suggested I reach out to Harry Fletcher, who lives a couple of streets over and is used to middle-of-the-night calls because he's a firefighter.

Harry arrived at the same time as the ambulance. I ushered Harry and the EMTs into the bedroom, where Pastor Mike was convincing Drew to stay calm. The paramedics went right to work and lifted Drew as easily as if he were a child. With all the lights on and the lighthearted banter that came naturally from our predicament, it felt like we were having a surprise party. Ha! I guess we were.

I apologized to the paramedics for the inconvenience, and they said with all sincerity that they would rather respond to a hundred calls like this than one of their customary crises.

December 20, 2018

Decorating a big Christmas tree seemed one tradition too many, and when I discussed it with Kim, she suggested a three-foot tabletop tree and offered it as their family gift to us. She sent me links to ones she liked online, and I chose a lighted one with snow on the needles. It came today, on a Thursday, just in time for our family dinner, so we trimmed it together with the smallest decorations I had in the attic: baby's breath, ribbon, little gold boxes, white beads, and fluffy red sprigs. It's adorable! And I didn't have to move any furniture around. Bigger is not always better.

I love this tree and the joy it represents in a household that is learning to scale back on the way we "always did it before." Priorities: loving one another, being sensitive to our changing needs, preserving the flavor of tradition but not the hassle, honoring the sanctity of the season, focusing on what matters, being together, and savoring the time we have.

December 21, 2018

Tonight, I realized we're quickly approaching the time when Drew will be fully bedridden.

I drove him to Burger King for dinner and parked right in front of the door. It took him forever to get out of the car. I brought the walker along for good measure, but that proved to be more cumbersome than helpful.

He shuffled and scuffed his way to a seat, and when it was time to go, he had trouble getting out of the booth. The walk back to the car was tortuous. Each step was slow and halting, and he almost fell attempting to get into the car. The walker clattered to the pavement, but I was able to catch him and get us home safely.

I'm not doing this again, I thought. It was too dangerous for him and too taxing for me. Most likely, this would be our last dinner out.

At 11:30 p.m., after I got his nighttime (extra-absorbent) incontinence underwear changed, his pajamas on, and had him all tucked into bed, I went to the kitchen to start the dishwasher. I was gone for no more than three minutes when I heard a thud and rushed back to the bedroom. There was Drew, looking sheepish, all sprawled out on the carpet between the king-sized bed and the hospital bed. Once more, he wasn't hurt because, for the most part, he had slid himself to the floor.

He insists his weak but restless legs will hold him and continually tries to get up to go to the bathroom. The more I caution him about the danger of standing, the more he wants to prove me wrong. I had to bite my tongue to keep from saying, "I told you so." Instead, I forced myself to keep a cheerful tone. I was frightened, frustrated, and on the verge of furious because he's incapable of comprehending the facts. The conversation went like this:

"So, you've gotten yourself in a fix, eh?"

"Yep, help me up."

"No, I'm sorry, hon. I can't. I tried to get you off the floor the day before yesterday and hurt my back. I'm not doing that again."

"Come on—you can do it. I know you can."

I shook my head. "Nope. Not smart. I'm not going to attempt to lift you. But what I *can* do is make you as comfortable as possible until we get somebody to come and help." I got him a pillow and blanket and called Dana. True to her word, she and John came immediately, and the two of them put him into the "baby bed" where we could put the rails up.

Drew and I thanked them profusely.

Life will look different to Drew now that he won't be able to get out of the house. It'll look different to me, too. But my silver lining is this: when you put your life on hold for another, it's like fulfilling John 15:13, *"Greater love has no one than this: to lay down one's life for one's friends."*

January 7, 2019

While I was sleeping last night, Drew went out in the cold in his stocking feet with no coat. Fortunately, from what I can gather, he went straight to Troy's house. I found out at 2:30 a.m. when Troy brought him home. Always the unexpected. Drew did that a year ago, and I thought his wandering days were over since his legs are so weak. Not so, apparently! I've gotten lax putting the board in the track of the sliding glass door and will install a child-proof lock pronto!

This time, Troy said his dad seemed more lucid and calm than a year ago when he was disoriented. Instead of shivering in a panic, he knocked on the door and asked, "Do you want to walk me back home?"

"Sure," Troy told him, "nothing like strolling in the dark in the wee hours."

Troy is savoring this impromptu father-and-son outing as one of the special moments he has been able to have with his dad.

I've had more interruptions than usual today. Drew is feisty and wouldn't take his shower when Ella came. We decided she will try again tomorrow.

I tried to get him situated in several different locations: the couch, the kitchen table, a chair in my office, and when I focused on my work, he moved himself to the bed where he stretched out on top of the covers. When I found him there, I covered him up.

"Have I been a good boy?" he asked.

I wanted to swat him and say *NO*, but I smiled sweetly. "Drew Abbott is a good boy," I said, and tucked the cozy blanket around him before going back to my office.

He stayed in bed for all of three minutes before he teetered and faltered his way back to me, forcing me to get up and guide him into the chair in the corner of the room. I'm trying my best to keep my publishing projects on some sort of schedule, but I have a cold, and my patience is short. I'm working on two children's picture books, and even though they are a delightful diversion, the interruptions are killing me. My other clients are being extremely patient with me.

One small advantage of having laryngitis is that I can hold up a sign that says, "I can't talk," point to my throat, and make a *sorry* face when he asks his dozen questions. But each time I hold up the sign, I still have to turn around, which means I've lost my train of thought *again*. His most recent questions were, "What time do we quit?" "When are we going to have dinner?" "What time are we leaving?" If only I could get closure on *one* thing.

When he's not asking questions, he's making comments. "Shoes are neat. I can wear a pair of shoes for a long time." And he's constantly drumming his fingernails on the end table, whistling, or doing his Donald Duck imitation. Constantly moving. This is a relatively new occurrence. I guess some part of him wants to "do" something, and the body parts that work are doing their best to accommodate him.

He can fold towels and sort socks, but he'd rather watch me do it. When paying bills, I found I could have him sit with me and affix the stamps to the envelopes.

He likes to pop air bubbles in cushioned packing sheets. "Pop, pop, pop," he says with glee. And then a shadow passes over his face. "That's what happened to me."

I had given him a *Kids Paint by Sticker* book for Christmas, so I pulled it out of the closet and thought he might be able to do some by himself. *Nope.* It surprised me that he needed help bending the page to release the stickers and couldn't place them on the page. I would be happy to see him place a sticker in the wrong place. After all, the goal isn't perfection; it's involvement. But he couldn't figure out how to get it off his finger. *Correction.* He did get it off his finger and stuck it on his nose with a big grin.

"Nice job, Dukie," I said, using the childhood pet name his dad called him.

We resumed playing, and I found he could identify the matching numbers, so I placed a few for him. It wasn't long before I realized he had stopped telling me the numbers and I was pretty much doing it by myself. Like a child, it doesn't take long before he's bored.

"All right, let's go," he said and made raspberry sounds.

I guess I've done enough work for one sitting. It's four o'clock, and I have my sister-in-law Shelly's homemade vegetable beef soup to heat up.

January 16, 2019

Drew's decline makes for an interesting discussion. He was resting in my office today and asked, "What's that thing on the wall?" I couldn't tell if he was pointing to the artwork, the clock, or the smoke detector, so I moved closer.

"This?" I touched the clock.

"Yes. What's it do?"

That took me back a bit. "What's it do? It tells time."

"What does that mean? Who does it tell?"

Hmmm. How do I answer that? "Well, it tells me or you or anybody who looks at it who wants to know what time it is."

"How does it do that? Does it talk?"

He had me there. I could see this spiraling into a conversation with a bottomless pit I couldn't dig my way out of. I decided to redirect. "That's a good-looking watch you have there on your arm. What does it do?"

"It tells time."

Voila! "It sure does. What time is it?"

He stared at his watch for a long while. "I don't know. What time is it?"

I glanced at the wall clock. "It's 2:15 in the afternoon."

"How could you tell?"

"The hands on the clock told me."

"I don't see any hands. How did it tell you? Does it talk?"

Time for a change of scenery. "How about a Coke and a nice ham and cheese sandwich?" I helped him into the transfer chair, and off we rolled to the kitchen for lunch. Maybe he'll take a nap afterward, and I can sneak back to my office and try to get some work done.

January 30, 2019

I wrote the following email to Cheryl Skid, one of my authors and a dear friend in Missouri:

> Drew continues to decline and requires more and more of my time. I am rarely able to work at the keyboard, so my publishing is crawling along, and I'm behind on tax preparation and stuff. Troy has neck cancer, and his chemo and radiation treatments are hard on him; although he's still helping out (shaving his dad every other day, taking out our trash, doing maintenance on my computer), the side effects are closing in on him, and he's not available to stay with Drew on short notice if I need to run to the store, bank, post office, etc. I have to do more advance planning for coverage. Drew doesn't know me half the time but gets panicky if I'm not in sight. At least he's not combative, just confused.

Cheryl gave me this brief but supportive reply: Candy, are you saying Troy, your son, has neck cancer? Oh, Candy! My love for you travels toward you, climbs up on your lap, and reaches up to kiss you on the cheek. Oh, sweetheart. I don't think I recall you ever mentioning Troy having cancer. This is such a horrific whirlwind time of pain for the saints of God.

We found out just before Christmas, and he asked me not to share it until after his treatments began. He's had three weeks of chemo and radiation so far. Another friend is going through similar fires, and the Lord gave her 2 Corinthians 1:3-7, which is ministering to me, too. Here's how it reads in *The Message*:

All praise to the God and Father of our Master, Jesus the Messiah! Father of all mercy! God of all healing counsel! He comes alongside us when we go through hard times, and before you know it, he brings us alongside someone else who is going through hard times so that we can be there for that person just as God was there for us. We have plenty of hard times that come from following the Messiah, but no more so than the good times of his healing comfort—we get a full measure of that, too.

When we suffer for Jesus, it works out for your healing and salvation. If we are treated well, given a helping hand and encouraging word, that also works to your benefit, spurring you on, face forward, unflinching. Your hard times are also our hard times. When we see that you're just as willing to endure the hard times as to enjoy the good times, we know you're going to make it, no doubt about it.

There is a purpose in everything God allows, and it is good. How do I know? Because God is good, and He knows just what it will take for us to grow in character and into His likeness.

February 11, 2019

Doris went with me to the support group tonight, and Dana stayed with Drew. When we got back, she told us she watched him walk down the hall to the bathroom by himself. As he strained to keep his legs moving and keep his balance, he kept saying to himself, "Push. Push."

She recorded their conversation. Here are snippets of some of the things he said:

"I'd like to have a set up where we'll all be a little closer; I'd like us to be more together."

"I don't feel like anybody. But maybe that's normal."

"You do a little thinking, like what I can do better. But I don't want to wrap myself up into something."

"Something's broke" (pointing to his head); "I'd like to finish this thing up with a nice warm feeling. I don't know how I'm handling that. I feel out of it. I don't know what's come in the picture. I don't like that all of a sudden I don't feel in charge so much."

About getting older: "Life's full of surprises." He pinched, then fanned his fingers out. "Surprise, surprise!" he said with a grin.

"There's been a big change from what I was. Help me figure out what I was."

The secret to having a good life: "Be honest and play your game right."

The conclusion Dana drew from their conversation is that her dad realized he was stumped and unable to solve the problem he and we are facing.

February 13, 2019

I haven't been able to spend any quality time at the keyboard, and when I do, I want to be entirely focused on the projects. Drew has severe separation anxiety and needs me by his side continually, so I'm very grateful for the many friends and family who have been lifting us in prayer. He's been increasingly agitated and insists more and more frequently that he needs to "go home."

Today ranks right up there in my top ten worst days as a caregiver. Drew's agitation began at 2:00 a.m. when he traipsed all around the house on legs that could barely hold him up, looking for a way to get out and go "home" until he fell in the bedroom and barely missed cracking his head on the corner of the dresser. That sobered and humbled him for a few minutes while I tugged and maneuvered him into the transport chair and got him back into bed. I strained my back in the process. BIG NO-NO! No sooner did I get him settled than he announced, "I need to go home," and began squirming to get up again.

I popped two Tylenol in my mouth and told him, "Good luck with that. You're on your own, Bud. My back hurts, and I can't help you."

I laid down and rolled over, listening to him roam around the house, bumping into things. At that point, I was too tired to monitor him. The hidden Door Guardian lock has been working well on the front door, but Drew could still sneak out the back, so I bought a childproof lock to attach to the sliding door in the kitchen. It's plastic and was easy enough to install (I did it myself). I figured it would do the job.

I underestimated his determination.

At 5:00 this morning, a loud crash woke me up, followed by the sound of the sliding glass door opening and closing. I jumped out of bed and ran outside, calling for him in the dark. With him being hard of hearing and the din from the downpour of rain, I realized he couldn't hear my tinny voice. So, I slipped my shoes on and grabbed a coat from the hall closet. Before I could turn to go back through the kitchen, I glimpsed a blur out the living room window that looked like Drew stumbling past. I moved toward the window for a closer look, and it was!

In the few seconds it took me to get to the front door and unlock the bolts, he had fallen in our front yard in the rain, face down in the muddy grass, arms flailing at his side—with a tree branch just inches from his face!

Mitch Cooper, our neighbor, had spotted him about the same time I did and came right over. Together, we got Drew off the ground, but his legs were useless to help. We carried him into the house and Mitch held him while I positioned the transport chair beneath his knees so we could lower him into it. I looked him over, and other than being cold and drenched, he didn't seem to be hurt. He thanked Mitch but immediately began rambling about needing to go home and asking for his help. Mitch and I exchanged sad, exasperated looks, and he reminded me to call if I needed him or Linda. (Later, I learned that Mitch had been experiencing heart problems and shouldn't have been lifting anything.)

Alone again with Drew, my husband began spewing ugly names at me I've never heard from his mouth before and kept asking why I was so "mean" to him. Then he would plead, thinking he could persuade me that way. Mentally, I've been able to process that this is Alzheimer's speaking and not my Drew, but emotionally, his words twisted my gut like a balloon being manipulated by a clown.

The insults and begging went on for *hours*. I wheeled him into the bedroom to clean him up and tried to get him to go back to bed, but he would have none of it. He peppered me with "go home" the whole time I fixed our breakfast and insisted I take him back to the living room to sit on the couch, where he continued his mantra. I tried redirecting by asking questions, using bridged phrases, and flat out changing the subject, to no avail. If I tried to walk away, he talked louder, and I didn't want to leave him alone. He was fixated—and stubborn.

Just as I was at my wit's end, Jodie came bouncing in expecting to work on publishing. But she took one look at my close-to-tears face and knew that I had more pressing needs. She intervened by trying to carry on a soothing conversation with Drew, but every word only served to make him more determined not to cooperate unless she would help him to get "home."

By 2:00 p.m., I managed to break away from him long enough to call Hospice and have them send a nurse who said this could be a progression of the disease but is more likely a urinary tract infection and managed to get a urine sample for testing. She provided medicine with instructions to give it to him at bedtime, and it worked like a charm, knocking him out within ten minutes. Maybe we'll both be able to get some rest tonight.

February 14, 2019

We had a family Valentine's Day dinner tonight with flowers, a *Love You* balloon, and spaghetti with Wyatt's homemade sauce. I made brownies and offered them first to Drew.

"Oh, brownies!" he said. "For me?" He clutched the plate and held onto it as he ate the top brownie.

It took a lot of convincing to get him to share. He finally relented, and after the plate made the rounds, we put the remaining brownies in front of him. He took a second brownie, took a bite out of it, and reached for a third. We all got a kick out of him because he looked so comical, and this is totally out of character. His "real self" would have been generous, always putting others first.

Later, Saige asked for another brownie. She even said please, and I wish you could have seen the scowl her granddad gave her as he grabbed the plate. Gentle persuasion didn't work, and we had to resort to a bit of a tug-of-war before he relented. Too funny! He was like a two-year-old saying, "MINE."

At the end of the meal, Kim and Dana stood up to chat, and I went to the other room to get the transport chair. While I was gone, Drew tried to stand up, but his legs collapsed. Dana caught him and was able to aim his bottom toward his chair, where he landed with a thud. Glad she has quick reflexes!

By the time I got there with the transport chair, he was too weak to get into it so Wyatt and Troy had to help me maneuver him. Now they know firsthand how closely he needs to be watched. Telling them about an incident like this is a lot different than experiencing it. This is the value of having weekly family dinners.

With all the commotion, I forgot to give Drew his Valentine's present until everyone had left but Dana. Together, we helped him open the variety of small gift bags I'd prepared, one for each of the five senses. Sight (a magnifying glass), Sound (a push-button sound machine with sixteen hilarious sound effects), Smell (Timberline cologne, more for my benefit than his), Taste (a heart-shaped box of chocolates), and Touch (Touch and Feel picture cards). He didn't show much interest in any of them, but the fart machine got a workout.

Oh, and for my special Valentine's bedtime gift for my beloved, I put a metal bar in the track of the sliding glass door. Now, both exits are secured.

February 16, 2019

I gave up leading our writers' group when Drew was diagnosed with Alzheimer's years ago, but I still attend the monthly meetings. I enjoy the sense of normalcy it gives me. People continue to look to me for direction, which is bittersweet. It makes me feel good to know that others value my opinion, but I don't relish the weight of additional responsibility that goes with it. Many times, it feels like work for me to have to think. Swinging between two worlds—the intensely personal caregiving role and the joy-filled cacophony of enthusiastic writers—I find it difficult to concentrate during the flow of multiple conversations.

Unfortunately, I made a communication blunder that resulted in hard feelings with one of the members, and every attempt I made to reconcile only seemed to make matters worse. At one point in today's meeting during a hot debate from confusion over something I had said, I blurted out, "Announcement, announcement; I have an announcement." It took a while for the group to quiet down.

"Candy has something to say," a voice rang out.

When I had their attention, I proceeded. "I have something to say, and it's important." I paused for effect. "I cannot be trusted."

They gave me stunned and horrified looks.

"That didn't come out right," I said, "which proves the point I'm trying to make. What I mean is that with Drew and all the stress I'm under at home, I sometimes say things wrong and don't even know it. I can't trust myself and wanted to caution you to take whatever I say with a grain of salt. Test it. Double-check it. Don't take the things I say at face value."

After a brief flurry of reassurances, the meeting continued, and I felt a baffling sense of freedom and relief.

Drew gave me a little comic relief when I got home. He tried to recite *Eenie Meenie Miney Mo, catch a bullfrog by the toe*, but it came out, "Eenie Meenie Miney Mo, catch a booger by the toe." He stopped and made a goofy face. "That's not right, is it? You don't catch a booger, do you?"

"Well, you could try," I said. "It might be easier than catching a bullfrog."

Every caregiver needs some silliness in her day.

February 25, 2019

The nurse came today and told me Drew could no longer put any weight on his legs. Although he is unable to get out of bed, he still tries. At 10:30 tonight, I had no sooner stepped from the bedroom into the kitchen than he called for me. I found him hanging onto the side of our bed, so I lowered him to the floor. *Now what?*

I called Hospice for advice, and they said to call 911 and tell them it was a non-emergency, that I just needed help lifting him from the floor to the bed. They came quickly. *Problem solved. For now.*

"Choose your attitude,
change your life."

— *Deborah Smith Pegues*

CHAPTER TWELVE

Bedridden

March 3, 2019

February 25th was the last of our close encounters with falls that could have ended in disaster. Since then, Drew has been confined to the hospital bed and will be from this point forward. Life looks different—for him, for me.

During the past week, I've been on an intensive learning curve with instruction and tips from nurses, aides, and friends who have experience with this aspect of personal hygiene and comfort. I'm learning to become proficient with things I never thought about before, including tools for handling someone who is bedbound (I found most of these items on Amazon):

- TOMI Turn – a quilted pad with grips that allows me to single-handedly turn, reposition, and slide Drew in the bed.
- Bed alarm with a magnetic pull cord so I can tell if and when he tries to get out of bed.
- Disposable washcloths (8 x 12) instead of flushable wipes
- Medline FitGuard Touch nitrate disposable gloves, powder-free.
- Balmex adult rash cream to guard against bed sores.
- Plastic basin for bedbath

- Now that he can no longer wear pull-ups, I've switched to AbMedline Extended Wear briefs with tabs. They last all night without leaking. Let me tell you, changing your husband's underwear and being in charge of poop patrol sure does bring a whole new meaning to intimacy in marriage.
- Disposable oral care swabs to clean his teeth (we dip them in mouthwash)
- Lorazepam, which the Hospice doctor prescribed for restlessness and agitation.
- Pill crusher
- Latex gloves

Often, I find myself telling him, "We're in a hard place; there's no question about that. But we're going to make the best of it because that's how we're built."

He's hungry for assurance that I'm going to take care of him and will never leave. I tell him I love him and that he's the most important person to me in the world—that I'm not going anywhere—that I'll be with him into eternity. I can never tell him these things enough times because he doesn't remember hearing any of it as soon as the words leave my mouth.

When I go out, I tell him where I'm going and say, "I may have to leave for a little while, but I always come back." He seems satisfied with that and sends me on my way without complaint.

We had to change our Thursday night family dinners to Sundays because of scheduling conflicts. And since we can no longer roll Drew to the dining room table, we decided to exchange our candles, china, and stemware for paper plates, and plastic cups so we can eat in the bedroom.

As we prepared the food and set up folding tables and chairs tonight, the commotion must have been too much for Drew. Kim went to his bedside to console him, but rather than respond favorably, he glared at her and snapped, "I wasn't talking to you."

I was in the kitchen, and she ran past me, bawling, and dashed into the bathroom—something I haven't seen her do since she was twelve.

My motherly instinct kicked in. I rushed after her to find out what happened. She told me she tried to hold back the tears but couldn't. She's been a brave and strong sounding board for us all for so many months that the dam broke. All her pent-up emotions came gushing out. I tried to offer soothing words in hopes of making things right. But she would have none of it.

"Mom, don't try to fix it. You're always doing that. Just let me cry. I need this."

Her words came as a slap in the face to me, but I saw the wisdom in it as she sobbed out the details of all she had bottled up in her.

"Don't let me mess up dinner," she said. "You go ahead and eat, and I'll get something later."

After Kim calmed down, she said, "Mom, how do you do it?"

"Do what?"

"Handle everything you have to deal with and not cry."

I don't really know. It's like my tears have been locked up and I've steeled myself. I was raised by parents who were realists and faced problems head-on, with no excuses, denial, or whitewashing, so facing difficulties objectively must be in my DNA. But I didn't think about that right then. As she sat there pouring her guts out, I wondered why I hadn't had an emotional blowout. *Was I out of touch with reality?*

"I almost envy you," I said. "I would like to have a good cry, but it's as if the Lord is holding me secure as I move about doing whatever needs to be done. I think this must be what the grace of God looks like."

Later, when I was reading *Why We Need the Gifts of the Holy Spirit* by Rick Renner, he opened up Scriptures that confirmed it is, indeed, the grace of God that I'm experiencing.

- God graciously imparts a special touch that *enables, empowers, and strengthens* the recipients.
- God's grace is an empowering touch that enables you to be and do what you could have *never* been or done before.

- Grace is *never* silent or invisible, and it is always accompanied by some type of *outward evidence or demonstration.*

I'm able to do what I do because I began learning how to keep in step with the Holy Spirit in 1983. I can tell a big difference when I try to do things in my own strength. It's not pretty: I'm confused, cranky, irritable, easily offended, selfish, defensive, judgmental, hard-hearted. You get the idea. Everything seems difficult, dark, and negative when I'm out of sync with the Spirit.

One of the things I love best about God is that He loves me even when I'm at my worst and is quick to forgive and help me get back on track.

March 8, 2019

While I was basking in tranquility and savoring a fluffy asparagus, ham, and feta omelet at Honey's Farm Fresh Restaurant in Lewes during my three-hour Friday morning respite, Tom was at my house trying everything he could think of to calm Drew down.

Ella came to bathe him and had to wake him from a sound sleep. *Uh*-oh. He fussed with her and complained the whole time, but she got the job done. Typically, Drew would go back to sleep so Tom could read, but he stayed wide awake and argumentative—big time.

Just before I returned home, Tom discovered the magic bullet: MUSIC. The Easy Listening channel on cable TV did the trick. If he hadn't told me about the nightmare he and Ella faced in my absence, I'd have never known.

When I was changing Drew's incontinence briefs tonight, he became agitated and seized my hands so tight it hurt. I managed to pull away.

He gave me his fiercest look, clenched his fists, and glared at me.

Fear shot through me for the first time. I backed away and put my hands up to my face with my elbows out, cowering in surrender. "Don't hurt me!" I said.

He continued to scowl at me with menace in his eyes.

And then, inspired to change the mood, I dramatized my fear by backing up as far as I could against the fireplace, assuming the role of a damsel in distress tied to the railroad tracks by Snidely Whiplash, the dastardly villain. "Pleeeease, don't hurt me!"

My antics jolted Drew from his angry place and brought him back to me. He didn't see the humor, but it did bring him to his senses.

"I never want you to be afraid of me," he said, remorse written all over his face.

I took advantage of his moment of clarity to reason with him. "I'm trying my best to take good care of you, and it would be nice if you could help me."

"I'll do anything you need," he said.

That sounded good, but I knew it wasn't realistic. No matter how much he wanted to, Drew had lost control of the ability to live his life as he wished. But I hadn't finished airing the grievance churning within me. "I can't have you lashing out at me. If you do, I'll have to leave the room, get help, or have you relocated. And I don't want to do any of that. I want to be right here with you, loving you and enjoying you."

He cooperated fully from then on. Maybe ten minutes later, just as I was about to finish changing him, he said softly, "I'm sorry."

That's my gentle, tender-hearted Drew. I hope he keeps coming back to me.

March 10, 2019

Dana, Troy, Kim, Wyatt, and Saige were sitting at folding tables in our bedroom enjoying one of my resurrected recipes from the '70s— Josiah Snelling's Fried Fish (black walnut-encrusted codfish)—and Drew and I were sharing one plate. The family talked about the scare we had in October with Drew's G.I. bleed and how grateful we are that he's still with us.

"I had an epiphany the other day," Dana said. "With all we've been through—what we're going through now and will be going through—I no longer see our family as individuals but as one unit."

"You mean like all of us rowing a boat together?" Kim said.

"Close," Dana said. "But it's more than that. Picture a cruise ship."

"Oh," I said. "You mean we're like crew members? The recreation director, captain, maitre d', cabin steward, that sort of thing?"

"No. It's not that we're on the ship together with each of us having different roles. It's more like we *are* the ship that's carrying Dad to his destination with Candy at the helm steering us in the right direction."

As devastating as Alzheimer's is, it's knitting our family together more than any other obstacle we've ever faced, and we've had plenty of them over the years. I hear accounts of too many families that are torn apart and estranged because of the pressures of dementia, and my heart goes out to them. We're so blessed to be able to recognize there is something good coming out of this nightmare we're living through.

I think we can always find something positive if we look hard enough. *Oh, yeah?* you're thinking. *Name one positive thing about the devil.* Okay. He works hard at his job.

A friend sent a text message asking how I'm doing, and it came on a particularly bad day when everything I touched seemed to fall apart. I didn't want to rehash my problems, so I replied, "I have many challenges, but they only serve to draw me closer to Jesus and depend on Him more." I felt better after I wrote that.

March 18, 2019

We have discontinued all of Drew's vitamins and most of his medications. He has difficulty swallowing pills, so I have liquid Lorazepam in case we need it, but I'll need to learn to use a syringe.

The nurse recommended Miralax because the disease causes his brain to stop communicating with his organs. He knows he has to go but doesn't know how to push, and we have to be careful to keep him from becoming constipated. But there's a fine balance. If I give the recommended dose, he has a blowout, and that's a mess for *me*, so I've found that a half-dose once a day is just right if he hasn't had a BM in two or three days.

Maria Johnson, a paid caregiver we have come to love already, saved me the agony of clipping Drew's toenails, and she's keeping them under control by filing them.

March 21, 2019

Between Sunday and yesterday, Drew celebrated his eighty-third birthday with a family dinner in the bedroom, lots of visitors, balloons, ice cream cake, and cards. He's adapting to the hospital bed nicely and hasn't tried to get up in a while. Having a steady stream of caring people has done us both good.

As for me, my heart is on a roller coaster ride as I'm frequently in A-fib with 122 HBM, then regular sinus rhythm which drops to 42 HBM. I saw the cardiologist on Tuesday, and they sent me home with a Zio Patch to monitor me for two weeks; in May, we'll discuss a cardiac ablation. If that doesn't work, I may need a pacemaker—all good options but most inconvenient. The adventure goes on, and I have tons of support. The Lord is refining me, for sure!

March 23, 2019

Conversations with Drew are a mystery. I discovered he was disoriented when he asked, "Are there people who oversee this establishment? I mean, is there someone I could talk to who takes care of everything here?"

"That would be me," I said. "I'm in charge of everything here. Stay close to me, and you'll always be fine."

He smiled and relaxed.

For a moment, I felt empowered. *Things are not as out of control as they appear. I'm in control! I'm in charge.* And then it hit me. Do I *want* to be in control? The secret to my ability to cope has been to trust the Holy Spirit to guide me moment-by-moment. The more I relax in His presence, the more I can release my loved ones and concerns into God's care. This is how I access my safe place of serenity, even amid upheavals and traumatic changes. Christ Jesus is constant, and no person or circumstance can take that peace and security from me. *No, I don't want to be in charge.* I want the One who holds all things together to be in charge.

March 25, 2019

Drew has been grumbling, restless, and argumentative all day. I think the reality is setting in that he's confined to bed with no change of scenery. On occasion, he says things that shock me, but never like this: "I think I'll just go out back and shoot myself."

I had no words of comfort or consolation for him. "Don't expect me to help you with that," I said as I turned on my heel and marched out of the room.

Allowing a few minutes to calm down, I returned and pulled up a chair beside him. I leaned in close, and said, "We have a bad situation, hon, but we're going to make the best of it. Because that's what we do. That's what we've always done when things are hard. It's how you and I are built. You have a whole lot of people who love you: Dana, Troy, Kim, and a whole lot more. Most of all, *I* love you, and I will *always* love you and be here to take care of you."

"No matter what?" he said.

"No matter what. I'm right here, and I'll be with you every day and every night. You're the most important person to me in the whole world. You live in a safe place, still have your wonderful personality, a beautiful home, and enough money for all the things we need. Besides, God is overseeing everything."

His shoulders relaxed, and he leaned back against the pillow. "So, I guess this isn't so bad, is it?"

"Not bad, at all."

About that time, Dana came in with a McDonald's bag, and he wolfed down the quarter pounder, French fries, and vanilla milkshake. We were so pleased his appetite was back.

Dana left, and I settled into the recliner to read. It felt so good to have a happy ending after a trying day.

I read two pages before he said, "Why is it so hot in here?" I took his sheets and blanket off, lowered the thermostat, and aimed a fan at him. Still, he was hot, and his face was flushed. His forehead felt clammy.

And then he threw up. Everywhere. Clothes, bedding, mattress pad, carpet, even the bed alarm monitor. My day was far from over, and the mess was so big I felt my eyes bulging as I stood there with no clue how to start cleaning up or even how to approach Drew since he was covered in slime. Immobilized, Drew's voice snapped me out of my stupor.

"Candy! Do something!"

"Sorry, hon. I'm thinking." I was staring, not thinking. But I needed to, and quick. My first rational thought was, *I need help!* I called Kim.

"Wyatt and I can come," she said, "but we're at Blue Water Grill, and our dinner just came out."

Having the assurance that someone was coming gave me courage, so I told them to relax and enjoy their meal. I hung up, offered soothing words to Drew, and gathered a basin and long-handled spoon from the utensil rack in the kitchen. Gagging my way along, I managed to scrape most of the goop out of the way before they arrived.

Together, we changed the sheets and Drew.

Fortunately, there were no further incidents, and he didn't have a stomach bug. Unfortunately, that will have to be his last McDonald's meal.

Oh, and for some reason, Wyatt looked under my bed and discovered a rifle I didn't know was there. I mentioned Drew's earlier remark about shooting himself and asked Wyatt to please take the gun with him, which he did. Not that Drew could have gotten out of bed and done anything with it—I just don't want guns in my house, not even unloaded.

On the other hand, years ago, I attended a "Tea and Target" event sponsored by the Delaware Family Policy Council. After a formal tea and half day of training on a 9mm pistol, I'm capable of handling a weapon if I decide to renew my interest in personal gun safety.

April 4, 2019

Pacemaker day. Kim drove me to the hospital and stayed with me during and after my surgery. Drew stayed at home, and I left the following letter to be read to him every time he asked for me:

Dear Drew,

I'll be at Beebe Hospital to have a procedure to guard my heart. It's a quick surgery (no more than an hour), and they'll keep me overnight for observation. Maria and Doris will stay with you, and Doris will be here overnight. Kim will bring me home on Friday, so I won't be gone long. Until then, be a good boy, and I'll be thinking of you every minute.

Only you, sweet Drew!

Love,

Candy

April 8, 2019

I've been home from the hospital for a few days (the procedure went well), but I'm not allowed to lift anything heavy for a while, which means I can't change Drew's briefs in the evenings by myself. Hospice has increased their CNA coverage, and I've made arrangements for two paid caregivers to help out.

Drew is doing well with the increased attention, asking where they live, how long they've been there, what school they attended. Every now and then, he glances my way.

"Look at her," he says. "Isn't she beautiful?"

I smile, and he runs through his litany of questions again, punctuated by compliments that I welcome no matter how often he repeats them. Why? Because he says, "Isn't she pretty?" with such enthusiasm and sincerity.

April 22, 2019

Drew is going stir-crazy in the bed and has been trying to climb out all day. The Delaware Hospice physician is in charge of his care, but

Drew doesn't know him. He *does* know and respect Dr. Palekar, our primary care physician, so I throw his name around a lot:

"You need to stay in bed, hon. Dr. Palekar's orders."

"What do you mean?"

"This is the hospital bed that Dr. Palekar ordered for you to have here at home in our bedroom."

"So?"

"So, there's one condition: you have to stay in bed. If you don't, Dr. Palekar said he'd have to put you in the hospital where he can keep an eye on you."

He stopped straining to get out. Worked like a charm. At least three times today I tell him about Dr. Palekar, and he calms right down.

Physically, all three of our kids and I have been having challenges:

Dana had the flu, followed by strep throat, so she was out of commission for quite a while, although she's on the mend now. Sometimes grief, whether denied or openly acknowledged, has a way of lowering our immune system.

Troy finished his chemo and radiation five weeks ago and is finally able to eat a little solid food. He has to keep water handy because his saliva glands don't work, but he's been brave and mature, staying optimistic throughout the whole process.

Since early March, Kim has been struggling with depression and anxiety triggered by the incident at our March 3rd family dinner when Drew snapped at her. I guess she'd been trying to be strong and positive for everyone (Wyatt's parents have health issues, too) while teaching full-time and doing all the right things that motherhood entails. But dodging stress, anxiety, worry, and grief isn't healthy. They can only be held at bay for so long before something gives. Her doctor prescribed medication that took a while to kick in, but it's working well now.

My heart. The pacemaker is functioning nicely, but my A-fib still flares up, so the cardiologist mentioned again that I may have to have an ablation. (I'll think about that another day).

April 24, 2019

Our first five-day respite is fast approaching. An ambulance will pick Drew up at 12:30 Saturday afternoon and take him to the Delaware Hospice Center in Milford. They'll bring him home on May 2nd. Dana is organizing a schedule for coverage by family, friends, and paid caregivers to keep Drew company from 9 a.m. to 9 p.m. each day. I'm a little concerned about him being alone at night, but I'm trusting the Lord for that.

I'm nervous and eager to have some quality "alone time" and am REALLY looking forward to these five days. I plan to spend the first two days at home catching up on my writing and the other three days at our condo in Fenwick Island. I'm not sure I'll know how to relax, but I'm eager to try. I can't remember the last time I had a stretch of undisturbed silence to sit with my Lord. I've been cautioned that I may still hear Drew calling for me even when he's not here, so I may close my office door and play soft music. I've already reserved two other blocks of time in June and July in hopes that this goes well for Drew.

Hey, good news: my heart has been in normal sinus rhythm for two days now!

May 1, 2019

Drew made the transition smoothly, without complaint. Maria helped get him ready and followed the ambulance to Milford, where she stayed with him for a couple of hours before the next volunteer relieved her.

Ahhh, time alone with nobody needing me. My respite plans went out the window from the first moment I had the house to myself. It's been four days and until now, my fingers haven't touched the keyboard. Packing to go to the condo seemed like too much effort—one more thing to do. And so, I didn't. Instead, I allowed myself "not to do." To discover what it means to "rest."

The weather was glorious with crisp, clean air. The first thing I did was brew a fresh pot of coffee and set up the wireless speaker on the deck. I sat in the wicker rocking chair for the first time in forever and tried to absorb the wonder of wispy white clouds as they played tag with one another. Interwoven silvery jet streams stretched their tendrils against the backdrop of a cerulean sky.

Calypso music to the rhythm of steel drums transported me to a tropical paradise. Instead of drinking my coffee black as usual, I pampered myself by pouring a generous amount of French vanilla creamer usually reserved for guests. Birds chirped as a soft breeze kissed my cheeks; fluffy-tailed squirrels scampered up tree trunks and leapt from limb to limb; Buttercup rested her Cocker Spaniel plumpness at my feet, snoring softly; Midnight purred and brushed her silky black body against my legs, while two small gray bunnies romped in the back yard. It's a regular menagerie around here, and I haven't appreciated it in years. I inhaled the aroma of budding trees and fresh-cut grass. It seemed God withheld nothing from me.

I gave myself permission to float through my days with no agenda: cooking simple meals; washing Drew's sheets and making his bed so it will be ready for him; tidying up areas that have been nagging for attention for months; paying bills, and doing whatever my mood called for. The farthest I strayed from home was to Walmart, where I leisurely roamed the aisles and made light conversation with strangers. Mostly, I read one book after another, watched movies, and napped. It is well with my soul.

I called Drew twice but decided it was best if I didn't contact him during our respite. Hearing from me confused him and drew me back into the caregiver role; afterward, he didn't remember I had called, and I fretted about how he would handle our remaining time apart.

Periodically, I got reports that he was doing well but had some incidents of not-so-good. Dana told me an aide came in to bathe and change him, and he called her "an asshole."

The aide, knowing this kind of behavior is not uncommon, went along with it. "Yes, I guess I can be an asshole."

Just then, a nurse came in and added to the litany, "That's right; she sure can be an asshole."

With that, Drew stiffened. "You can't talk about her that way!"

May 7, 2019

Drew insisted his mother was alive, and he wanted to talk to her. "She's not home," I said, thinking that would deter him.

"How do you know? Call her anyway. The number is 856-6649" *(our number).* I told him if I called that number, it would ring here, and not her house.

"Try it anyway."

Doris was here, listening, and pulled out her cell phone. "I'll call." She dialed and handed the phone to Drew.

"It's ringing," he said.

When the phone rang, I answered. "See, it's me. This is our phone."

Drew didn't comprehend any of that. His face lit up! He was sure he had his mother on the line and talked to her enthusiastically. Then he said, "Let me get Candy."

"Caandeee," he yelled.

Standing across the room from him and waving my arms to get his attention, I said into the phone, "I'm right here on the phone with you. I'm Candy. And I'm right here."

"Caandeee," he yelled again.

I hung up, and he continued talking on the phone. "I'm trying to find Candy so she can say hello." But nobody responded. "Are you there?" Still no response. "Hello? Hello?" He shook the phone and stared at it. "Something's wrong with this phone."

But, for a brief time, he had a nice chat with his mother, who died in 1985.

May 9, 2019

Last night, Drew was restless and woke me up off and on from 11 p.m. until 5 a.m. Every time I was about to doze off, he'd ask a question. His chatterbox was in high gear, and his monologue was punctuated with questions he expected me to answer. After too many times to count of deflecting, "Are you ready?" "Let's go home," "Where are my shoes?" I stopped answering him.

"Why won't you talk to me?" he wanted to know.

"I'm trying to sleep," I mumbled.

"What? At this hour? What time is it?"

I peeked at the clock. "It's 4:15 in the morning."

"So?"

"So, you've kept me awake all night long and, if you're not going to be quiet so I can sleep, I'm going to have to move to the couch."

"I'm sorry." He sounded sincere. Four seconds later, he said, "Can I ask just one more question?"

"Okay, just one."

"When are we going home?"

"Tomorrow. No more talking, okay?"

"Okay"—pause—"How far is it from here to Georgetown?"

The badgering continued. "Come on, let's go." "Are you ready?" "Let's get out of here." "We need to get home."

"That's it!" I shouted and threw my covers back. "We can't GO home. We ARE home. You have to stop talking. I can't take it anymore." I stood over him with my hands on my hips. "I'm leaving." And then I realized how that sounded and added "for ten minutes. I'm going to the other room, and I'm not coming back for ten minutes, so don't ask me anything because I won't be here to answer you."

"Go, then," he said with a grunt. "I don't need your bullshit. Get out! I'll find my way home without your help."

Good luck with that, I thought as I stomped out of the room. *This is the disease. This is the disease. This is the disease.* My thoughts raced in time with my pounding heart.

It's difficult to guard your peace with only a few hours of sleep. Try as I might to speak softly, answer with kind words, and rebound from my husband's sour disposition, my patience was hanging by a thread. Gone was Drew's gentle personality. Hello, horrid person.

Isn't that just like the devil? *Kick 'em when they're down—Drew is at his most vulnerable, and Candy is sleep deprived. Strike now!* Well, that may work with some couples, but this wife knows spiritual warfare when she sees it, and Satan's tactics will *not* break the harmony Drew and I share.

I stood in the kitchen until I calmed down and then moved to the living room. I could hear him calling, "Candy . . . Candy," but I steeled myself not to go to him. Instead, I watched the clock. Four minutes, five minutes, seven-and-a-half minutes. Ten minutes to cultivate my peace seemed like an eternity. I had visions of him squirming around and getting hung up in the bed rails. *Devil, the jig is up. My husband needs me, and you have to get out of the way.*

Finally, with my exile over, I returned to the bedroom and found him scrunched down at the bottom of the bed, uncomfortable but safe. I figured he wouldn't remember what had just transpired, so I approached him with a smile. "Hi, handsome. Looks like you got yourself all tangled up in the covers. Let me get you situated."

I tilted the foot of his bed up with his head down, enlisting the aid of gravity, and positioning myself at the top of the bed to pull him toward me.

"Lift your knees, hon. That will make it easier."

He lifted his shoulders. I stood there, amazed at how little his mind could communicate with his body parts. I moved to the side of the bed and put my hands beneath his knees to urge them upward. Even with my touch, he couldn't comply. Instead of bending his legs, he straightened them and lifted his feet. *So much for having his help.*

"Never mind; it was a nice idea," I said, forcing myself to sound cheerful. "I think I can handle this alone."

Returning to the head of the bed, I pulled him forward, patted him on the shoulder, and kissed his forehead.

"I like that," he said—his first words since I had entered the room.

I got the bed realigned, and as I was smoothing the covers, he reached for my hand, pulled me close, and gazed into my eyes.

"I'm sorry if I said or did anything to upset you."

He was lucid. He remembered! Or, more likely, he didn't know what transpired but felt the discord. Emotions register more vividly than facts.

He struggled to find more words to express his remorse, trying to get his mouth to say what he was searching for. I saved him the agony with a flurry of all the words I could think of that would make him feel better.

"It's okay, Drew. I forgive you. And I'm sorry, too. I lost my patience. I love you. You're the most important person to me in the whole world."

"But you left me."

"I only left for ten minutes, and I was just in the other room. Here's something you need to know: If I ever go away, I always come back."

I think the need for reassurance increases in direct proportion to the progression of the disease.

He asked what he had done wrong, and I told him about our sleepless night. "We both need to get some rest," I said. "We just had a little argument, and we made up, so everything is totally fine between us. It's five o'clock in the morning. If I turn the light out, do you think you can close your eyes and get some sleep?"

"Yes," he said. "I'm tired."

He rolled over, and I got four hours of blissfully uninterrupted sleep. Maybe I should have gotten mad sooner.

"It is often just as sacred to laugh
as it is to pray."

— *Charles R. Swindoll*

CHAPTER THIRTEEN

Mystery Words & Imagination

May 12, 2019

Who knew we had the perfect music therapy for Drew right in our own family? Our niece, Lora, and her husband, Frank, live in Harrisburg, Pennsylvania, and perform under the name "The Faves." Frank plays the guitar, and Lora sings. Their light harmonies of pop, jazz, and blues impressed us when we first heard them play at Tim and Myrna's anniversary dinner. Drew was attentive the whole time and said with a sparkle in his eyes, "He's the best I've ever heard."

Lora said they would bring the guitar and come to see us when they came back to Georgetown. True to her word, they came this afternoon and were set up in no time at Drew's bedside.

"This is an 'important gig,'" Lora said, and it warmed my heart that she would make us a priority. Flipping through her notebook of three-hundred-plus selections, she and Frank chose songs that I could tell resonated with Drew.

Too soon, they were saying their goodbyes, but Drew's joy and contentment were still evident at bedtime. *Yes, indeed.* This had all the earmarks of an important gig.

May 17, 2019

Hospice delivered an oxygen tank today. Drew's breathing has been erratic when he sleeps, intermittently alternating between snoring and not breathing. The nurse thought it might be good to introduce oxygen during the night. I tried to put the tube in his nose, but he squirmed and brushed it away. Well, at least we're set up if the time comes when we need it.

May 18, 2019

I heard there was a bit of commotion at home today while I was at the writers' group. Donna, a hospice volunteer, was reading when I left. Doris was planning to relieve her but came by early, and things were still quiet. The trouble began when an enthusiastic Certified Nursing Assistant (CNA) breezed in and woke Drew abruptly. *Big no-no.* But I wasn't there to caution her that Drew responds best to quiet, gentle, and slow. The last time she was here, she bathed Drew in the shower. A lot has changed since then.

From what Doris and Donna told me, this is how things unfolded:

The CNA went to the foot of the bed and asked Drew, "Are you ready for your bath?"

He stiffened, frowned, and gave her the evil eye. "No," he said loud and sternly.

Doris thought it might be helpful if she intervened since Drew is familiar with her. "Do you want her to give you a bath?" she asked.

Drew reared up and leaned toward her. "I said, NO!"

The CNA stood aside, and Doris hugged her. "Don't take this personally. He doesn't want to be bothered."

"I just want to sleep," Drew added loudly.

Doris and the CNA stepped into the kitchen, while Donna stayed in the room with Drew.

"So, he's declining?" the CNA asked Doris.

She said yes, and the CNA said, "Shouldn't you call his wife?"

About that time, Wyatt and Kade came in to say hello, and Doris filled them in on what was going on. Here's what Wyatt told me:

"I'll make the judgment call," he said and went to Drew's bedside. "You want a bath?"

Drew glared at him. "Do *you?*"

"No," Wyatt said. "Do *you* want a bath?"

Drew pointed his index finger at Wyatt. "Do *you* want a bath?"

"No," Wyatt said, "maybe tonight I'll get one. I asked if *you* are ready for *your* bath."

"What ails you?" Drew said.

"What?" Wyatt asked.

"What ails you?" Drew repeated. "You're smart."

"*You're* smart," Wyatt countered.

Drew glared at him. "You're a smart (pause)"

"A smart what?" Wyatt said.

"A *smart ass!*" Drew looked pleased with himself for spitting out a bad word.

Wyatt squeezed his shoulder. "Love you."

"Love you," Drew said.

Stepping into the kitchen, Wyatt announced, "We're declining."

By the time I got home, everything was as quiet as when I left. If they hadn't told me, I'd have never known. Glad that was one time I didn't have to oversee or referee.

May 22, 2019

Drew and I have had several disjointed conversations lately. Here's how this one played out tonight:

"Go down to your office," he said and pointed.

"Okay, then what?"

"Go straight down this street, cross the railroad tracks" (which are on the other side of town), "and you'll end up" (long pause) "at the nicest place."

"Who lives in this nice place?"

"Peedump."

"Peedump?"

"Uh-huh, Peedump."

"Who's Peedump?"

"He's a man, and if he wants to talk, we'll go in one of the back doors. Or maybe we shouldn't enter. We'll think about that. It might be too early. But we should get off this road."

How do you respond to this sort of circular thinking? You do the best you can. "Okay. That sounds like a plan," I said.

"Good. Let's go."

"Yep, in just a few minutes. I have to take care of a few things."

"Where's the end of this road, right at the end?"

"Definitely. The end is at the end."

"We might want to fix something to eat." This was the first clue Drew had given me in days that he may be hungry.

"How about hamburgers?" I suggested.

"Yeah, hamburgers would be good. You ready to go?"

"I thought we would fix them here."

"Um, uh" (pause) "how much do people use?" he asked and waved his hands in the air.

"How much do people use of what—hamburger?"

"No, you know. How much do they use?"

"I'm sorry, but I don't know what you mean."

"I guess we need to find somebody smarter."

"Good idea."

May 22, 2019

Drew is continuously calling for Candy but often doesn't know who I am. I was sitting in the recliner, and he asked, "Where's Candy?"

"I'm Candy."

He laughed with a grunt. "No, you're not."

The debate went on until I realized that nothing I could say would convince him. "You know what?" I said. "Candy should be home any minute now. Let me see if I can find her." I went into the other room, made a little noise, and breezed through the bedroom doorway with my most enthusiastic greeting. "Hi, hon. I'm back! Did you miss me?"

"Where've you been?" he wanted to know. "I've been waiting for you."

May 29, 2019

Doris stayed with Drew while I went to the grocery store. When I got back, she beamed and could hardly wait to tell me about the plans Drew had made. Day in and day out, unable to even put his legs over the side of the bed, he looks at the same view of the wall and bookcase in our bedroom. Waving his hand toward the dresser, filing cabinet, and bookcase, he invented a solution for the boredom.

"First," he said to Doris, "we need to get rid of this clutter, and then there'll be enough space for a nice little room—a room for kids."

"What kind of room?"

"A reading room."

She immediately latched onto his imagination, and together they came up with plans to construct a low wall that kids could see over, a place for old-fashioned schoolhouse chairs with attached desks, and children's books on the lowest shelves. He would hire a well-qualified reading specialist whose desk would face the children with her back to the bookcase (very specific).

It would be Doris's responsibility to get two-by-fours and other building materials.

"My wife will be in charge of checking everyone in and giving them nametags."

Sessions would be once a week for groups of two to six and would last twenty to thirty minutes, depending on the attention span. The parents would be responsible for bringing the kids in and signing permission forms, and there would be a place where the adults could sit and socialize while they waited.

Doris asked what we would charge for this program, and he stared her down. "No charge!"

The whole time the two of them brainstormed about the project, he was animated and bright-eyed. *Oh, the value of imagination!* There's no way either of us would have thought to mention anything to Drew about a library or children's reading room.

"Tell me about the reading room for kids," I said to him, and he launched into a vivid description with Doris coaching him on some of the details. Better entertainment than a 3-D movie!

May 31, 2019

"What's that? Is that dried blood on his cheek? And in his hairline? Doris, come here and look at this. It's all over his fingers, too!" I was alarmed.

She confirmed it looked like black blood. "I don't know how that could have happened. He hasn't been out of bed, and I've been with him the whole time."

I got some warm, soapy water and gently began wiping it from Drew's face and fingers, expecting to find a cut. There didn't seem to be any skin broken, and then I got a whiff of chocolate. I brought the washcloth to my nose for a closer smell.

"Ha! Doris, it's a Peppermint Patty!" Drew's favorite snack. I buy a bag every time I buy groceries, and Doris feeds him a few whenever she comes. This one must have melted.

June 1, 2019

We've had several nights in a row of deep, restful sleep. Oh, what a difference that makes.

Yesterday, when Drew awoke, he had difficulty making his mouth form words—only a mumbled mishmash of consonants and vowels, but he was trying hard to say something. His fingers fluttered over his lips, temples, and forehead, and finally, he got the words out: "Something's not right in here."

I squeezed his shoulder and said, "I know, but I'm right here to take care of everything you need, so you don't have a thing to worry about."

This morning when he woke up, he asked, "How much have you had?"

Huh? "How much what?"

"Drink."

"Oh, I try to drink eight glasses of water a day. Is that what you mean?"

"No. I feel drunk," he said.

This, from a man who has only had two beers in the last twenty-plus years, and certainly nothing alcoholic recently. I guess it's an indication that the disease has his equilibrium off balance, so he feels unsettled.

"You're fine, hon. You haven't had too much to drink, but you might feel better if you lay on your side. Want me to help with that?" He agreed, so I tucked a pillow next to his back, repositioned him, and straightened his sheets. Before I got to the foot of his bed, he was asleep again, snoring gently.

June 6, 2019

I'm on day four of my second five-day respite and am relaxing at the condo in Fenwick Island. The freedom and change of scenery are intoxicating. This is probably the first time in ten years that I've stayed here overnight. It's such a peaceful place. I feel like a little girl playing house as I search every nook and cranny for things that could be better organized or replaced. I'm ordering odds and ends from Amazon whenever I see something we need. When everything arrives, I'll have fun coming back to put them where they belong.

Doris stayed overnight on Monday, and we went to Nick's House of Ribs and then to Harris Teeter's for groceries. She was one of five Christian sisters I invited for lunch on Tuesday to introduce them to *The Path*, a book by Rick Joyner. We decided to meet monthly at my house, and they're going to order the book so we can discuss the first four chapters next month. Before they left, they laid hands on me and prayed.

On Wednesday, I went to the beach at 8:30 p.m. and had the whole place to myself at that hour. I had visions of taking a long walk by the water but only got as far as the top of the dune where I could soak in the view. I was short of breath and my legs felt weak, so I turned around and wobbled back to the car. My legs aren't used to maneuvering loose and shifting sand. Enough huffing and puffing for one visit. Plus, it was getting dark, and I realized it wasn't very smart of me, a woman alone, to be out there all by myself. On the way back, I stopped at Fisher's and indulged in a tub of caramel popcorn.

This afternoon, my friends Susan Wingate and Pat Bennett brought salads, and it was so nice to be able to visit without a deadline to get home.

Ah, the value of an opportunity to truly *rest*.

June 7, 2019

I signed up with the Bible App to receive a Verse of the Day in my email. Look what I got today for my birthday:

Thou wilt keep him in perfect peace,
whose mind is stayed on thee:
because he trusteth in thee.

(Isaiah 26:3 KJV)

And that's where I am at this moment—trusting God at a deeper level than ever before, immersing myself in His perfect peace.

I've done a little writing, and that's satisfying. Most of my time has been spent reading, playing Christian music and basking in the presence of the Lord. The weather has been glorious! This afternoon I'm going to soak my feet and give myself a pedicure. Kim will pick me up tonight to take me to Ocean City for dinner at Red Red Wine/Dry 85.

I plan to drive home after dinner. Troy and Dana are doing a great job of caring for Drew, Buttercup, and Midnight. I'm getting regular reports that Drew is making out fine at the Hospice Center, and I'm eager to see him tomorrow when the ambulance brings him home.

I'm filled to overflowing with joy and gratitude, so it seems that turning seventy-two is not so bad, after all.

June 13, 2019

Doris was here yesterday, helping as usual. Before she left, she took a few minutes to sit in the recliner in the bedroom. Her husband is exhibiting unruly behavior, and feeling overwhelmed at what she might face at home, she put her head in her hands and wept quietly. Drew noticed and asked what was wrong.

I came into the room just as she answered, "I'm just sad."

Immediately, Drew said, "We've got to get Candy in on this." He may not know or understand words or situations, but his emotional thermometer is working at 110%.

"Come over here," he said. "Both of you." When he could make eye contact with us, he went into fix-it mode. He reached his hand out to Doris, and she held it. It took him a while to get his words out, so he had us hanging on every one. "If you could have . . . anything . . . something that would . . . make you happy . . . something that would . . . make you . . . feel good . . . feel happy . . . what would it be?"

She thought for a moment and said, "Highlights. If I could get my hair done, that would make me feel happy."

"Candy," he said, "can you take care of it? Make sure she gets that?"

"Absolutely," I said. "Doris does so much for us; it's the right thing to do."

Drew's sensitivity, compassion, and generosity are fully intact.

That was yesterday. Today, when Ella came to bathe and dress him, Drew was fully uncooperative. I was half an hour late giving him his dose of Lorazepam and ran to get it. He swallowed it willingly, but it usually takes ten minutes to kick in.

Ella began by cleaning his feet.

"You don't do this on a Sunday!" he shouted.

"But this is Thursday," I said.

He frowned and spat out, "I know what day it is."

"Okay," I said, convinced he had no idea of what month it even was. "What day is it?"

"It's *Thursday*," he said triumphantly.

Ella and I burst out laughing, and that set a better tone. We bragged about his sense of humor, and I carried on a running dialogue with anything that came to mind while Ella continued her work. By the time she had to ask him to roll on his side, he was wonderfully cooperative.

June 16, 2019

Last night, I finished reading *Mike & Me*, a book written for couples who choose to face Alzheimer's together at home. I learned so much and was comforted that it confirmed many things I'm doing right. One major thing I hadn't thought of was to PRAY TOGETHER. With all the prayer support going on for me—for us—why didn't I think about praying *with* him? I vowed to change that and make it a part of our daily routine, especially at bedtime.

Tonight, after changing his briefs and tucking him in, he was disoriented and unnecessarily worried.

"Did you know worry is a sin?" I asked.

"No, I didn't," he said. "Why?"

"Because if we're worrying, it means we're not trusting the Lord to take care of everything that concerns us."

"That makes sense."

I asked if he would like to pray with me, and his eyes brightened more than I'd seen in a while. "Yes, I'd like that."

And so, I prayed, "Thank You for my precious husband and for this safe place. Thank You, Lord, that You always know just what we need and want us to rely on You, not on ourselves. Thank You for teaching us to trust You so we don't have to worry."

Drew said, "Amen," and I asked if he would like to pray. He nodded, and I was astounded by his clarity and how smoothly the words flowed from his mouth:

"Master, thank You for tough times and that we don't have to worry because You make everything okay." He got it!

June 27, 2019

I lost fifty pounds between January and December 2018 and regained twenty-five of them in the first six months of 2019. Try as I might to get back on track by eating right, all the no-no's keep finding their way into my mouth. My bad eating habits began accelerating when Drew became bedbound in February, and my health will suffer if I don't get a handle on this. I haven't spent much time in the Lord's presence listening to what He has to say. Maybe I don't want to hear. Maybe I've forgotten how. This morning while Drew was sleeping, I picked up a new journal and wrote:

All the cells in our bodies answer to You, Lord! And I'm going to do my part by staying out of the sweets and away from the carbs that are harmful to me.

And then, as smooth as a hot knife slides through butter, the still small, gently piercing voice of God spoke, and I captured these words:

You have questioned your ability to hear My voice. The problem is that hearing what My Holy Spirit has to say to you is not dependent upon your ability to hear, to listen, or to discern. I AM your source, your strength, your joy, and I AM the One who opens the eyes of your heart and the ears of your spirit.

Your role is to be still, as you are now, and My words will flow because I live in you. My thoughts are as close to you as your own thoughts. You do not have to grasp or strive to hear what I long to impart. You simply have to be still long enough to give Me your full attention.

Be still and know that I am God (Psalm 46:10).

Come near to Me, and I will come near to you.

Draw near to God and He will draw near to you (James 4:8).

It is my joy to commune with you through My Word and My Spirit. For you are My precious child, and I love you with an everlasting love. I AM with you continually, leading and guiding you.

If only I could stay in this quiet spiritual place for days at a time and not have to reenter the world of trials and temptations. Sometimes I just want to do what I want to do. Thus, the weight gain and self-condemnation. I'm grateful that His mercies are new every morning. Great is His faithfulness (Lamentations 3:22-23).

June 28, 2019

My journal was on the table. Dare I pick it up and write what is on my heart? Yes.

Oh, Lord! I had the most wonderful day in Your presence all day yesterday. Until 6:00 or 7:00 p.m. when my mind kept drifting to the Chocolate Fudge Ripple ice cream in the freezer. I reminded myself that I had promised: "to do my part by staying out of the sweets." I resisted the temptation for an hour but then deliberately, intentionally, willfully grabbed the container and a spoon—to give some to Drew. He ate three or four bites, and then I sat down and polished off the rest.

Mmm, chocolate—which whetted my appetite for Peppermint Patties. Drawn to them like a magnet to silvery-metal wrappers, I stuffed one after another after another into my mouth as fast as my fingers could tear them open.

It occurred to me that I shouldn't have junk food around. What else do I need to get rid of? Oh! The Reese's peanut butter thins. So instead of throwing them out, I ate the rest of the bag. And then opened the box of Cheese-Its and ate those, too. Is my gluttony greater than You, God? Heavens, no!

It was a choice I made. Like Eve, I listened to the tempter and gazed at the forbidden fruit with my eyes. Then, I touched it. And tasted. And it was good. My conscience whispered to me the entire time, but I ate faster. Not until all three were empty (the container, the bag, the box) was my appetite satisfied and my regret overwhelming.

This is why you have been having difficulty hearing My voice: because you are reaching out for comfort with your flesh rather than turning to Me with your spirit. I planted the Tree of Good and Evil in the Garden, where

Adam and Eve would have a constant reminder that it was their CHOICE to obey or disobey. Foods will always be nearby to tempt you. What I want is for you to exercise self-control, and that will come when you draw so close to Me that you no longer desire those things that will harm you. When you eat and fill yourself with the bounty of healthy foods I have made available, you will feed your soul as well as guard your body. This will be an act of worship and a way to draw closer to Me. Day by day. Moment by moment. In the evening, when TV ads lure and your self-control is at its weakest, turn to Me—not to the kitchen.

But, if you do fill yourself with "forbidden fruit" that you know is damaging to your physical body, there is no need for self-condemnation. You are going through a difficult time, and there is grace for this.

This all made perfect sense to me this morning when the day was fresh and the Lord's presence was palpable. But then evening came, and old habits die hard. At least Eve reached for an apple—and look at the damage *that* caused. I can only imagine the sin ensnared in an apple dumpling. God, help me.

June 29, 2019

Our forty-fourth anniversary! It was a great day with family and friends stopping by. The flowers that Kim and Wyatt brought made a great backdrop for photos of our candlelight bedside dinner. Doris helped me coordinate everything and joined us for the meal of Chicken Marsala that Bella Capri delivered. Drew stayed alert and engaged throughout the evening, and after Doris left, he and I whispered sweet nothings to one another for about fifteen minutes, then we kissed like honeymooners and settled in for a good night's sleep. Another memory to add to the bank of special occasions I will always cherish.

July 2, 2019

Communication has become more difficult because I can't understand what he says. He tries hard to find the right words by combining random consonants and vowels, which makes a "word salad" that is sometimes fascinating but equally frustrating for both of us. Occasionally, it sounds like he's speaking in tongues. At other times, he looks at me expectantly. I'm never quite sure how to respond, but I do my best.

- "Scooch-a-watch." He looked at me intently as though I should do something.

  "Scooch-a-watch?" I repeated.

  "Yes."

  "What's scooch-a-watch?"

  "You know."

  "It's fun to say, but I'm sorry, I don't know that word. What's it mean?"

  He waved me away. "Forget it."

- "Want me to cass-a-pate?"

  "Cass-a-pate," I repeated. "Hmm, no. I don't want you to cass-a-pate."

  Sounds disgusting.

- "We're in our regular telephone now?"

  "Did you mean, 'Are we in our regular house?'"

  "No. We're in our regular telephone, right?"

  "Sorry, hon, I don't know how to answer that."

- "Can you help me?"

  "With what, hon?"

  "It's my steam-it melon that I lost in a show."

  The only thing I did with this was run for pen and paper to write it down.

- "Are you a pecker?"

  "No."

  "Do you want me to be a pecker?"

  "No."

- "How could I use my" (pause)
  "Your what?"
  "I forget."
  Oh, well.
- "What just walked by compared to what we do?"
  I didn't attempt to respond to that one.
- "It's high time in the angel house."
  Is he foreshadowing heaven?
- "I wouldn't want to live in a house without a coffin." He looked puzzled. "That didn't make any sense, did it?"
  "No, it didn't." I was puzzled, too. "Do you want to try again?"
  "I'll have to think about that."
  Me, too! I never said one word about the funeral home papers and coffin pricing I reviewed just hours before. Coincidence? A sign of readiness? An emotional connection to what I'm thinking?
- "Why did they put us in a junkyard?"
  I evaluated the stuff he pointed to and moved the stack of supplies and a pile of pillows to another room. When his bureau and the corner by the bookcase was clear, I asked if that was better. The uncluttered space did the trick.
- "Resta ann."
  "I'm sorry, hon, I don't know what 'resta ann' means. Can you say it another way?"
  "Resta ann?"
  "No, I still don't understand. I have no idea what that means."
  He shook his head. "I've got it all messed up. Never mind."

Lately, he feels compelled to talk constantly, and very little of it makes sense. He gets aggravated if I don't give him my full attention. Here's a sampling of the strangeness that goes on for hours: "The fighter is convertible." "Skazzle!" "How far are we to Chipawink?" "Who owns this flood zone?" "I don't think we can see the panzer thing." "We're going to be—um, uh—moonshiners." "I don't want to mess with skeeter-break." "The biggest samareese is hammerheist; can you stop it?" "Are we sleeping in a single edge trail?"

After a few hours of this, along with his normal, tiresome repetition, I'm certain I've entered the Twilight Zone. No doubt about it.

July 8, 2019

Okay. Let's talk about the house.

I finally lined up someone to resolve the wet rot in our crawl space. The company is scheduled to begin work on September 30th and will approach it in phases. The first step will be to clean out the moisture, sagging insulation, rotted beams, and whatever else they find. And they will dig. A lot. So after they haul the gunk and junk away, I'll have a big pile of dirt to figure out how to spread or dispose of. When they've cleared out enough to be able to get in there to assess the damage, they'll tackle phase two, reconstruction. The third step is to encapsulate everything and install a dehumidifier, so we're looking at a long process. Hopefully, it won't be too disruptive for Drew as our bedroom is at the far end of the house.

And then there's the bird in the chimney situation. The fluttering worried me. Had a bird fallen in and was struggling to find its way out? To my relief, I learned that it's a chimney swift known for nesting in chimneys, so I don't need to fear the bird will die on my watch.

But, the birds (yep, more than one) have nested there to have babies, and I think they've hatched. What was once a soft fluttering sound is now a symphony of chattering, chirping, and squawking. And it's *loud.* Wouldn't you know, Drew, who gets upset at any little noise, has his hospital bed right beside the fireplace, which serves as a loudspeaker for the bird activity. I've tried to think of some way to relocate his bed, but that's not feasible. Even if I could figure how to shoo the chimney swifts away, they're protected under the Federal Migratory Bird Treaty Act, so I can't bother them until the hatchlings reach maturity. So I guess we'll have to figure a way to enjoy the ruckus of our fine feathered neighbors until they decide to vacate the premises. After they migrate, I will look into having a chimney cap installed.

I never imagined I'd have to take care of homeowner things like chirping chimneys and creepy crawl spaces. Drew always made things like this look so effortless. Oh, how I miss him.

July 11, 2019

It's amazing how many people I encounter who are caring for someone with dementia. One of the things they often say as they talk about coping with the irritation of repetition and memory loss is, "I have to work on my patience." The thing is, we can "work" on having patience, and that approach can actually add to our tension and frustration. True patience is not a matter of gritting our teeth and *being patient if it kills me;* patience is a companion of peace. "How do you do it?" they ask.

Oh, it was helpful that I grew up under the influence and example of a mother who was the epitome of peace and patience. But that isn't the real source of my ability to exercise patience.

Patience is a fruit of the Spirit of God. My ability to be patient didn't happen overnight. It began in 1983 when I sought a personal relationship with the Holy Spirit. Right away, He made my top priorities: love, joy, peace, patience, kindness, goodness, faithfulness, gentleness, and self-control. Ever since, Galatians 5:22-23 Scripture has been my life verse.

During the ten years it took me to write my first book, *Fruitbearer: What Can I Do for You, Lord?,* I became acutely aware that people were watching to see if I lived up to what I wrote. *If you're going to put yourself out there as a Christian,* I thought, *you'd better act like one.* Even when nobody's watching, I yearned to be authentic. After years of intentionally inviting the Lord into every situation, being authentic and practicing patience became second nature to me, effortless—a way of life, a part of my personality. The stress and strain of trying to imitate my mother's patience was replaced by peace and relinquishment that came from God doing it in me and through me.

Sometimes, walking away to get some breathing room provides the reset I need to be able to exchange my anger and frustration for a creative and loving response. But most times, a quick reminder that I can tap into the calming presence of the Holy Spirit is all I need to fill me with genuine patience, not the kind I attempt to manufacture. *Since we live by the Spirit, let us keep in step with the Spirit* (Galatians 5:25).

Little did I know that one day, I would write books about Alzheimer's where the fruit of the Spirit would be front and center. Developing patience can't be done in a rush. As you learn to practice patience, slow down. Bathe yourself in the inner peace that comes each time you reflect on the presence of God in the midst of the chaos.

July 12, 2019

I spent my third five-day respite by tackling a publishing project. What fun to be able to stay at the keyboard and work uninterrupted on a children's picture book.

I received good reports on Drew while he was at the Center, but he came home different this time—disoriented and slurring his words to the point where I couldn't understand him at all. Several times, he lifted both arms to the ceiling as though reaching for something or climbing a ladder. He was also hallucinating, talking about the four cars behind us (in the bedroom) and how we needed to get out of their way. But that was Tuesday, and he was better yesterday.

During the last several months, he's had spells when he would get agitated and be verbally ugly. Sometimes he would call nursing aides names ("son of a bitch") or say hurtful things to kind volunteers ("don't need your bullshit"). I've become accustomed to tolerating a string of foul language that I never heard him utter the whole time we've been married.

A pattern has developed. Often, when he cusses at an aide, I will come alongside to intervene. He'll turn toward me with a hateful face, but the instant he recognizes me, his expression softens, and he says to the aide, "Isn't she pretty?"

The aide agrees and adds, "You're a lucky man."

I take that as my cue to launch into the love story of how we met, and from that point on, as long as I stay nearby, he cooperates with the aide.

The flip-switch when he cares about someone is astonishing. Yesterday, when he yelled "Jesus Christ!" in anger over some nonsensical thing, I made sure we had good eye contact and said, "You know one day we're going to have to answer to God for every careless word we say. I don't think He'll be very happy with you using His Son's name in vain like that."

Immediately, remorse washed the anger from his face. "I'm sorry, Master. I didn't mean it." At least his spirit is still coherent, and he's not only capable of repentance but eager to set things right.

For the remainder of the evening, I gave him my full attention with lots of assurance and some passionate kisses. That was the turning point, and we both slept peacefully.

This morning, he awoke calm and alert.

Late this afternoon we have a thunderstorm brewing, and it seems to be keeping pace with Drew's sundowning symptoms. The rain hasn't shown up yet, but the lightning strikes and low rumbling in the air compounds Drew's grumpiness. I don't know what set him off, but he said, "God damn," as he squirmed in bed.

I scolded him before I could stop myself. "God's not going to like you using His name as a cuss word."

And at that very moment, lightning struck nearby, and the heavens crashed with a loud *CRACK—BOOM—POP—SIZZLE—ROAR—RUMBLE.*

"See that?" I said. "You made God mad."

I wish you could have seen his owl-eyes and the way he held his expression for the duration of the rumbling as if God had him in a choke hold. Maybe *that* got through to him. We'll see if his irreverence improves. Or not. Time will tell.

July 18, 2019

Doris is at it again. She encouraged Drew's creative fantasy while I was shopping for groceries. She met me at the door, eager to tell me that he made plans to surprise me with a weekend getaway. Moving to the kitchen, we unpacked the bags, put them on the shelves, and she revealed the whole "secret" plot.

She beamed as she told me he had it all packed down in his mind, and the more he talked about it, the more excited he got. "I want you to reserve an ocean-front room for my wife and me," he told her, "at the Henlopen Hotel in Rehoboth."

He asked if she knew the number. When she said no, he said, "Go get the phone book." She did, flipped through some pages, pretended to find the listing, dialed a pretend number, and had a pretend conversation.

"I'm sorry," she said after hanging up. "They said with such short notice, they're all booked up this weekend."

"Did you tell them it was for Drew Abbott?" *(Ha! Apparently, he has no problem with self-esteem.)*

"Yes," she said. "Everybody knows Drew Abbott, but all the rooms are spoken for." When his whole countenance dropped, quick-thinking Doris added, "But they said they'd call if they have a cancellation and a room becomes available."

For the next fifteen minutes, he kept asking, "Did the call come through?" "Did they call yet?" and made sure Doris understood, "This is strictly between you and me—a surprise for my wife."

There was a little lull. He stared at Doris. "You're looking at me like I've never done this before."

"You probably have," she said.

He nodded. "Many times." *(Which is true; he used to enjoy planning weekend trips for us.)*

Doris said he became more and more enthusiastic as she asked about the details and they pinned them down. The ideas for how things were to unfold were *all his*. He thought everything through.

Doris was to secretly pack my clothes, and he would pack his. Drew would dress in his best suit, take the suitcases to the room, and see to it that he arrived in the restaurant at the hotel ahead of time. Doris would bring me there for dinner and make sure my seat faced away from where he would be waiting in the wings. As soon as the server brought our salads, he would come up behind me, rest his hands on my shoulders, lean down, and whisper into my ear, "Hello, pretty wife. Is there room at the table for one more?"

By the time Doris finished telling me about Drew's imaginary romantic interlude, both of us had bittersweet tears rolling down our cheeks. *If only his fabrication could be real.*

Funny thing. To Drew, it *WAS* real. This is how I know: Doris helped me fix dinner, and the three of us watched several episodes of Andy Griffith. After two or three hours, she said, "Drew, it's time for me to go home to Piney Grove. I'll see you tomorrow."

"No, you won't," he said adamantly.

Doris was on the left side of Drew's bed, and I stood by his right. She and I exchanged puzzled glances over him.

"Yes, I *will* see you tomorrow," she said. "I come just about every day."

"No." His eyes locked on hers. "No. You won't," he said, followed by an exaggerated wink, wink.

Doris and I were a little slow to comprehend, but with the double-wink, we "got it." He was so invested in their secret scheme that he remembered it more than two hours after they had mapped it out. This, from a man who can't recall anything else for more than ten seconds at a time.

Drew's starry-eyed plan may not have materialized as he had hoped, but it is fully complete in his spirit and mine.

This is the man I fell in love with forty-four years ago—and a perfect illustration of why *I will never love him less.*

I pray that God, the source of hope,
will fill you completely with joy and peace
because you trust in him.
Then you will overflow with confident hope
through the power of the Holy Spirit.

— Romans 15:13 (NLT)

CHAPTER FOURTEEN

We're In a Tough Place

July 21, 2019

The changes continue as the disease advances. Relentlessly. In the last few days, Drew has begun having more and more issues with spatial awareness. He has trouble bringing a cup to his lips because he gets a vice grip on it and will only bend his elbows partway. When I put my fingers over his to guide him, he stiffens even more. If I try to hold the cup to his mouth myself, he reaches for it and often bumps it. To avoid spills, I don't fill it too full. Maybe it's time to switch to a sippy cup, but I don't suppose that would help with the spatial issues that prevent him from bringing it to his mouth.

When I feed him, he often clamps his mouth shut before I can get the whole forkful in. Then he bites off the excess and throws it on the floor or smears it on his sheet. I have to be Johnny-on-the-spot to scoop it off his fingers before he makes a mess.

If he reaches for toast or a cookie, he has difficulty estimating where it is and grabs at open air even if I touch the food to his fingers.

It's more than spatial awareness, though. He doesn't know the difference between fabric and food. The other day, he stuffed the blanket in his mouth and tore into it like a piece of tough meat.

And what should we do about his frenzied, fluttering fingers? They're on the move all the time, usually worrying the sheet by bunching, pulling, or twisting it. I gave him some blue slime as a hand exerciser that Doris's grandkids made (modern-day Silly Putty composed of white glue, Tide or shaving cream, Model Magic, and paint). Always before, he had fun stretching, squeezing, and balling it up. But today, before I could stop him, he tore off a piece with his teeth. Try as I might to get it out of his mouth, he clamped his jaw tight, staring at me with an ornery grin. He chewed. When he did open up, the only thing left was the blue stain on his teeth. I guess one swallow of the stuff won't hurt him.

Oh, my. This is a wake-up call for being more diligent in safety measures.

July 24, 2019

"Have I paid you?" he asked.

"No," I said with a smile. "You don't have to pay me. You bought a marriage license forty-four years ago, and you *own* me."

Oh, how he laughed at that! It thrilled me to see him comprehend my little joke.

Then tonight, we caught another glimpse of the authentic Drew Abbott. After supper, I was putting dirty plates in the dishwasher when Doris came to tell me what just happened.

"Drew called me over to him," she said. "He gave me one of those looks—you know, when he's calm and focused on something."

"You want to know what you're good at?" he said to her.

"Of course," she said. "What am I good at?"

"You're good at standing by my wife. And I mean it. You're a good friend."

The real Drew Abbott is quick to notice positive qualities in people and delights in telling them.

Oh, for more good days like this one.

July 26, 2019

The nurse always asks about Drew's ability to swallow when she checks his vitals on Fridays. This time, I reported that he had choked a few times, usually when swallowing his pills. Months ago, I bought a container of *Resource Thickenup*, clear instant food thickener (unflavored) because I anticipated the day would come when we would need it. That day has arrived.

Jena said to put it in all liquids from now on. The first beverage I added it to was Drew's orange juice, and he drank it all. The pills went down easily this time. Maybe I should have tried it sooner.

His teeth need attention. Since he became confined to bed, the aides and I have been using mouth swabs with mouthwash; he can't tolerate flossing. Without actual brushing, his teeth are looking pretty bad. I use a battery-operated toothbrush that signals me every thirty seconds for a two-minute brushing, and it works for Drew, too! After I finish my two minutes, I run it with the leftover toothpaste for another two minutes in his mouth. (Hey, after forty-four years of marriage, I figure we can share a toothbrush.) He opens his mouth wide, and because it's a soft vibration, he doesn't balk at it, and his teeth are beginning to shine again. We sure don't want him to develop a toothache.

July 27, 2019

Throughout last night and most of today, Drew mumbled softly, carrying on conversations with people I couldn't see. It's the first time I've noticed prolonged hallucinations. Always before, they've been isolated incidents.

I couldn't understand what he was saying because his words were muddled, but I could tell he was asking questions and making emphatic statements. Sometimes, I knew he was on the receiving end because he'd say, "Huh?" or "How'd I do that?" Once, he said, "Drew," and I took it that someone had asked about his name.

It's like he was dreaming and talking in his sleep, but his eyes were open. Maybe it's a form of sleep-walking without the walking part. He gestured with his arms and hands and shrugged his shoulders.

More often than not, he gazed upward toward the ceiling (or maybe beyond it) with parted lips, and his mouth curled into a soft smile, a look of wonderment. Some of the phrases I could understand were: "Thank you for setting me straight." "Yeah, it's gonna be hard." "All right, we'll wait on that." "Your worst enemy . . ." "If I put my body safe into the subject, can I come through?"

This behavior went on for hours, all night and into the next afternoon. He wore a look of awe and fascination. I'm envious to see what he saw. Frequently, he fully extended one or both arms above his head and clawed with his hands as if reaching for the rungs of a ladder. Whatever was going on, he seemed to be in a happy place. Maybe they are not hallucinations. Maybe he's having a conversation with angels or departed loved ones. But it's too soon for that. *Isn't it?*

His hands are busy (interlacing his fingers, touching his face, folding his hands) but not frantic and frenzied like before. It wasn't long ago that his grip was vice-like. Today, his grasp was hesitant and unsure. He couldn't clutch anything I gave him to hold. When I changed his briefs, he was compliant and willing to roll to the side but had trouble stretching his arm out to reach the railing.

Some things change as this disease advances, and we miss the milestones. I can't remember the last time Drew sang to me or recited Eenie Meenie Miney Mo. When did it stop? Would I have savored it more if I had known it would never happen again? Or maybe it will.

At this point, I'm not focusing so much on who Drew *was* but who he *is*. I'm thankful for whatever part of him that remains and want to make sure I do my best to love him through *every* moment. No regrets, that's my goal.

Sometimes his capabilities surprise me. Chaplain Marjorie celebrated communion with us the other day, and Drew joined in when we recited the Lord's Prayer. Who knew he was able to do that?

Marge confided later that when she offered him the elements of bread and grape juice, she noticed a look of holy clarity in Drew's eyes that told her he realized the significance. He was remembering Jesus.

She told me that she pictures Drew's face when she ministers to others who are unable to express their awareness.

August 3, 2019

Dana brought two-year-old Jax for a visit today, and after they left, Drew asked, "Where's the little boy?" Even though he was only here for a brief time, Natalie and Anthony's two-and-a-half-year-old made an impact on his great-granddaddy and brought a smile to his face.

We'll have an opportunity to see Brooklynn at her second birthday party later this month, and a chance to celebrate the news that Trevor and Jill are expecting a son in December. They're naming him after both grandfathers, Andrew David.

"Trevor is naming your great-grandson after you," I told Drew. "Andrew Abbott." He had a hard time comprehending how the family tree worked, so Troy wrote a note:

Troy (son)

Trevor (grandson)

Andrew (great-grandson)

It would be so wonderful if Drew could live long enough to hold Andrew. Even if he doesn't, there is comfort in knowing that his namesake will carry on.

August 14, 2019

Drew cried today. I stroked his cheek, and his lips quivered. His eyes filled with tears.

I leaned over to kiss him, and he drew me close, holding me tight as if he would never let go. When he tried to speak, everything came out garbled. He knew it. And he sobbed openly.

"I don't know what you said, but I love you. And I'll be right here with you." My eyes watered, but I didn't cry. I was too focused on assuring him that I understood.

He sobbed more, and all I could say was, "I know, I know," the way my mother did when there were no other words.

If trying to comprehend what he's saying was difficult for me, I can only imagine how frustrating, how maddening it must have felt to him to lose control of the most basic elements of life, to not be able to express himself.

Jena, Drew's nurse, told me difficulty with speech and swallowing are interconnected (it's called dysphasia), so I'll be mindful of feeding him small bites and allowing as much time as he needs to swallow. I crushed two of his pills and mixed them into applesauce last night, which worked well.

We're definitely in the Very Severe Decline stage of Alzheimer's. It's a hard place, but I'm grateful that he's not experiencing physical pain, and there are no signs of bedsores.

August 17, 2019

Jesus Calling by Sarah Young is my go-to devotional. I have read it almost every day for the past several years, but today's passage truly spoke to my heart of hearts:

Find Me in the midst of the maelstrom. Sometimes events whirl around you so quickly that they become a blur. Whisper My Name in recognition that I am still with you. Without skipping a beat in the activities that occupy you, you find strength and peace through praying My Name. Later, when the happenings have run their course, you can talk with Me more fully.

Accept each day just as it comes to you. Do not waste your time and energy wishing for a different set of circumstances. Instead, trust Me enough to yield to My design and purposes. Remember that nothing can separate you from My loving Presence; *you are Mine.*

August 21, 2019

Well, this is embarrassing.

I arranged for Doris to stay with Drew while I went to the hospital for my ablation; my lab work was ready ten days ahead, and I had prayer teams interceding for me. Kim picked me up right on time at 5:15 a.m., and we arrived at Beebe Hospital in plenty of time for my 6:00 a.m. appointment.

But the lady at the desk couldn't find my name on her computer. She made a couple of calls to no avail and kept searching the monitor while she was on hold. I began to suspect it might be my fault when it occurred to me I hadn't received the pre-op call the day before.

"Oh," the receptionist said. "I see the problem," she told the lady on the other end of the line. She smiled at me. "Candace Abbott's ablation is scheduled for *November* 21st at 6:00."

We all let out healthy belly laughs. "Hey, Mom," Kim said. "You got the day and time right, just the wrong month—you're three months early!"

Kim and I went to Bob Evans for an early mother-daughter breakfast, and I kept shaking my head the whole time we ate. How could I have messed up like that? The best I could figure was that when the cardiologist's office called to relay the date of the appointment, the phone must have clicked or crackled when she said the month. *Couldn't have been that I'm on tilt or anything, right?* Must have been the phone's fault.

There is some consolation that my A-fib must not be urgent. And, I'm banking those advance prayers.

August 23, 2019

When I got home from breakfast after my three-hour respite this morning, Tom told me Drew was alert, and they talked a lot about Jesus (Drew mostly listened, of course).

Before that, Drew had gotten into one of his broken-record ruts about needing to go home. Tom said he fielded it the best he could for as long as he could stand and then tried something new: "Okay, you go on home," Tom said. "I'll be right here." And he resumed reading.

Since Drew is pretty much immobile now, he couldn't wiggle himself out of bed, but he had permission and gave it the All-American try. When he finished squirming, he settled back and didn't mention going home again. That same approach worked for me a couple of times, but I'd forgotten about it. It's a valuable tool I'll use again.

It's not uncommon for Drew to think he's in the house where he grew up. I catch on when he gives me clues like, "Mom will have supper ready soon."

Sometimes, I'm able to embrace his world and enter in, but tonight when he said, "Let's go upstairs to bed," I blurted out, "You don't want to go upstairs because there's no bed there. It's an attic, and it's filled with a bunch of junk." For once, I wanted him to grasp reality in MY world instead of me having to enter into the warped perception of HIS world.

He tried to convince me his bedroom was on the second floor.

"Nope," I said. "Not anymore. Your bedroom *used* to be on the second floor when you were a boy, but now you're all grown up and your bedroom is here on the ground floor. How about that? You're already here—in your bedroom, right where you belong—in your home in Georgetown."

My rambling monologue may or may not have registered. Probably not. He still maintained eye contact, and his body language screamed *tension*, so I ended with my go-to phrase, "Everything is just as it should be. It's all good."

Those last few words caught his attention. "It's all good?" he asked. "All good," I said.

He smiled and rested his head on the pillow. Having the assurance he craved, he settled down for the night with no further issues. Maybe next time, I'll skip all the commentary and jump right to the punch line, "Everything is just as it should be. It's all good."

August 26, 2019

Nurse Eileen came tonight to check on Drew before he goes to the Center tomorrow for our scheduled respite. She was here last year when he was in bad shape and, although he has lost his mobility and a lot of weight, she was pleasantly surprised by his radiant complexion, bright eyes, and responsiveness.

I stepped into the kitchen while she checked his pulse and blood pressure. But I came running back as soon as I heard Drew wailing like a wounded child. His bottom lip quivered and was pushed out and curled down in a massive pout. He squinted his eyes tight.

Eileen looked alarmed and asked, "Did I hurt you?"

"Yes," he whimpered with his eyes still shut, and his siren wail continuing louder, longer, and higher pitched.

"Open your eyes and look at me, hon," I said.

He didn't and kept howling.

"He's kidding," I said to Eileen but could tell by her expression that she didn't believe me.

"Drew," I shouted above his long, drawn-out squeal. "That's enough."

No let-up.

I leaned over, so my face was close to his and spoke into his right ear. "This isn't funny. She thinks you're serious and that you're hurting."

He wailed louder.

"Where does it hurt?" Eileen asked.

"Hey, it's time to stop the funny business," I said and leaned close again, with my lips next to his.

"I don't think he's joking," Eileen said.

"Yes, he is," I insisted. "Hey, Drew. You want a kiss?"

Instantly, his eyes popped open, his face transformed into a goofy grin, and he puckered up.

"You goofball!" I kissed him soundly.

Eileen shook her head, and the three of us burst out laughing. "You got me!" she said. "You got me good."

"You made his day." I was laughing so hard I could hardly get the words out. "There's nothing he likes better than to fool somebody. Usually, I'm the one who falls for his funny business."

But never has he gone on so long or so loud or been so convincing. I think he liked the entertainment of the sounds he was able to make.

Or it could be that the little bugger is perfecting his acting skills.

More likely, though, it was a way of releasing the frustration of not being able to find the words to carry on a conversation or communicate as he once did. Wailing doesn't require the synapses to connect with any neurons. It must have given him a feeling of being in control. And, hey, if he could work it into a "gotcha," all the better.

September 8, 2019

Drew went to the Hospice Center for a five-day respite last week. Overall, he made out well, but communication continues to be difficult. Alice came back with a story: When it was time to feed him, she couldn't find the bed controls. Drew watched her as she lifted covers, patted them, reached, bent, and stretched with no sign of the remote control.

"What are you looking for?" he asked.

"I'm trying to find the button to raise the head of your bed," she said.

Drew tilted his head and replied fluently, "Why don't you get somebody who knows what they're doing?"

This reminds me of when Doris was with Drew and he kept asking her questions that she couldn't understand. He was attempting to talk, but the words weren't coming out right. She tried to pretend that she knew what he was asking and said, "I don't know," again and again. After the fourth time, Drew said, "You don't know much, do you?"

Amusing to us. For him, not so much.

Since he got home, he's been sleeping more, and I've seen another overall decline. Hospice sent him home with a handmade Alzheimer's busy quilt. Sometimes called an activity blanket or fidget quilt. I call it a "worry quilt" because Drew frets a lot, and it seems to allow him to worry in a productive way that keeps him calm. This one is lightweight with squares of different fabric—no zippers, buttons, or anything hard—and it's just *perfect* for him. I bunch it up and tell him I need him to hold onto it while I'm changing him, which keeps his hands busy and gives him something to focus on instead of trying to grab my fingers or tug at the sheet.

His legs are beginning to atrophy, and it's painful for him to straighten his right leg, so I'm helping him exercise it a fraction of an inch at a time several times a day.

Although his grip is strong, he's unable to open and close his fingers without assistance; we have to pry them loose. This makes it much more difficult to get him to hold onto the rails of the bed when we turn him to change his briefs.

He's having increased difficulty swallowing, so we're switching from an unrestricted diet to more soft foods. I may need to begin thinking of pureeing his meals. Applesauce, pudding, smoothies, and mashed potatoes seem to provide a texture he can tolerate nicely and swallow effortlessly.

I've been using ThickenUp (Clear) to thicken Drew's liquids to the "nectar-like" level (1 scoop for four ounces of water, juice, coffee, and tea) but may soon have to move to the "honey-like" level (2 scoops) and eventually the "pudding-like" level (3 scoops).

I read that it sometimes helps to massage the throat muscles to encourage swallowing. Jena said she doesn't know if it would be effective because there's a flap in your throat that closes off access to your lungs when you swallow, preventing food and fluid from going into your lungs. With Alzheimer's, the flap doesn't get the involuntary signal to swallow. But she encouraged me to give it a try by tilting his head backward to open his airway and then stroking the sides of his neck in a downward motion.

Verbal skills continue to lessen. Drew is rarely able to say actual words because they mostly come out as grunts and syllables. I do a lot of guesswork and take cues from his facial expressions. It warms my heart that he reaches for me, and his face still lights up when I come into the room.

He's taking very little medication now but seems zoned out most of the time. Yesterday, I knew he wanted to say something, but the words wouldn't come out. I told him to take all the time he needed and kept looking at him as he struggled to put it together.

"Please . . ." he said.

I held his hand in both of mine and encouraged him with my eyes. "Be . . . "

"Please be," I said, studying his face as it contorted with the effort. His brow furrowed, he pursed his lips, whispered several unrelated vowels, and sighed. As he looked up at me with longing, confusion, and frustration, I squeezed his hand. "You can do it," I said. "Please be—?" Waiting is so hard.

It took him a full minute and a half to say those first two words. The last word came with equal difficulty, but finally, he got it out: "Near." He relaxed, his message finally delivered. *Please be near.*

He had been clutching my hand so hard I thought he might break my fingers. When he loosened his grasp, I pulled our entwined wrists up to my face and kissed the back of his hand. "I'm here, and I'll always be near. I'll be with you every minute." I thought about saying "until the end" but left that part out. Instead, I forced a smile and hoped it looked convincing.

"You and me, babe. You and me and Jesus. We're in this together. And whatever comes, we'll get through it just fine."

September 13, 2019

Drew's right leg is flexible again! Maria and I have been exercising it for him, a fraction of an inch at a time, putting a pillow under his knees, and applying CBD oil to his kneecap and tendon.

His face had gotten dry with red patches around his nose, lips, and chin, so I put CBD oil there, too. I'm hoping it has an overall calming effect as well as moistening his thirsty, irritated skin.

Yesterday his words were mostly a whispering that I could barely hear, let alone decipher. Today, he looked at (or beyond) the ceiling and said softly but clearly, "Mom . . . is here." Regardless of whether this was a hallucination or an actual visit in the spiritual realm, the expression on his face of awe, love, peace, and recognition was priceless.

Howard and Kelly stopped by this afternoon. Drew said very few words while they were here but listened actively, making good eye contact. He's been mentioning Howard quite a bit lately, so it was a satisfying visit for Drew.

As is our habit, I gave him a small dish of ice cream at bedtime. "Last bite," I said as I glided the spoon into his mouth. "Unless you want more."

His face beamed.

"You want more ice cream?"

He nodded and said, "I think . . . it would be . . . good for me."

Okay, then! One more dip of ice cream, coming right up!

September 13, 2019

Last Monday's support group was especially satisfying.

I took advantage of the chance to vent, and others vented, as well. Two of them are dealing with their loved ones' hygiene problems (like being unwilling to bathe or change clothes) and combative issues that border on abuse (like the caregiver winding up with a concussion). We talked about medicating, reluctance to see a doctor, and how important it is for caregivers to protect themselves. There is a time to take care of your loved one at home, and a time to entrust your loved one to the care of professionals.

Drew gets agitated and lashes out on occasion, but not to the point where he has become a danger to himself or me. I came home from the meeting more appreciative than ever that he willingly takes his medication, has Hospice bathing him daily, his temperament is fairly stable, and I have all the help I need to keep him here at home.

Last month, Dean, Drew's youngest brother, became concerned about my stress level and health, especially after I mixed up my ablation appointment. He began a little phone campaign to see if our kids could persuade me to consider placing Drew in a facility with a dementia Alzheimer's unit. Dana, Troy, Kim and Wyatt talked with me about it, but they all agreed that I'm doing the right thing by keeping him here.

"Dean hasn't seen how you two interact on a daily basis," Kim said. "He hasn't seen the way Dad calms down when you're in the room and the joy it gives you to reach out and touch him whenever you want.

Instead of giving you comfort and relief, being apart would be even more stressful for you."

Oh, back to the support group. Another thing I learned at the meeting is that stuffed pets are good companions for people with Alzheimer's. Pam Halter sent Drew a stone figurine of a beautiful Cocker Spaniel recently, and Drew was fascinated, but it was too heavy for him to hold. But a plush animal wouldn't be too heavy, so I came home and ordered a lifelike stuffed Cocker Spaniel the same color as Buttercup. It was delivered today, and Drew was enthralled. He pets it and holds it tenderly. A little while ago, he turned it around and looked at the tag on the dog's bottom. "Is it alive?" he asked.

I could see the hope in his eyes, so I said, "It sure is," and then squeezed it, so its ears flopped forward. Therapeutic fibbing? Yep, it's all about emotional stability and flickers of joy, even if only fleeting. I wish you could have seen the way his eyes lit up when he thought he was holding a live puppy.

The last words he said before he dozed off were, "Are you gonna take over?"

With all sorts of thoughts swirling through my mind about how much I'd already taken over, I answered, "Absolutely. You trained me well."

He smiled. "That's good." He nodded and is sleeping soundly with the stuffed puppy under his arm.

September 17, 2019

Drew crooked his finger for me to come closer to him. He wanted to tell me something and did his best, but every word came out distorted. His expression twisted in frustration as he tried again and again. The worst part wasn't that he couldn't get the message across but that he knew something was dreadfully wrong. Fear was written all over his face.

I lowered the metal railing on his bed so I could lean in, cupped his face in my hands, and fluttered tender kisses from his forehead to his cheeks before giving him a solid kiss on his lips.

The fear in his eyes gave way to tears, the second time I've seen him cry since last month. I think he's coming to grips with his situation, maybe to the point of acceptance. He's grieving. So am I.

Holding his hand, I encouraged him to let the tears come.

Chin quivering, and tears trickling down his cheeks, he gazed upward with a look that implored me to give him some assurance.

"We're in a tough place," I said as I caressed his face. I let that sink in for a few seconds and then added, "But we've been in tough places before. We got through those difficult times, and we'll get through this one."

Again, I paused as he seemed to collect himself. "You don't have to worry about a thing. I've got it all covered. I'm working hard to make sure everything is just right. The kids are helping me. You are going to be fine. It's all good."

"All good," he repeated.

"Real courage
is when you know you're licked
before you begin,
but you begin anyway
and see it through no matter what."

— Harper Lee
To Kill a Mockingbird

CHAPTER FIFTEEN

How Long Do We Have?

September 25, 2019

Drew's clothes and snacks are all packed for his five-day respite. The ambulance will arrive at 10:00 a.m. to pick him up and transport him to the Hospice Center in Milford. (See Appendix IV for the letter to family, friends, and nursing staff I sent along.)

October 12, 2019

Some things have recently changed that are noteworthy:

I'm thickening his liquids and feeding his drinks to him a small spoonful at a time, even Coke. Two months ago, one scoop of thickener was sufficient, and he could still drink from a glass. Last month we needed two scoops. When he began choking on that, I added a third scoop to pudding texture and introduced the spoon, keeping portions small. I'm surprised by how quickly he's progressed to this stage.

His biggest agitation is when we roll him from side to side to change and dress him. Ella suggested I slit the back of an undershirt and one of his tops (from the hemline to about three inches from the neckline). It's so much better for him that I'm about to go scissor happy and cut up more (maybe all) of his shirts.

The "worry quilt" that he used occasionally has become a "must" both day and night. If he doesn't have it in his hands to wad up and keep his fingers busy, he pulls on the sheet and blanket until they're all balled up. It also keeps his fingers from touching his face or scratching his head, which is his nervous habit.

He doesn't speak much because it's too hard for him. And the words he strings together are muffled and spoken too softly to understand. Every day is a guessing game.

Jena comes every Friday to check Drew's blood pressure and other vitals, and we always talk about his medicine and sleeping pattern. One good thing is that he sleeps all through the night, praise the Lord! Not long ago, he was a light sleeper, thrashing in the night and stirring at the slightest sound. Now his sleep is deeper, more restful, with less snoring.

All day yesterday, Drew's hands were very cold, and last night they were hot. I asked Jena about it, and she said the disease, as Drew approaches the end stages, will mess with his ability to regulate his temperature, and he might spike a fever. I see a hint of this already.

October 18, 2019

For a few days this month, Drew was listless, slept most of the time, and ate very little. The silver lining was that he was compliant when Ella did her work, pretty much sleeping through the bathing, turning, and changing of clothes rather than his usual resistance. I was concerned that maybe "the end" was coming more quickly than I expected.

He rebounded and has been responsive for the past week and a half. He can't tell if he's hungry, so I offer him food and drink as often as he's willing to accept it. I've gotten into the habit of pureeing his vegetables and meat in a blender. He's awake about five of twenty-four hours. I rejoiced the day I saw the fight come back into him, the spunk he showed when he gave Ella the evil eye and told her, "No!" A bad day seemed better to me than watching him fade away.

But tonight, he was fired up and got agitated when I tried to get him ready for bed. He didn't recognize me. "What's your name?" he asked with a scowl.

I gave him my sweetest smile. "I'm Candy, your wife."

"No, you're not," he barked. "Get away from me."

That stung, but I wasn't surprised. It's part of the disease, and I've noticed that he doesn't brighten up as much as he used to when I come into the room. Instead of beaming, he gives me a pleasant look as if he knows I'm someone he should recognize.

I turned away from him to pull on latex gloves in hopes of gently moving toward the goal of getting his underwear changed. He allowed me to undo the tabs from both sides of his briefs with no objection. I opened them up and, sure enough, there was a BM in there—a messy one— confirming the sour aroma permeating the room. So, this is what "in sickness and in health" looks and smells like.

He snarled and grabbed my wrist. "Don't do that! You're not supposed to see that! That's *private!*"

"It's okay. I'm your wife." My words came out soothingly, masking the panic I felt as I tried to free my hand from his grip so I could get the messy briefs out from under him before he smeared poop all over both of us.

"Liar!" he shouted. "You just want to look at it."

His fingers released my wrist and he grasped his private parts. In what should have been an act of modesty, his fingers squeezed with the same strength he'd used on me, turning his vice-like grip on himself. His eyes nearly bulged out of his head. "You're hurting me! You're hurting me!" he shrieked with hatred in his eyes.

I stepped back with my hands held high, fingers wide apart. "It's not me. I'm not touching you. My hands are right here."

In what must have been excruciating pain, he looked confused. His brain won't tell his fingers how to release his grip. "Why are you doing this to me?"

"I'm not hurting you. See?" I wiggled my fingers in the air. "You're hurting yourself! Open your fingers. Let go!"

Poor guy. He couldn't comprehend the strength of his hands. If I tried to pry them loose, he may have felt even more threatened and squeezed himself tighter.

I stood there, paralyzed as to how to help him.

Just when I feared he might maim himself or pass out from the pain, he released his fingers. We both breathed a sigh of relief—me, emotionally and him, physically by peeing a nice stream.

"You might be bruised," I said, "but it's nice to see your plumbing still works. Let me clean that up for you." With a flurry of wet wipes, lukewarm soapy water, Balmex, and fresh briefs, I worked quickly. He cooperated fully and recognized me, thanking me again and again.

I stepped outside to dump the stinky trash, and when I came back in, Drew was already snoring. Poor baby. He had fought a good (nevertheless unnecessary) fight he brought on himself, and he was exhausted.

The devil might think this is funny, but we get the last laugh: Love never fails.

October 30, 2019

This is day six of my chest congestion and coughing spells. My eyes were crusty yesterday, and my fever broke last night, so I went to the Beebe walk-in clinic. I felt better when I saw the familiar, smiling face of Melinda Ricker, who said my mucus was clear and I had signs of wheezing.

After giving me a nebulizer treatment, she said, "Sometimes viruses like to bring their bacterial friends along," so she handed me a prescription for an antibiotic to fill later in case I start coughing up yellow gunk.

I went immediately to the pharmacy to pick up my prescriptions. The cashier checked the computer and said they could fill the order for Prednisone, but insurance wouldn't cover the inhaler.

There at the counter, at that very moment, I tried to say, "But I need it—" and the effects of the nebulizer must have kicked in. I got into a violent coughing fit that was so bad I ripped open the package of cough drops I hadn't yet paid for and shoved one into my mouth, only to spew it out on the floor. As if things weren't already bad enough, in a coughing moment of insanity to find some relief, I did something no person in her right mind would do: I bent over to scoop it up off the floor, where dozens of other sick customers had stood, and popped it back in my mouth. *Ewww! Gross! Yuck!* Somewhere in the white noise of my mind, I heard the clerk say, "You think you should go to the restroom?"

I caught a glimpse of customers' distraught faces as I coughed and propelled my way out of the spotlight. Choking and gagging in the restroom for what felt like ten minutes, I was so consumed with trying to catch my breath between coughs that I never even closed the door. That meant the scene that began in public was reverberating off the private tile walls, echoing throughout the store. How mortifying for everybody!

A clerk came to check on me as I began to recover and said my prescriptions were ready. I splashed my face with water, managed to finalize the sale, and drove home. The inhaler was in the bag—guess I convinced them I needed it, and they did somersaults to find an affordable generic.

I pray that Drew doesn't catch this virus as it could prove deadly for him. A few days ago, I asked the nurse what precautions a sick person needs to take when caring for someone with Alzheimer's. "Should I wear an antiviral mask?"

She said I could if I wanted, but droplets spread germs, so a mask isn't necessary as long as I keep my hands washed, use gloves, and am careful not to cough and sneeze around him.

With his compromised immune system and inability to get up and move around, he would likely wind up with pneumonia, which is often the cause of death for Alzheimer's patients.

Drew's youngest brother Dean and I were talking on the phone tonight, and I told him the nurse said if Drew caught my cold that I shouldn't feel guilty.

He burst out laughing. "Honey, you don't have the luxury of feeling guilty. You've done so much more than most people would ever think of doing, guilt shouldn't even be in your vocabulary!"

I think guilt has a way of creeping in and nagging at those who care for their loved ones. *What could I have done better? What did I do that I shouldn't have done? If only . . .*

If you're doing the best you know how, if you mess up but not on purpose, or even if you do something hurtful on purpose that you deeply regret, guilt is a trick of the devil and a waste of time. To keep in line with my motto of "no regrets," if I have reason to feel guilty, I confess it, forgive myself, and move on.

One of the reasons I can do that is because of a conversation Drew and I had early in our marriage. I was berating myself over something horrendous I had done before we met, and he asked, "Have you asked God to forgive you?"

I remember how the question caught me off guard because I was so preoccupied with my monologue of self-rebuke. "Yes," I answered.

"And has He forgiven you?

"Of course."

And then he asked another question: "Have you forgiven yourself?"

It took me a little longer to answer. "No, I guess not."

"So why don't you?" His eyes probed mine.

"I don't know."

"Why not?"

Before I could answer, he added five words that have stayed with me all these years: "Are you greater than God?"

It took a while for me to be able to breathe again as that sank in. "No, of course not." I can still remember how hot the tears felt trickling down my face.

"Then, why don't you?" He put his forehead to mine and wrapped his arms around me. "Go ahead. Forgive yourself—right now."

As deep sobs came from the core of my being, the seething anger I had harbored toward myself dissipated, never to return.

As I sit here this evening with a cinnamon-scented candle burning, a cup of hot herbal tea at my elbow, and soft music playing, I watch Drew while he sleeps. I'm grateful he isn't in pain. He looks so peaceful. Peace begets peace. I feel serene.

I think it must be a blessing that he doesn't have the same awareness of the passage of time as the rest of us do. Whenever he opens his eyes, he's in the present. He doesn't know what time it is, what day it is, what season it is, or what year it is. To him, it doesn't matter.

When I open my eyes at the beginning of the day, each tick of the clock requires me to be alert for who's coming next, where I need to be at any given moment, when medication is due, which appointment may need to be rescheduled, and how I can guard some personal time. So, I strive for peace while trying to make every minute count.

His world is simple, uncluttered, compartmentalized.

My world is fragmented, fatigued, and frazzled.

His body is imprisoned in a hospital bed, but his mind is protected from awareness of it by a mysterious fog.

My body can get up and go, but my mind is keenly aware of more than I wish to know as I watch and wonder how long the process of dying with Alzheimer's will take.

He is preparing for his journey to heaven.

I am preparing for the void that will remain, which no one else can fill.

November 5, 2019

So far, Drew appears to be virus-free. His pattern lately is to sleep most of the time and he is typically awake a total of four out of twenty-four hours, so he's eating and drinking very little. During his few waking hours, he's drowsy and sometimes dozes off between bites.

Being around someone sleepy can be contagious. I take frequent naps in the recliner and try to be near him as often as I can so he can sense my presence. This puts a crimp in the work I need to do, but I don't want to be too far away when he wakes up.

Yesterday, he barely spoke at all—mostly inarticulate puffs of air. It took too much effort for him to form the words. So, I didn't do much talking either.

Instead, I tried to set an upbeat tone by using my style of sign language: I puckered my lips like a fish. He smiled and puckered up, too, so we blew kisses to one other for a while. Then, we passed the time by making funny faces. With Golden Oldies music playing softly, I took his hands in mine and danced with him (or more accurately, danced for him). And then I sat down, exhausted from my efforts to pep him up.

He's speaking better today. When I tried to give him one last spoonful of thickened orange juice, he clamped his teeth together and said clearly, "I don't like it." Real words—music to my ears!

November 9, 2019

The stiffness in Drew's legs has become excruciatingly painful, so last night, I replaced his evening meds (Lorazepam, Benadryl, and melatonin) with 0.25 ml of the morphine. I got it from my Hospice "Comfort Pak" in the refrigerator, which contains a variety of items to be used when new symptoms emerge or current symptoms worsen, requiring an immediate response. He handled it well, and I noticed that his breathing throughout the night was more regular than usual.

Drew's older brother Howard and our sister-in-law Kelly stopped by when Dana and Troy were here today, so we had a quality visit. Drew recognized Howard and gripped his fingers so tight and for so long that Howard told Kelly, "I think I'm going to be here a while; you might have to come back in a couple of days to pick me up."

Drew tried very hard to tell Howard something but couldn't get it out. Whatever it was, it was important to him, and we could all feel his frustration as he realized something was going on in his brain that he couldn't do anything about. Kelly said he looked like he was crying but without tears. My guess is that he wanted to tell his brother he was dying or maybe that he had seen their parents. During his few waking hours, he spends more time gazing past the ceiling with a look of wonder on his face than seeing things in the room.

November 15, 2019

New symptoms have cropped up that indicate an acceleration in decline.

Drew's hands and arms involuntarily twitch and jerk. On Thursday, Ella said his fist flew up, and he hit himself in the forehead so hard she thought he might develop a bruise (which he didn't). Jena says it's typical in late-stage Alzheimer's and goes hand-in-hand with the inability to speak. I think it's called myoclonus: a brief, involuntary twitching of a muscle or a group of muscles, usually caused by sudden muscle contractions.

Two days ago, I discovered he had a scrape on his right hand that bled a little, so I put some Neosporin on it and covered it with a Band-aid. I have no idea what he did to get that. Maybe he scratched himself with his nails.

He was gripping the blanket in the night, and I tried to pry his fingers loose but couldn't. I mentioned it to Jena, and she said it's because the confusion makes him fearful, and he's trying to hold onto anything that can give him a sense of security, even when sound asleep. In my attempt to help him relax by loosening his grip, I accomplished the opposite by threatening the refuge he had found in holding tight.

He also gets hiccups frequently, another common late-stage symptom. It's a neurological thing.

And he's developing yucky secretions, so I'm giving him mouth care more often than morning and night. I'm using a sponge swab, and he bites down on the stick. This stuff is thick and sticks to his teeth like glue. The electric toothbrush is helpful, but he doesn't tolerate it well anymore.

A week ago, Drew was awake about four hours a day. Today, it was just one and a half hours. He gave Troy a broad smile but went back to sleep immediately. While he was awake this evening, his mouth moved, and wisps of air came out, but no words at all.

His humor is still going strong. Kim stayed with him on Monday night while I was at the support group. He stuck out his tongue at her and scrunched up his face. She stuck out her tongue, too. They exchanged silly, goofy communication without words for quite a while. Precious memories for her to savor.

This happy exchange is quite a contrast from the discussion the support group had that same night. A new member said it's a matter of "quality of life," and when that goes, he believes it should just "be over."

The rest of us looked at each other wide-eyed, and one asked, "Are you talking about euthanasia?"

He said he *was*, that some states have legalized it and that we "put dogs down," so why not people?

I resisted the urge to begin a debate about dehumanizing our loved ones or the ongoing value of a person after life loses its desired quality. I yearned to say something about the sacred times that can be experienced even after the person can no longer communicate and how satisfying it can be for them—and us. But I wouldn't have been able to do it justice because I only had a few minutes before I had to go home. So, I kept quiet.

As I stood up to leave, I was surprised to hear myself say, "I hope you'll come again," and he said, "You can count on it. I'll be here every month." Maybe he will. Maybe I'll have the opportunity to express my views—primarily that God is God and I am not.

It was the first time I left the group feeling agitated instead of uplifted. Instead of lingering as I usually do, I hurried away as if to escape the anxiety that had risen in me. But it followed me home.

These are heavy issues, and we all face them the best we know how.

November 17, 2019

What a difference a day or two makes. Instead of grimacing and gripping the blanket like a lifeline, Drew smiles in his sleep, and his fingers are relaxed. He could plateau like this for a while or decline quickly, and I'm emotionally prepared either way—or at least I think so.

I have him scheduled for a five-day respite at the Delaware Hospice Center on Wednesday because I'm having my cardiac ablation on Thursday. I'll be in the hospital overnight, and that will give me a few days to recuperate before he comes home.

November 19, 2019

Jena came to check Drew's vitals and evaluate him before he goes to the Center tomorrow. He slept through her visit, and we discussed his decline and symptoms to look for as he approaches his last days.

She said we're probably "looking at weeks now" rather than months. I was glad Troy was with me to hear all she had to say. It was a sobering moment for both of us and made me cherish all the more each day I have with Drew.

November 24, 2019

My cardiac ablation on Thursday was supposed to take two to three hours. Kim was in the waiting room watching the monitor about my status, which read "ongoing procedure" well into the four-and-a-half-hour mark. Other families came and went, and new families came and went. She texted Wyatt, "I'm beginning to get worried" (an understatement). She was trying to stay calm, but the cardiac unit receptionist couldn't give her any information until someone from the operating room came out.

About that time, a lady who was equally frustrated said she was going to go back to the cardio prep room and check on her husband. She came flying into the waiting room with her face flushed and blurted out, "I just saw an old lady with gray hair and glasses, and they put her down."

"What?" Kim shouted. "What did you say? They *put her down?*" Trying not to freak out, she speed-clicked through some facts:

The guy at the support group had said those very words.

Mom doesn't look "old" like other old people.

Mom's hair isn't gray. She colors it.

Mom doesn't have her glasses on. She grabbed her purse and looked inside. *I have them right here.*

Just as she was figuring out I couldn't possibly be the old lady who got put down (or sedated or shocked or whatever), a nurse came out and called for, "Abbott."

Kim jumped up and introduced herself.

"Your mother's out of surgery, but it's still going to be a while." And that's all she could tell her.

After another hour, trying not to worry, the doctor came out but walked over to another family and stood there as he talked with them.

Then he turned and came over to Kim and sat down across from her. Her mind was still racing. *But you stood up to talk to them. Doctors sit down with people when they have bad news. Stand up. Please stand up.*

Dr. Islam was gentle and straightforward. "We had some complications," he said and explained that parts of the procedure that should have taken fifteen minutes took an hour and a half, that there was some minor internal bleeding, and that they would have to continue applying pressure to both incision sites. He suggested she get something to eat, that it would probably be a couple more hours.

Kim was back in plenty of time to greet me in the recovery room when I woke up. She said there was a line of people outside my curtain: nurses, a phlebotomist, technicians, a radiologist, two anesthesiologists, a lady with a doppler ultrasound, and a guy to put pressure on the site again. He also put a contraption on me to sustain the pressure that Wyatt later described as a medieval torture device (and felt like it). At 7:30 p.m., Dr. Islam instructed the nurse to transport me to ICU, a full twelve hours from when they had wheeled me into the operating room.

I spent three nights in ICU where they triple checked my hemoglobin, blood pressure, and oxygen levels in addition to my heart rhythm, which was perfect until A-fib showed up the second day (apparently this can be normal while the heart is adjusting). I had to lay flat on my back, which gave me renewed empathy for Drew. I wound up in excruciating pain that morphine wouldn't touch, so they gave me Dilaudid with anti-nausea medication by IV. I am now officially a fan of Dilaudid.

Kim texted, sent emails from her phone and mine, and posted Facebook messages to keep everyone updated and solicit prayer support. She kept on top of things, and it took a toll on her. It's not easy to sit beside someone you love while they go through something you're helpless to do anything about—whether it's moms in hospital beds or husbands with Alzheimer's.

On Saturday evening, when I was able to sit up and use the phone, I spoke with Dana while she was with her dad at the Hospice Center. "He acts irritated with me," she said. "It's like he thinks I'm keeping something from him."

"You are," I said.

She sounded surprised. "I am?"

"Yes. You're not telling him what's going on with me, and I'm sure he's overhearing bits and pieces about how concerned everybody is."

I thought about it after I hung up. After a few minutes, I called Dana back and told her that if Drew could just hear my voice to know I was okay, he would be at peace.

She held the phone to his ear. "Hey, Dad. It's Candy."

"Hi, hon," I said.

He made husky sounds communicating that he knew it was me. I explained that I'd had surgery and would be in the hospital for a few days. That I knew he wanted to be with me. That it was hard to be apart. That we were both getting the care we needed. That we would be together again soon. Then, putting as much emotion as I could into three little words, I spoke slowly, "I *love* you."

After a brief pause, he gathered himself as best he could and uttered the most heart-warming breathy expression of affection I will probably ever hear: "Ahh *wuff* ooh." I didn't know it then, but these were the last words he would say to me.

November 29, 2019

I brought Drew home from the Hospice Center on Friday and felt whole again having him here with me.

During my recovery, I talked with several people who spent time with him, who told me that he looked up at (or beyond) the ceiling a lot. I already knew that, of course, but it came as a surprise to them.

My brother Mike said Drew gave him a big smile when he came into the room and ate a good dinner that night. Maria, our private-pay certified nursing assistant, was there at the time and said the recognition was genuine, that his face lit up when he saw Mike. Drew had rallied, something that often happens as death draws near.

On Thanksgiving, Dana was with him, and she said he was alert that day, too, and ate well. She gave him a thumbs-up sign and said, "Good job," and he asked as clear as a bell, "What's that mean?"

Later on, he was looking up as he often did and said, "All ready." Those would be the last words Dana would hear from him.

Here at home, he seems content and has been resting comfortably. He continues to look skyward. I believe the spiritual realm is becoming more real to him than the earthly realm.

November 30, 2019

All of Drew's foods have been pureed for the past week because he's lost the ability to clean out the inside of his mouth with his tongue. Oh, the simple things we do all the time without even realizing it. In late-stage dementia, people with Alzheimer's forget how to swallow and they store or "pocket" food in their cheeks and under their tongue and lips. When this happens, they open their mouth for another bite and another bite, pocketing food until they're in a choking situation. Mealtime is a long and slow process. I'm keeping a supply of baby food on hand. That, and mashed potatoes.

This "pocketing" situation makes mouth care all the more important. Not only do the inside of his cheeks need to be swabbed to clean out excess food, but the moisture from the sponge helps with hydration.

I got lemon-glycerin swabs in addition to the blue oral care sponges we've been using. Drew doesn't like either and clamps his teeth on the stick. I've given up trying to pull it out of his mouth because he bites down harder when I do. But I've found I can put an end to the tug-of-war game if I let him lay there for about forty-five seconds with the stick hanging out of his mouth and watch for his jaw to loosen up. Yep, asleep again, and the swab is out. I win!

When my mom was dying, I remember her request for a popsicle and how satisfying it was in quenching her thirst. I don't think it would be a good option for Drew, though, because the juice would be too thin and could choke him.

Maria suggested swabbing his lips and tongue with cold, thickened water to help alleviate the dryness. But when she tried it, Drew choked on the dab of thickened water she gave him and was unable to cough it up or swallow it because of the mucus in his throat.

I called Hospice, and the nurse directed me to the refrigerator for the Comfort Pak, where I found a pill to dry up the secretions. I placed it under his tongue to dissolve. He can have one every four hours if needed. A second one seems to have done the trick. I'll want to keep a supply of those little pills on hand.

After the choking incident this morning, he hasn't been awake at all. I tried to give him a teaspoon of thickened orange juice, but it just pooled in his mouth and trickled down his chin. I had hoped to at least get a dose of Miralax in him, but no luck. I opened a container of sweet potato baby food, but he showed no interest, and the risk of aspiration was too great for me to attempt to feed him even one bite.

This is his first full day with no food or liquids.

He's been sleeping comfortably the entire day and into the evening. Since I'm not supposed to do any heavy lifting for a while, Maria changed Drew's briefs and repositioned him in the bed with lots of pillows. He slept pretty much through the whole process and is all snuggled in for the night. He didn't seem to need any medication tonight.

When Howard came for a short visit this afternoon, I tried to rouse Drew, but the only response I got was snoring. It was truly a comfort to have Howard and Kelly here to commiserate together.

December 1, 2019

This is Drew's second day with no food or drink. He has lost all ability to swallow, opens his eyes just long enough to close them again, and it's clear that we're facing a matter of days now, rather than weeks.

Dana came and asked if I had talked with Jena.

"No," I said, "it's Sunday, and I won't see her until tomorrow, but I'll call to keep her informed."

As I dialed Jena's number, the reality hit me that Drew's death is getting close. I could feel the emotion crawling up my throat, and by the time I heard Jena's voice on the answering machine, I was so choked up, I could barely speak. I did manage to croak out the message and then called Kim. When she answered, I was in full-blown tears.

"I'll be right there, Mom," she said. "We'll have a good cry together."

I was looking forward to a good sobbing episode, but in the fifteen minutes it took Kim to get from her house to mine, my tears had gone back into hiding.

December 2, 2019

This morning, Drew was in the exact position Maria and I had placed him at 9:00 last night, on his left side. He had yucky brown slime drooling from the side of his mouth and pooling on the pillow. I swiped at it with a cloth and had to run into the kitchen to gag where he wouldn't hear me. I've done all right with everything to this point—urine, poop, even vomit—but this slimy stuff just about did me in. Lord, help me to steel myself for the ongoing job of swabbing his mouth that needs to be done.

The nurse will come every day now. Jena said Drew's death is imminent, maybe days or a couple of weeks. Dana pressed her for her best guess, and she said possibly by the weekend but not to hold her to it.

The three of us were standing next to Drew, talking about the supernatural, and I urged Dana to share a dream she'd had the previous month.

"In the dream," she said, "a woman was giving me a big bear hug—the most calming, reassuring hug I've ever known. I couldn't tell who she was until I stepped back, and it was Mom Mom Abbott. She was *beautiful,* so beautiful—in her early thirties and absolutely radiant. She spoke, but her mouth didn't move. It was like she spoke straight to my heart rather than to my ears, assuring me that Dad's going to be fine. 'You don't have to worry. I'll take good care of him.' Then I said—and my mouth moved even though hers didn't—'Oh, Mom Mom, you don't know how much that means to me. That's such a comfort. It's just what I needed to hear.'"

I watched Drew, who smiled the whole time Dana spoke, and when she finished, he grinned as if to say, *Ah, you get it.*

After talking about how this was "day four" with no food or drink,

Dana turned to Jena and choked up so badly she could barely get the words out. "When is it the right time to—you know—give Dad 'permission' to go?"

Jena said today would be a good time.

Before Jena left, Drew looked as though he had gone back to sleep, but she touched his shoulder and said, "Mister Drew, are you playing 'possum on me, or are you really sleeping?"

He took short, shallow breaths, and the corners of his mouth turned up into a silly grin.

"There you go, playing your tricks on me again," she said. "I'll see you tomorrow."

Even then, his humor was still evident.

After Jena left, family and friends spent one-on-one time by Drew's bedside. It's all about the love, and it's overflowing and saturating this place.

I met with my cardiologist this afternoon, and I'm amazed at my energy level. Dr. Islam said there's an 80 percent chance I will never have A-fib again. I like those odds.

Alice stayed with Drew while I was gone, and she said most of the time, his eyes were open, primarily looking up and beyond the ceiling with an expression of peace and awe. He said, "I see you" to somebody Alice couldn't see, and "I understand."

Most of the afternoon and into the evening, he slept or stared upward, but he had several lucid moments. When he did, I candidly talked with him about what his body was going through as it shuts down.

For the past several days, Buttercup has crawled under the hospital bed and laid there to be close to Drew. No doubt, she senses what's going on and is grieving like the rest of us.

Dana, Kim, and Troy took turns being alone with their dad, saying, "It's okay for you to go; everything's good, and we'll be fine."

Trevor sat beside him yesterday and today for a few hours, and the two of us had deep and meaningful conversations. He picked up one of the books from Drew's bookcase, *The Power of Positive Thinking*, by Norman Vincent Peale, and randomly opened it to Chapter 16, "Prescription for Heartache." It was almost like Granddad Drew said, "Here, read this."

Select excerpts from the chapter (pages 247-249) spoke to me (emphasis mine):

> Whatever the character of your heartache, one of the first steps is to resolve to escape from any defeatist situation which may have been created around yourself, even though it is difficult to do so, and return once again to the normal course of your life. *Get back into the mainstream of life's activities. Take up your old associations. Form new ones.* Get busy walking, riding, swimming, playing—get the blood to coursing through your system. *Lose yourself in some worthwhile project. Fill your days with creative activity and emphasize the physical aspect of activity.* Employ healthy mind-relieving busyness, but be sure that it is of a worthwhile and constructive nature.
>
> *It is natural to cry when pain or sorrow comes. It is a relief mechanism provided in the body by Almighty God and should be used. To restrain grief, to inhibit it, to bottle it up, is to fail to use one of God's means for eliminating the pressure of sorrow.* Like every other function of the human body and nervous system, this must be controlled, but it should not be denied altogether. *A good cry by either man or woman is a release from heartache.*
>
> *The deeper remedy for heartache, of course, is the curative comfort supplied by trust in God. Inevitably the basic prescription for heartache is to turn to God in an attitude of faith and empty the mind and heart to Him* . . . It is not advisable to attempt to carry the burden of sorrow and mental pain without Divine help, for its weight is more than the personality can bear. *The simplest and most effective of all prescriptions for heartache then is to practice the presence of God. This will soothe the ache in your heart and ultimately heal the wound.*

I didn't take my turn saying goodbye to Drew until that evening, and the experience will stay with me forever. Maria was in the other room but had come to change him. I came up to his bedside and said, "Hey, hon." He was gazing upward, and the sound of my voice startled him.

I watched as he slowly, very slowly—as gradually as a sloth, with its low metabolism and deliberate movements—pulled his stare from above and willed his eyes toward mine. They were glassy, and I could tell he was trying hard to find me. At last, his gaze located my face and continued searching until he found my eyes. In the instant our eyes met, his look changed from vague to focused, and he was lucid.

"Dying is hard work," I said. "It's a big job, and you've never done it before, but you're doing everything just right. You're brave and courageous, and I love you more than I can say."

He kept his gaze steady, and I knew he could comprehend each word.

"You're doing it just right," I told him again. "You're leading by example as you've done all your life. Now it's time to show us how to let go of earthly things and embrace the heavenly. It's okay to leave me because I know where you're going. You'll be meeting Jesus face-to-face, and I'll join you later. Between now and then, I'll be fine. You don't have to worry about a thing. It's all good."

Drew was seeing the spiritual realm and the earthly realm at the same time. We all live in parallel realms, but we only see the visible one. He saw both. Eternity isn't for later—we're living in it now, and what we do on earth carries over. Watching him look from the invisible realm to the tangible world and back again has cemented my belief that heaven is a real place filled with goodness and joy beyond what we can fathom.

But as it is written:

Eye has not seen, nor ear heard,
Nor have entered into the heart of man
The things which God has prepared for those who love Him.

(1 Corinthians 2:9 NKJV)

December 3, 2019

When I awoke, his breathing was faster and shallower than yesterday. There wasn't as much drool as I expected, so I didn't attempt to clean his mouth, opting for Ella to do that when she came to bathe and change him around 10:30.

Marjorie, the chaplain, came in at the same time, so I sat with her in the kitchen, and we chatted over coffee while Ella went about her work. I told Marge that I felt a nervous sense of anticipation all morning—butterflies in my stomach like I have when I'm standing in line to go on an amusement park ride. *(I found out later that Dana had the same sensation.)*

Suddenly, Ella shouted, "Call Jena! *NOW!*"

I grabbed my phone and tried to find Jena's name in my contacts. My hands shook, and my eyes wouldn't focus.

"I can't find the number," I said, holding the phone out to Ella. "You do it."

She called Hospice for me.

Marge and Ella kept the conversation going with me until Jena got here. She was planning to come at noon anyway, so she was in the vicinity and arrived within minutes. She breezed into the bedroom like the angel she is and said to Ella, "Is he—"

Ella nodded. "He's gone."

Drew passed away at 11:20 this morning.

That was the first time I looked at Drew since Ella's shout. I knew from the urgency in her voice that he was in trouble, but I didn't know he was *gone!* It seemed surreal. In many respects, he's been "gone" for years, but this time he was really gone—the ultimate "gone." Except it didn't *feel* like he was gone.

Ella's words came to me as muffled sounds, like I had cotton balls in my ears, but I could still hear her saying, "I had finished and was pulling the blanket up to his chin when I noticed his jaw had gone slack, so I listened to his heart and stomach, but there were no sounds at all."

By then, I was standing beside Drew, caressing his cheek, and her words were less muffled. My hearing was coming back to normal.

"He's totally clean," she said. "I got everything done. Shaved, shampooed. Everything. He bit down on the stick of the sponge as usual when I cleaned his mouth, but he didn't fight me, not even when I turned him." She smiled. "I guess this was his way of saying, 'I win.'"

Ella had her hands right on him when he died, and the transition was so peaceful, she didn't even know. What solace it brought me to have Ella and Marjorie right here with me when it happened.

I called Dana first, so she was here when Jena declared the official time of death as 11:56. I had to leave a message for Troy, who was at a doctor's appointment, and for Kim, who was teaching, but they arrived quickly and had their private time with their dad. Then Wyatt and Saige arrived. Then Natalie.

Saturday seemed to be the best time for the funeral because Kade had exams in North Carolina and could drive up by them but had to be back by Monday. I showed Marge the draft of the funeral program I'd been working on and asked if she could sing a solo. She said she could if we could make it 2:30 p.m. because she had another funeral that morning.

Rev. Egger came over to extend his condolences and say a prayer. He knew we wanted to have the service at the Presbyterian Church and told me the sanctuary would be open all day on Saturday, and Tunnell Hall would be available to us until 7 p.m.

Harry Fletcher, our dear friend and funeral director with Pippin Funeral Home, called to see if I was ready for him to come for Drew's body. He said there was no rush, so I asked him to wait until 4:00. That gave others like Natalie, Trevor, Drew's middle brother Tim and sister-in-law Myrna, Doris, and Tracey (Kim's childhood friend and second cousin) a chance to say their final goodbyes here at the house. During the afternoon, Dana, Kim, and I made calls to let people know about the arrangements. I was in my comfort zone: making plans, reviewing the format for the service I had sketched out using my dear friend Wilma's program as a guide, and consoling others even as I received consolation. I felt like I had it all together.

And then our friend and funeral director Harry arrived. I very matter-of-factly informed him that the funeral would be on Saturday at 2:30 at the Presbyterian Church. His face fell.

"What?" I said. "Is there a problem?"

"Well, yes," he said, "there is. We have two other funerals on Saturday, and even if we were able to do it that day, we'd have to be at the cemetery no later than 2:00." He explained that it was a safety issue for the vault company employees. After the graveside service, the workers had to take down the tent, place the lid on the vault, then fill in the grave, and clean all around the grave before dark.

Holy cow! *Who plans a funeral without consulting the funeral director?!* Um, I do. Everything was falling apart before my very eyes. I blew it.

"Not to worry," Harry said.

I could see he was trying his best to mean it.

"We'll work something out." His wheels were turning as he suggested one alternative after another, but Kim, Dana, and I kept coming back to Saturday and didn't want to extend our emotional resources beyond one day.

"Let me make some phone calls," Harry said. "If I can get extra helpers, an available hearse, and the equipment for the cemetery, could we aim for the visitation to be from 10 to 12 and the service at noon?"

"YES!" we agreed. That would be great.

He reminded us it was a BIG "IF" with all the loose ends he had to wrap up. He made the calls, and it looked promising.

When it came time for Harry to put Drew on the stretcher, he asked me to keep Buttercup in the other room so she wouldn't be underfoot. Kim did her best to keep her in the living room, but she kept trying to ease her way back to Drew. I had to put her on the leash to restrain her, and she couldn't get close to him to say goodbye. *How do you help a dog grieve?*

Harry gave us private time with Drew before he wheeled the stretcher outside. His body served him well and loved me fully. I caressed his face and kissed his forehead. His skin felt soft to my lips—no longer warm, but cool, not cold. That was the last time he would be here in the house with me.

After the others left, Kim, Wyatt, and Saige lingered. That old commercial, *Calgon, take me away,* ran through my mind. They took me to dinner at the Georgetown Family Restaurant, and it did me good to be out and about with others in the land of "normal."

Alone in the house that night, I picked up the towels and shirts that Ella had left after bathing and changing Drew. I put them in the washer and looked around for anything else that might need attention. Pulling the baggie out of the wastebasket beside the hospital bed, I tied the strings, took it outside, and tossed it into the trash barrel. As I heard the thud when it hit bottom, it struck me that I had been on caregiver duty 24/7 all these years, and just like that—*thud*—my responsibilities had ceased. Abruptly.

Nobody needs me, I thought.

At that very moment, Buttercup barked, and Midnight scampered over, purring and wrapping her tail around my ankle.

"*You* need me," I said, ushering them into the house. "Come on, guys, let's get you fed."

"When death,
the great reconciler, has come,
it is never our tenderness that we repent of,
but our severity."

— *George Eliot*

Arise, Let Us Go From Here

December 4, 2019

Wonder of wonders, miracle of miracles, Harry managed to pull everything together for the funeral to take place on Saturday! Harry did his part. Now, the remaining challenge was for me to find another soloist and remember all the people we had given wrong information to. I'll think about that tomorrow.

I had the most wonderful day with Kim chauffeuring me around from 8:15 a.m. to 6:15 p.m. I got a clean bill of health from Dr. Palekar in Lewes; we went to Honey's Farm Fresh restaurant for my favorite omelet; then to the outlets for shopping where I found an outfit for the funeral; then drove an hour north to the funeral home where Harry guided us through casket selection and all the other details; then around the corner from Pippin's for an impromptu visit with my brother Jim and sister-in-law Shelly where we laughed our heads off for a couple of hours telling family stories; then home again where everything was fresh because Brandon and Jillian had come to do their monthly cleaning, and the hospital bed had been removed. Doris waited to say she had greeted visitors throughout the day (our neighbor Mitch even cut the grass and mulched the leaves) and had dinner waiting that my friends, Betty and Judi, had brought; then Richard, the caterer who is doing the luncheon on Saturday, came to go over menu choices; then I went to bed with a smile on my face and happiness in my heart.

It will take me a while to get used to being able to go where I want without having to make caregiving arrangements, but already I feel a sense of freedom. Making decisions is like trying to think through molasses, so I'm grateful that Kim guided me along.

I'm surprised and pleased with my energy level since the heart procedure two weeks ago. The cardiologist told me on Monday, the day before Drew died, that I could resume normal activities. All this is beyond "normal," of course, but somehow it seems right that things are unfolding this way.

I'm amazed at the joy that is bubbling up within me. For seven years, I poured out, and I guess this is what it feels like for God to pour in. It's almost euphoric! But I'm wondering if I should share that. This is not how widows are supposed to behave, and people may think I'm bonkers. But, if this is bonkers, bring it on! I think it must be *the joy of the Lord*. I remembered the Scripture, "The joy of the Lord is your strength," and looked it up to find the chapter and verse. Imagine my surprise when I looked it up and discovered the first three words of that verse:

> *Do not grieve,*
> *for the joy of the Lord is your strength."*
> (Nehemiah 8:10 NIV)

Of course, this verse was written for the Israelites under different circumstances than a woman whose husband just died, and the Lord surely intends for us to grieve. But it gave me permission to embrace the strange joy that has overtaken me.

December 5, 2019

My dear friend, Linda Mason, agreed to play a flute solo, and somehow, all the misinformation about the service timing got straightened out—or, at least, I hope all the people we talked with were notified.

I busied myself with funeral bulletin details and floated through the day. I'm enjoying the ability to start and finish a task without anyone calling me away from it. It's so freeing to be able to put a load of laundry in the washer, add the detergent and softener, and turn it on without hearing, "Caaaanndy."

I've been sleeping soundly and waking refreshed—quite a contrast to the last many months and years.

December 6, 2019

Talk about an emotional roller coaster. This morning, the Abbott brothers (Howard, Tim, Dean, and I representing Drew) and my sisters-in-law Kelly and Myrna had settlement on the former mobile home park in Fenwick Island we've been trying to sell for years. Look at how the Lord arranged the timing of Drew's death so it wouldn't interfere with this long-anticipated milestone. Dean came from Ohio for the closing, so he didn't have to make another trip for the funeral. He picked me up and drove to us Rehoboth where we joined the others. After the flurry of paper-signing with the buyer and attorneys, the six of us celebrated over lunch at Baywood.

Even though Drew is no longer here, he is still taking care of me, thanks to his father's foresight in purchasing "swamp land" so many decades ago. I breathed a sigh of relief that I'll be able to pay all the bills and take care of the wet-rotted crawl space that has been getting worse by the day.

I arrived home just in time for my hair appointment, which Michele had graciously rescheduled on her day off, so I was able to relax in her salon—I'm particularly fond of the shampoo chair.

Alice and Dana worked on the photo display here at home. I finalized the funeral bulletin, and Doris and Alice helped me fold and staple them. The church would have taken care of this for me, but I love pushing papers and working side-by-side with faith-filled friends. The joy of the Lord is all over me!

I keep expecting sorrow to sneak up and overwhelm me, but with so many blessings being poured out and the activities in front of me, it will most likely come when I'm alone. Or maybe not. After all, I've been grieving off and on for seven years. The Drew I would have yearned for has been absent from me for so long that the deep grief I anticipate may not come. Little weepy sessions, perhaps. Or maybe the dam will break when I least expect it. Others have told me it hit them six months or fifteen months later. I guess grief is like ocean waves, sometimes gentle, sometimes knocking you down and flipping you over. I'll find out how it affects me in due time.

Buttercup seems to be adapting well to Drew's absence, but Midnight is exceptionally affectionate and almost clingy—if that's a word that can be used to describe a cat purring at my feet and nuzzling to be petted day and night. This is out of character for her, but I hope it lasts. A purring kitty is good for what ails you.

December 7, 2019

The day of Drew's funeral dawned crisp, cold, and bright with no wind or other distractions.

We had to have eight pallbearers instead of six because they needed to carry the casket up the eight steep cement steps of the Georgetown Presbyterian Church. It worked out well because we had two of Drew's brothers, Tim and Dean Abbott; two grandsons, Trevor Abbott and Kade Bullock; two sons-in-law, Wyatt Bullock and John Painter; and two brothers-in-law, Mike and Jim Fennemore.

Reverend Gerald Egger, the interim pastor, officiated, and Sallie Horner, co-director of music, played the organ. My friend Betty Kasperski read the Old Testament Scriptures, and my sister-in-law, Shelly Fennemore, read from the New Testament.

I chose three of Drew's favorite hymns: "Jesus Loves Me," "How Great Thou Art," and "When Peace Like a River" ("It Is Well with My Soul").

Linda Mason's flute medley started and ended with "In the Garden" and included "What a Friend We Have in Jesus," "Abide with Me," and "Great Is Thy Faithfulness." How refreshing it was for me while she played. It felt like I had been transported to another place of total peace and comfort as if nobody else was around. It was truly an anointed time for me.

The service went smoothly and flowed into a time of remembrance for those who wanted to speak.

Dana's Tribute to Her Dad

Dana managed to keep her emotions in check as she read her tribute:

Dad was an incredible father. He was the best dad a child could hope for—a teenager could hope for—an adult could hope for. In the fullest sense of the words, he was full of unwavering love, strength, and loyalty.

Dad was genuine and gentle, and if you noticed his easygoing personality, that was him each day. He was always the same and truly caring and loving to all people. He had a wonderful sense of humor, and almost every day was filled with laughter. But he could also be very serious when a situation presented itself. He was the greatest of problem-solvers of complex situations. Not only could he quickly assess the challenges but arrive quickly at solutions and always know the best one to choose.

He had a beautiful life and enjoyed each day and loved Candy with his whole heart. He would want me to tell you today how very, very grateful he was for her steadfast love and meticulous care, and that he is so proud that she was his wife beginning in the month of June, forty-four years ago, until now. He would have told her, "You did everything just right." He loved his family and his friends.

He enjoyed golf, dinners out, a bright starry sky with a gorgeous full moon—and music. Some of his favorite songs were "Only You" by the Platters, and with his fun-loving nature, I can still see him doing his happy dance in the kitchen to the Bee Gees. His favorite Christmas carol was "Little Drummer Boy." He had great respect for athletes like Jesse Owens and Jack Nicklaus. His favorite month was September. Dad was a morning person. He loved animals, books, nature, walks in the woods, and simply being content in his own back yard.

He taught us all about how to enjoy the simple things in life. Even as Alzheimer's had begun to affect him, and even when it had taken a toll, we had great conversations. When I looked back over the videos of these conversations, I wasn't surprised by his words—not how we laughed but how many times we all laughed.

I wanted to leave you with some of his words. Many of our conversations began with me asking, "Dad, what is the secret to having a good life?" His answers gave such a true testament to the man, and these were the words he lived by all his life. He would answer:

- "Be kind to others."
- "Treat everyone fairly and with respect."
- "And, if someone needs help, help them if you can."
- "Take each thing as it comes; don't worry about things; don't fill your days with worry."
- "Let things go that you can't do anything about."
- He would often say, "I've had a great life."
- I asked him, "How did you get through hard times?" He'd say: "I would tell myself, 'I got through something before, and I'll get through this, too.'"

- He shared, "Don't think that you didn't do enough."
- "Take care of yourself."
- I would say, "Dad, life can be so hard." And he would say in a second, "Yes, but it can be so good, too."
- I asked him, "Dad, if someone loses someone they love very much, what would you tell them to do?" He answered, "I'd say, I'd tell them, go backward; think of all the good and all the great times—how much you meant to one another, and that will last forever."
- His overarching answer to life was: "Believe in the Lord, our Lord and Savior, Jesus Christ, Big Time. He is real. That's number one. And, then, that takes care of everything else."
- In summary, his words were, "Have peace; love and help others; enjoy the simplicity of each day, and fully rely on the Lord."

He would tell you how very much each of you meant to him, and how thankful he is that you're here today.

It never surprised me he was born the first day of spring, and it doesn't surprise me he passed during the season of the year of peace.

I have no doubt where my beloved dad is. He's experiencing the greatest love and joy we could ever imagine.

As those of you know, Dad loved home. He was a total homebody. He's now reunited with his mother and father and many other family members and friends. Ironically, his last words to me were, "All ready." Dad is home. He is in paradise, and we will be with him again for eternity.

Troy's Tribute to His Dad

Troy stood up next, and he, too, maintained his composure as he relayed an almost poetic recollection, entitled, "I Love My Dad":

When I think of my dad, he reminds me of a day at the beach—a warm, sunny place full of good times and awesome memories.

A stroll down a wooded train track behind the old Button Factory in Georgetown.

A walk down a dirt road with our 22s on our routine Saturday adventure as we did so many times before, behind my great-Grandmom Jarvis's house in Harbeson, Delaware.

A drive to Seaford Woolworth's on a rainy Saturday to get that brick of 22s, then stop in at Hardee's for a flame-broiled quarter-pounder before heading back to town.

Together on a snowy winter's day in Dad's old truck checking on this and that.

A day at the golf course when every now and then, he would reach down in his golf bag and pull out a fresh pack of Titleist golf balls so my shots could go a little farther.

Sometimes we spent Saturdays in the backyard piddling with this and that.

Riding together, going to my son Trevor's baseball and football games as we never missed a one.

And all the family dinners through the years. *(Here, Troy looked up from his notes and straight into my eyes to thank me for all I did to make his dad happy through the years and for taking such good care of him.)*

Dad, thank you for everything. You are the best dad a son could ever ask for. I love you.

Kim's Tribute to Her Stepdad

Kim got as far as the word "reliable" in her first paragraph before choking up. It was probably a good thing because I could tell others wanted to cry, and her tears gave them permission. Somehow, she pulled herself together and managed to relay her entire tribute articulately and well-paced:

> As many of you know, Drew became my dad when I was three, thanks to Mom Mom Fannie. He wasn't just a dad, but an outstanding pillar of the community. Many knew him as an athlete, the person who sold them their favorite vehicle, a town council member, classmate, brother, uncle, grandfather, great-grandfather, landlord, golf buddy, church family member, and friend. He was always dependable and willing to go the extra mile. He loved to hear about you, ask about your life, and then would joke about his to soften the mood. He was God-driven, loyal, reliable, supportive, encouraging, kind, funny, and a model man who believed in all that was true, right, and good. What a legacy he has created!
>
> Dad would quickly turn today into an event about you. That's who he was. He raised Dana, Troy, and me to always give our best, stay true to our word, to never look back unless there was a lesson to be learned or a silly tale to be told, and to use those things to make our world a better place. He was a huge believer in second chances. That is who Dad was!

We will continue to see him with us: in the fifth row of the Presbyterian Church, at the restaurant enjoying a meal, on the blue couch facing the door and the TV, and always next to Mom. He is here today and will always be a part of our lives as we share him with each other. Carry him with you and remember, he's with God, looking down, probably making his Donald Duck sound right now because he never could resist being silly.

We love you, Dad. Thanks for loving Mom, for being such a caring father, and for sharing your life with every one of us.

We all have Drew Abbott memories and stories. He would want us to share them with each other, so this time as a gathering with friends and loved ones would be more about us than about him. So, I leave you each with this: God is good, all the time. Thank You, God, for Dad and for Your goodness in him!

Others came forward with tributes: Elizabeth Boerner, Betty Kasperski, Cat Stenger Martin, Grace Lowe (on behalf of the class of 1954), and Pastor Mike Williams.

My Turn to Speak About Drew

After the tributes were finished, I stepped to the lectern and was surprised at the absence of anxiety. It felt natural and right for me to stand in front of an audience of people who knew, admired, and loved my Drew. I spoke of his childlike faith and how he always wanted to keep things simple.

"There's a lot of little boy in that man," I said, and that it seemed appropriate to share something he wrote.

One day, about fifteen years ago, he got up from the kitchen table and disappeared into his office, which wasn't unusual. I assumed he was working on an appraisal, but it was more than that. He'd had a wave of inspiration about how to condense the entire Bible into a few lines. Without soliciting my help, he had typed it on his computer, printed it out, and then cut around it and presented me with a scrap of paper.

"Read this and tell me what you think," he said.

I told him it was fabulous and should be published.

Several months ago, I wondered where that same scrap of paper might be. And there it was, taped to his office wall right next to the light switch.

"It's printed in your bulletin," I announced, "and I thought maybe we could read it together," which we did:

THE BIBLE
According to Drew

OLD TESTAMENT:
    God created everything.
    Man and woman messed up big time.
    God cleaned up their messes, again and again, and again.

NEW TESTAMENT:
    God has a new plan.
    He sends His Son to help.
    Together they both clean up messes.

    Jesus goes back to heaven and sends a Helper.
    God is pleased with many faithful servants.
    The Helper is still here cleaning up.

Trevor's Tribute to His Granddad

While Trevor didn't speak during the funeral, he posted the following eulogy on Instagram:

On Tuesday, my grandfather was called to heaven. Today, we celebrated his life in the same church he attended since he was a young boy. Many knew "Drew" as the owner of the Pontiac dealership, residential appraiser, town councilman, golfer, member of Sussex Pines golf club, or church member. To me, he was who I've always looked up to and never wanted to disappoint. I admired his kindness, wisdom, and problem-solving ability. There wasn't a situation he didn't know how to handle. He would talk, and I would listen. He taught me many valuable life lessons. There were times out on the golf course when he may chunk a shot, but you knew that the next shot was long and straight, right down the fairway (a mulligan was acceptable on our Saturday afternoon rounds). With everything he did in life, it was long and straight, right down the fairway. Granddad, you were the best!

December 8, 2019

What a glorious day we had yesterday! I was so pleased with how the service flowed. Several people said it was "the best funeral" they had ever attended. I thought they were just being nice, but after hearing it so many times, it must be genuine, especially after someone said, "It will be a service that will be remembered for years to come."

Dana said one man told her "the service changed my life." She didn't know what he meant exactly, but he looked deep into her eyes when he said it, as if he wanted her to feel the impact of his words. Another man told me he planned to frame "The Bible According to Drew" and hang it on his wall. Loretta Rogers summed up the service in five words, "It was a love story."

Love has many facets. As the crowd was thinning at yesterday's luncheon, I saw Dana laughing with Barbie, who was always at our house when they were growing up.

"What's so funny?" I asked.

"Go ahead," Dana said. "Tell her." And she laughed again.

Barb giggled. "We were remembering how you and Drew would both come home from work for lunch. You'd go into the bedroom and, just before closing the door, tell us you were going to take a short nap. About twenty minutes later, you'd both come out looking refreshed. You did that a *lot*, and we never thought anything of it. Until now that we're old enough to understand. *Now* we know what you were *really* doing in there. You had more sex than anybody I know!"

I doubt we "napped" as often as they remembered, but there was enough of a pattern that it made an impression. Drew would have been pleased that they thought he was so virile. Ha! I do recall Drew and I winking at each other in 1976 every time we heard "Afternoon Delight" on the radio.

Kim and Wyatt invited me to dinner at their house tonight with Saige and Rosco, their Shih Tzu. Wyatt made beef stew, Caesar salad, and homemade biscuits, and I enjoyed a beverage and conversation in front of their crackling fireplace.

I've slept soundly the past few nights, no longer waking in the wee hours with to-do things running through my head. I'm hoping this is my new normal.

December 12, 2019

It's been overcast and drizzly the past few days. The intense joy I experienced initially seems to have developed a slow leak, and that's as it should be. The gloomy weather is appropriate. I'm mellow today. Numb, actually. I think grief can be numbing. I've been sleeping eight, nine, and ten hours a night and still need naps. Is too much sleep helpful or harmful? It's difficult to concentrate.

Last night, I suddenly felt alone. For the past few years, Drew was here with me but helpless and wouldn't have been able to protect me if an intruder broke in. In essence, I've been "alone" for years. I reminded myself of that fact and felt a little braver, but the awareness that I am "a woman alone" gave me a chill. I'm not afraid, just aware of the need to be alert, practice safety measures, and keep my phone nearby.

This morning, I went through the motions of having my teeth cleaned. Afterward, I treated myself to breakfast-for-one at IHOP, followed by a few errands. I opened my Kindle but mostly stared at the words on the page instead of reading.

It was as I was standing at the counter in the Register of Wills office, filing Drew's death certificate and will, that I felt my throat constrict and tears well up. *Not here. Don't let me lose it here.* I accepted kind condolences from the clerk and was surprised to find I was still relatively composed by the time I left the building.

On a mission to get things done, my last stop was Chardon Jewelers on The Circle, where I brainstormed ideas of what to do with Drew's wedding band. Donna suggested hanging it loose from a gold chain so I could wear it close to my heart. More almost-tears came, and I would have let them flow, but other customers came in, so I made a quick exit to the comfort of my car. Sitting there, I remembered a diamond-cut chain and Celtic cross I had at home that would be a good companion for Drew's ring.

At home, after feeding Buttercup and nuzzling the kitty, I took care of a couple of other things on my to-do list, threaded Drew's ring over the chain so it dangled next to the cross, put it over my head, and then settled into the recliner.

Enough *to-do*. It's time *to be*. To *feel*. My emotions felt ragged and raw but suppressed. Was I intentionally holding them back, avoiding the pain of grief? Was I trying to force my feelings to the surface? Could I even do that?

I turned on Pandora radio, turned up the volume, and let the soothing, romantic melodies and voices of Andrea Bocelli, Josh Groban, and Il Divo wash over me. Music Drew and I loved to listen to together. By the time the Stylistics, Barry White, and the Platters evoked sweet memories, tears began to trickle down my cheeks. It was just the release I needed. I had just gotten to the point of freeing a deep sob when I heard footsteps and the cheery voice of a friend, "Candy, are you back here? Ready or not, here I come!"

Poof! There went my grieving session. Bless her heart. I couldn't bring myself to tell her that she had interrupted a tender moment of personal grief. Besides, there will be other private times for weeping. I'm grateful to have so many dear friends who know my door is always open to them.

But I'm in a new season of life now—a season of bereavement. There will be times when I'll need to be alone and undisturbed. I'll also need to find a way to communicate this to those who love me. Maybe locking the door and posting a sign, "Grieving in progress."

My brother-in-law Dean goes back to Ohio tomorrow, and he took me out tonight for a lovely dinner at the Back Yard in Milton. On the way home, as we drove around the Circle in Georgetown, three blocks from my house, the community-led live nativity was on full display, warming my heart and bringing the true meaning of Christmas to the forefront of my mind. Check it out on YouTube. (Search for "Nativity on the Circle 2019").

December 15, 2019

With everything that's been going on, I haven't given much thought to Christmas, but my friends are extending invitations. First, Jena's having a luncheon featuring Frito pie, board games, a photo session with props, and a tour of her well-decorated home. On the 28th, Betty will host a dinner party at her house, and she's sure to have some happy assignment for us. The last thing on my girlfriend-party agenda is celebrating the New Year at Judi's for lunch at her house. It will do me good to get out, and I'm already developing an appetite for the food.

Kade and Saige will come over on Thursday to bake cookies with me, and we'll probably watch a movie.

On Saturday, Delmarva Christian Writers' Fellowship will have our Christmas meeting, my brother-in-law Tim and his wife Myrna are having an open house on the 26th, and my brothers and their families will have our annual Fennemore family get-together on the 27th.

I've been told that holidays are especially difficult after losing a loved one, but the busyness is helping. I think one of my biggest challenges will be to pace myself and not over-commit. If I feel overwhelmed at any point, I'm prepared to bow out, but so far, I've had the energy and desire to accept the kind invitations that have come my way. I'm beginning to feel sweet anticipation for Christmas and its memories and nostalgia.

December 17, 2019

And what better Christmas gift than the arrival of our great-grandson, Andrew David Abbott! Trevor and Jill announced that he was born today at 8:07 p.m., 9 pounds 7 ounces, and 22 inches long (ironically, the very same measurements as his big sister, Brooklynn).

In Hebrew/Aramaic, Andrew means "brave." How beautiful because his namesake Drew braved his situation with grace and faith and showed us all how to navigate with courage the journey we traveled with him. What an enduring tribute this child is to Drew, and what a legacy little Andrew Abbott has inherited!

December 24, 2019

Troy went with me to the Christmas Eve candlelight service tonight, and it was just what I needed. Afterward, I lit candles in the living room and sat on the couch the way Drew and I used to, with a cup of coffee, the TV tuned to Christmas music, and Buttercup at my feet.

I closed my eyes as four decades of happy memories of Christmases past washed over me. After about a half hour with visions of Drew and I sitting cross-legged on the floor with our heads together, assembling a doll house, train set, or other multi-part present, I decided to prepare the dough for tomorrow's sausage balls.

Humming "I'm Dreaming of a White Christmas" along with the TV as I moved into the kitchen, it occurred to me that I hadn't once heard

Drew's favorite "Little Drummer Boy" this season. No sooner had I reached for the Bisquick box when "pa rum pum pum pum" came to my ears. Was that my imagination because I wanted to hear it, or was it really playing?

I hurried back to the living room, and sure enough, our favorite version of "Little Drummer Boy" was coming through the speakers. Of all the Christmas carols, what are the odds of the very next song being the one I longed to hear? The sausage ball dough could wait. I lowered myself to the couch and savored each note, each word, feeling closer to Drew than ever. And then the last part of the last verse came with fresh meaning:

> I played my drum for Him, pa rum pum pum pum
> I played my best for Him, pa rum pum pum pum
> rum pum pum pum, rum pum pum pum
> Then He smiled at me, pa rum pum pum pum
> Me and my drum.

I gave my best for Drew and for Jesus, and I could see them smiling at me from heaven—me and my faith, my perseverance, my devotion.

Thank You, Lord, for my beloved's presence with me tonight . . . and Yours. For communicating his pleasure . . . and Yours.

Gentle tears flowed, cushioning my grief. *What a gift!*

December 25, 2019

We kept our forty-four-year tradition of Christmas brunch at noon, and I set the tables in the dining room and kitchen for seventeen. It was relaxing this year because the family divided up our standard menu. Instead of cooking everything myself, Troy baked the turkey, Kim and Wyatt brought the breakfast casserole, Dana made Mom Mom Abbott's snow-whipped mashed potato casserole, and Natalie brought the green bean casserole. That freed me up to focus on the extras: appetizers, fresh fruit salad, stuffing, gravy, relish tray, rolls, and dessert.

I made copies of a poem Alice had given me, and it provided the perfect Christmas brunch devotional. We read it aloud together:

Christmas in Heaven
(Author unknown)

I see countless Christmas trees around the world below,
With tiny lights, like heaven's stars, reflecting in the snow.
The sight is so spectacular—please wipe away that tear,
For I am spending Christmas with Jesus Christ this year.

I hear the many Christmas songs
That people hold so dear.
But the sound of music can't compare
With the Christmas choir up here.

I have no words to tell you the joy their voices bring,
For it is beyond description to hear an angel sing.
I know how much you miss me; I see the pain in your heart,
But I am not so far way; we are really not apart.

Be happy for me, dear one; you know I hold you dear.
And be glad I'm spending Christmas with Jesus Christ this year.
For, after all, love is a gift, more precious than gold.
It was always most important in the stories Jesus told.

So please love and help each other
As my Father said to do,
For I cannot count the blessings
Or the love He has for you.

So have a Merry Christmas and wipe away that tear.
For I am spending Christmas with Jesus Christ this year.
I can't tell you of the splendor or the peace here in this place.
Can you imagine Christmas with our Savior, face to face?

I'll ask Him to lift your spirit as I tell Him of your love,
So then pray for one another as you lift your eyes above.
Please let your hearts be joyful, and let your spirits sing.
For I'm spending Christmas in heaven,
And I'm walking with the King!

January 15, 2020

The New Year is well underway, and I've settled into a comfortable routine, pacing myself so I'm not doing too much or too little, enjoying lunch with friends, and easing myself gently back into the publishing saddle.

I slept until 9:30 this morning and awoke rested, but my ordered world was rocked when I saw blood on Buttercup's face. Apparently, she'd had a nosebleed in the night. It didn't look too bad at first, but then she sneezed, which removed a clot and blood gushed out—all over her, all over the kitchen floor. Somehow, I managed to grab some bath towels and get her out the back door and onto the deck where she laid down and continued to hemorrhage.

After ten or fifteen minutes, the bleeding subsided enough for me to go into the house and call the vet. He said to bring her in immediately. "Prepare yourself," he said. "It isn't good."

I hung up and turned to go back outside. There was poor Buttercup standing at the sliding glass door looking in at me and bleeding all over the glass. Oh, my aching heart. She needs me near her.

That's what Drew told me, "Please be near."

"I'm right here, baby. Stay right there, I'm coming out." Cell phone in hand, I slid the door open just enough to ease myself through and keep her from coming into the house. I sat in the rocking chair on the deck and called her to my side so I could rub her head and back.

"I'm right here, baby," I repeated, because it calmed me down to say it. How would I ever get her to the Georgetown Animal Hospital with all this blood?

Troy. He'll know what to do. I dialed his number, and he answered right away but had just gotten out of the shower. While I waited for him to dress, I sat with Buttercup, talking to her in soothing tones, telling her what a good girl she was and how much I loved her.

Troy came as soon as he could and drove his car right up next to the deck so we wouldn't have to carry Buttercup too far.

It was a little after ten o'clock, and Alice arrived for her workday. She took one look at our situation, and began praying, "Jesus, Jesus," then offered to clean everything up.

I collected cleaning supplies for her while Troy wrapped Buttercup in more towels.

"You drive," he said, "and I'll hold her."

Buttercup trembled but never even whimpered once as we maneuvered her into the car. We covered her face with a towel to keep the blood contained, and she tolerated it well. I drove gently so she wouldn't get bounced around. Fortunately, it took less than five minutes to get to the vet's office.

The nurse ushered us into a vacant office right away, and Troy got down on the floor beside Buttercup so he could pet and comfort her while we waited for the doctor.

When Dr. John came in and saw her, he said it was one of five things (brain tumor, aneurysm, etc.), and none were fixable. Our only choice was to put her to sleep.

I had years to condition myself for Drew's death. And now this. The end? So soon?

Dr. John asked if I wanted to hold her while he administered the shot to calm her, but I declined. I had done that before, and it was more than I could bear to do this time. He assured me that he would comfort her and she would know she was loved right to the end.

I knelt down and rubbed her ears, put my face next to hers and said, "Goodbye, Baby. Goodbye, Buttercup." I had trouble getting the words out. Tears that had been bottled up in me for weeks, months, and years threatened to flow, but I held them back.

The nurse put the leash around Buttercup's neck and handed it to Dr. John. My precious eleven-year-old puppy followed him out the door without hesitation or reluctance, as trustingly as if she were going to the groomer. Such a good dog.

A vision of Drew's body being rolled out of the house on the stretcher flashed through my mind. At least Buttercup was walking on her own accord. And she wasn't in pain. If pets go to heaven, and I believe they do, Drew and Buttercup will soon be frolicking together.

At 11:00, I pushed through the exit to the parking lot swallowing sobs that threatened to overtake me.

Troy drove me home. I tried to tell him how grateful I was that he was there for me so I didn't have to do this alone, but the words caught in my throat and only a few vowels and syllables squeaked out.

Alice was waiting with open arms when I came through the door. I walked into them and she held me close.

"Let it out," she said. "Go ahead, let it out."

And I did. Buttercup's death triggered the deep, soaking release I've been needing since December third. Alice continued to hold me, and her tears flowed, too. At last, my sobs turned to quiet sniffles, and I was spent.

I blew my nose on a paper towel (tissues wouldn't have been strong enough) and withdrew to the bedroom to settle into the recliner for a nap. Midnight usually spends her days outside, but I noticed she was still in her bed and hadn't gone out all day. She was sound asleep, so I didn't disturb her. I think she knew Buttercup was in trouble and was grieving in her own way. The two of them were fast friends.

When I got up around noon, Alice said, "It's a lovely day," and suggested I go outdoors for some fresh air. She asked if there was a body of water nearby—like a lake—where I could go to be alone, and I thought of Trap Pond State Park in Laurel. Drew and I used to take Buttercup there when she was a puppy, and it's a place with fond memories of family picnics and playground fun.

On the way there, I stopped by the deli and picked up a sandwich and bottle of water. When I arrived at Trap Pond, there were very few cars, and nobody nearby. I chose a picnic table by the water and enjoyed lunch with a flock of geese and friendly squirrel.

About ten times, the little squirrel would jump on the end of the table and stand up straight showing his white belly, with his tiny hands crossed in front. He'd stare at me for about thirty seconds, cock his head sideways, and then scamper off, only to come back and play the same game again—about eight times. If he was hoping I'd share my sandwich, he must have been sadly disappointed, but he didn't show it. In fact, he was a happy little fellow, and his antics were uplifting.

Nature has a way of renewing and replenishing us. The solitude and fresh air did me good, and I came home refreshed.

I may be a woman alone now, but I am never alone. In good times, and especially in hard times, love is what matters. And love comes from the God who never leaves or forsakes me. I have learned that whatever my circumstances, whatever "this moment" may bring, I am committed to being fully present in it and loving my way through it.

Drew lives in my heart, and I will never love him less than when he was here physically, enveloping me in his arms and holding me close.

As the Holy Spirit gives me eyes to see, I will be looking for the joy. I hope the same for you.

"Arise, let us go from here."

(John 14:31c NKJV)

With Gratitude

This book has the fingerprints and heart-prints
of many who prayed, helped me along the way,
and are helping me still.
Consider this a blanket thank you
for the love, support, and skills
generously shared and eternally appreciated.

Candy

Meet the Author

Candy Abbott is a widow, grandmom, author, publisher, and inspirational speaker. Most of all, she considers herself a "fruitbearer" because it is her life's goal to exhibit the fruit of the Spirit as described in Galatians 5:22-23 (love, joy, peace, patience, kindness, goodness, faithfulness, gentleness, and self-control). Candy's award-winning independent publishing company, Fruitbearer Publishing LLC, was established in 1999. She founded Delmarva Christian Writers Association (www.delmarvawriters.com) and Mothers With a Mission (www.motherswithamission.org). Candy lives in Georgetown, Delaware, with cat, Midnight. Her three children, grandchildren, and great-grandchildren are all nearby. For more information, visit www.fruitbearer.com.

Resources I've Found Helpful

Books

Mike & Me: The New Alzheimer's and Dementia Home-care Guide by Rosalys Peel with Dan Zadran – An inspiring guide for couples who choose to face Alzheimer's together at home.

The Unseen Gifts of Alzheimer's Disease and Dementia: The Greatest of These is Love by Wendy Chanampa – People can live fulfilling lives with this disability. We, the caregivers, are the solution as we learn to embrace and enjoy the journey. There is no easy route, and there will be setbacks and crises. I offer this book as simply another tool to assist you along the way.

When Reasoning No Longer Works: A Practical Guide for Caregivers Dealing with Dementia and Alzheimer's Care Angel Smits' bulleted lists clearly explain: How to avoid a catastrophic reaction, Specific approaches for aggressive behavior, How to deal with disruptive behaviors, Ways to diminish wandering, What to do when a wanderer is missing, When to look for outside help

Elder Rage, or Take My Father . . . Please! How to Survive Caring for Aging Parents by Jacqueline Marcell – A Book-of-the-Month Club selection (a caregiving book first), receiving five-hundred-plus 5-star reviews. It is a riveting, often LOL humorous, non-fiction novel chronicling Jacqueline Marcell's trials, tribulations, and eventual success at managing the care of her aging parents. *Elder Rage* is also an extensive self-help book with creative solutions for effective management medically, behaviorally, socially, legally, financially, and emotionally of challenging elders who resist care.

Look, I Shrunk Grandma: A Psychiatrist's Guide to Nursing Homes, Dementia, and End of Life by Karen Severson, M.D. – As a geriatric psychiatrist who spent twenty years wandering the halls of those dreaded destinations called nursing homes, she became mentally exhausted from watching people with Alzheimer's disease decline and suffer. She writes about the unnecessary suffering caused by doctors, nurses, and families who are on totally different pages regarding end-of-life issues. This book helps families understand dementia and its associated behaviors in a down-to-earth manner. Dr. Severson uses a great deal of humor and discusses other important issues, but mainly how we can better allow families to learn to let go of those with end-stage illness. Dr. Severson hopes to prevent unnecessary and potentially harmful medical interventions as well as allow more geriatric patients to die in peace.

The 36-Hour Day: A Family Guide to Caring for People Who Have Alzheimer Disease, Other Dementias, and Memory Loss (A Johns Hopkins Press Health Book) by Nancy L. Mace and Peter V. Rabins – This classic gives a thorough overview of all stages of the disease and valuable tips for caregivers.

Ministry with the Forgotten: Dementia through a Spiritual Lens by Kenneth L. Carder. Dementia diseases represent a crisis of faith for many family members and congregations. Ken Carder draws on his own experience as a caregiver, hospice chaplain, and pastoral practitioner to portray the gifts as well as the challenges accompanying dementia diseases. He demonstrates how living with dementia can be a means of growing in faith, wholeness, and ministry for the entire community of faith. He also reveals that authentic faith transcends intellectual beliefs, verbal affirmations, and prescribed practices.

Seasons of Goodbye: Working Your Way Through Loss by Chris Ann Waters – Writing can be therapeutic when going through painful transitions or grief. For those who don't know how to begin,

Chris Ann offers instruction, as well as tips for where to write and what to write. *Seasons of Goodbye* will give the reader the courage to say goodbye to yesterday and the strength to say hello to tomorrow.

The Power of Positive Thinking by Norman Vincent Peale—In this timeless bestseller, written with the sole objective of helping the reader achieve a happy, satisfying, and worthwhile life, Dr. Peale demonstrates the power of faith in action. You'll learn how to:

- Believe in yourself and in everything you do
- Build new power and determination
- Develop the power to reach your goals
- Break the worry habit and achieve a relaxed life
- Improve your personal and professional relationships
- Assume control over your circumstances
- Be kind to yourself

Online Resources

AlzAuthors.org—Your go-to place for exceptional Alzheimer's Disease books and dementia books. "We're confident you can find a resource here that will help you on your journey."

The Alzheimer's Store (alzstore.com) has helpful resources such as calling cards that say: "The person I am with has Alzheimer's. Please be patient." https://www.alzstore.com/please-be-patient-alzheimers-cards-p/0187.htm

Tepa Snow on YouTube—brief instructional and informative videos for caregivers of people with dementia—https://www.youtube.com/user/teepasnow

YouTube: Suffering Artist Self Portrait—A series of self-portraits from the Alzheimer's patient's perspective on YouTube. When American artist William Utermohlen was diagnosed with Alzheimer's in 1995, he decided to make the best use of his limited time and memory. For five years, he drew portraits of himself before he completely forgot how to draw. This visual perspective is eye-opening.

Spiritual Resources

Fruitbearer: What Can I Do for You, Lord? by Candy Abbott—
The author's search for the Holy Spirit and the early years of Drew
and Candy's life together.

Jesus Calling: Enjoying Peace in His Presence by Sarah
Young—Experience a deeper relationship with Jesus as you savor
the presence of the One who understands you perfectly and loves
you forever.

Come Away, My Beloved by Frances J. Roberts—A devotional
classic, this book has given Candy strength for many years.
Featuring Scripture from the New King James Version of the
Bible and the heavenly Father's ministering spirit, it brings
encouragement, hope, comfort, and conviction, challenging you to
a deeper intimacy with God.

*Sparkling Gems From The Greek Vol. 1: 365 Greek Word
Studies for Every Day of the Year To Sharpen Your
Understanding of God's Word* by Rick Renner—An amazing
cache of rich, enduring treasures mined from deep within the Word
to unveil a wealth of brilliant wisdom and sound counsel that will
enrich and redefine your life.

Why We Need the Gifts of the Holy Spirit by Rick Renner – Are
you hungry to know and experience more of the supernatural
workings of the Holy Spirit in your life? This book will ignite
your heart with a fresh desire to see His grace and goodness
supernaturally manifested in your life.

*Encountering Our Wild God: Ways to Experience His
Untamable Presence Every Day* by Kim Meeder—Our God is
extreme. Our God is unstoppable, unfathomable, and untamable.
Our God is wild. And He is beckoning us to pursue Him beyond
our circumstances, beyond our emotions, and beyond our logic into
the glorious mystery that is Him.

Appendix II

5 Holiday Tips for Alzheimer's Caregivers
(National Institute of Health on Aging)

Although the holidays can be especially stressful for families living with Alzheimer's, maintaining or adapting family rituals and traditions can help all family members feel connected. Follow these tips to help you have an enjoyable holiday season:

1. Celebrate holidays that are important to you. Be sure to find time for holiday activities you like to do, even if you have to go by yourself.

2. Involve your loved one with Alzheimer's as much as possible. Participating in and observing you prepare for the holidays will familiarize them with the upcoming festivities.

3. Simplify when possible. Don't feel like you have to cook an elaborate dinner or decorate the entire house. Consider hosting a potluck or putting up a few simple decorations.

4. Encourage friends and family to visit. If that feels overwhelming, try scheduling one or two visitors at the times of day when your loved one is at his or her best.

5. Try to avoid frustrating or confusing situations. Limit loud noise and music or lighting that is too bright or too dark. Also, make sure there is a space where the person can rest when he or she goes to larger gatherings.

APPENDIX III

7 Ways to Stay Calm This Christmas

(The Upper Room)

1. Get some sunshine and fresh air.

2. Squeeze the space between your index and middle fingers for thirty seconds.

3. Say no to extra activities.

4. Enjoy a big belly laugh.

5. Focus on your breathing for three minutes a day. Repeat these words to yourself: "Thoughts will come and go; my mind will wander. Even so, I have only one thing to do for the next three minutes: breathe."

6. Give up on the idea of doing it all.

7. Listen to your favorite music.

<u>APPENDIX IV</u>

Letter for Drew's Respite
at the Delaware Hospice Center

September 25, 2019

Dear Family, Friends, and Nursing Staff,

Thank you again for your loving-kindness in filling the gap while I'm gone. This is my fifth respite, and I hope it will be as refreshing as the others. Here are some tips you may find helpful:

- When he asks, "Where's Candy?" tell him I'm on a writing assignment and will be home on Monday.

- Help yourself to the refreshments in the kitchen and the snacks in Drew's room (peppermint patties, applesauce, etc.). He also has ice cream and fresh fruit in the kitchen with his name on them as well as Cokes, Gatorade, and Boost. (Thicken liquids with two scoops of Thicken Up.) The Center provides his regular meals. Swallowing is an increasing problem, so soft foods are best, but he can still handle small bites of a normal diet. When feeding him, watch him closely in case he spits.

- He can no longer hold a glass or cup but will try (and probably bump it). I gently place my hand over his (both, if possible), and put the beverage to his lips. Small sips, please. And watch out that he doesn't spit a mouthful all over himself. (Keep a cup handy for him to spit into.)

- Drew can no longer read, but he likes to be read to. Try the kids' joke book on for size.

- Don't ask him questions because he won't know answers to even the simplest things. One thing he does know is that he's from Georgetown and will likely ask (many times) where you're from, if you grew up there, and where you went to school.

- Background info:
  - He's eighty-three years old
  - He and Candy have been married forty-four years
  - He has three children: Dana, Troy, and Kim; four grandchildren: Natalie, Trevor, Kade, and Saige; and two great-grandchildren: Jaxton and Brooklynn (and another due in December)
  - He is retired. He used to own and operate Bedford Motors (Pontiac and GMC Truck) and was a certified residential appraiser for twenty years.

- He may say he has to go to the bathroom. Tell him he's wearing "special underwear, like the astronauts," that have gel in them, and he can go right where he is.

- If he asks what's wrong with him and sincerely wants to know, you can explain that he has Alzheimer's disease, which does two things: steals his memory and the strength in his legs. Be sure to stress that he still has his wonderful personality and a whole lot of people who love him. After all, "Love is all that really matters."

- He responds well to soft music: Easy Listening (channel 448), sitcoms like Andy Griffith on TV Land (60), and golf (34).

Nurses and CNAs:

Drew craves sleep, so don't wake him for meals or to change him. I have provided extended wear briefs that are very absorbent and should last most of the day and all through the night.

Please be GENTLE, move SLOWLY, and speak SOFTLY. Drew has always been a soft-spoken and gentle man, but now he's fragile and delicate. He doesn't like to be startled or rushed, so take as much time as you can with him.

Swallowing is an increasing problem, and soft foods are best, but he can still handle a normal diet in small bites. He can no longer feed himself. When feeding him, watch him closely in case he spits or smears food around. He prefers to sip from a small glass or cup rather than a straw.

You will need to hold the glass for him. Place your hands over his so he doesn't reach up to "help." His liquids need to be thickened (two scoops of Thicken Up).

MEDICATIONS: His normal meds are Lorazepam, Benadryl, and Melatonin at 8 p.m. Crush the medications and put them in applesauce. The goal is to keep him calm, so if he becomes agitated during the day, give Lorazepam right away, and then every six hours until bedtime.

Give him a capful of Miralax with his breakfast or lunch beverage.

Please change his clothes daily, but don't wake him up to do it. I packed five sets of pajamas. Don't worry about washing anything; send the dirty clothes home in a plastic bag.

He has limited peripheral vision, so be sure he sees you before speaking to him. If you have to wake him, touch and speak gently.

Don't ask questions. If you say, "Are you ready for your bath?" he will tell you NO and resist you from then on. Better to give him calm instruction as you do each thing, i.e., "I'm going to wash your face, okay?" or "Put your knees together now, we're going to roll over." Sometimes he responds well if you ask for his help. But you might want to change his briefs and clothing in silence. And tell him, "You're doing great" as often as you like!

He has Meniere's Disease (vertigo and hearing loss). Turning him too quickly can make him dizzy and panicky.

Gratefully,

Candy

Book 1 of the Abbotts' Alzheimer's Journey

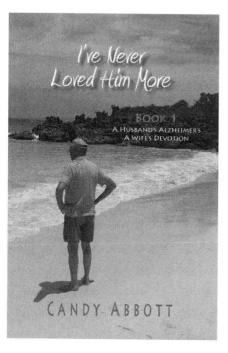

I'VE NEVER LOVED HIM MORE

I've Never Loved Him More is one wife's story of what it means to live out her vows, "in sickness and in health." As her husband's caregiver in his struggle with Alzheimer's, this story takes the reader through discovery, acceptance, adjustment, and battle against the ravages of what is often seen as a soul-crushing disease. Armed with faith, humor, and a history of spiritual victories, Candy demonstrates how she is loving her way through the mind-maze that would steal her husband of four decades. Displaying peace under pressure, she never pretends to have the answers as she navigates unfamiliar waters while also dealing with her own health issues, financial uncertainty, and more. She finds strength in her faith, family, friends, and the kindness of strangers. She engages Scripture, prayer, and spiritual support to combat this disease, weapons which can inspire others who are fighting chronic illnesses. Far from depressing, this is a worthwhile, helpful read for anyone struggling with anything.

Candy's First Book

FRUITBEARER: WHAT CAN I DO FOR YOU, LORD?

If you've ever cried out, "Help me, Jesus!", or "Use me, Lord!" then you are in a good position to become a fruitbearer. If you've ever responded to God's call when it made no sense, then you may already be a fruitbearer. If you hunger for a closer relationship with God, then you will be inspired by Candy Abbott's journey from a casual believer to a bona fide, undisputed fruitbearer.

With back-to-back natural disasters, financial stress, global chaos, and personal trials at every turn, it is more important than ever to trust Christ to empower you for service. Consider this a guidebook to fruitful living in a sour grape society. Invite the Holy Spirit to speak to you between the lines of these pages, and you will discover a new depth and fresh appreciation for Christ's work in your life. Rather than ask, "What can God do for me?" let the Holy Spirit prompt you to ask, "What can I do for YOU, Lord?"

Fruitbearer is the book for you:

- if you long for the power to live your faith joyfully and make God your top priority.

- if you long to recognize the voice of the Holy Spirit and sense a "call" on your life but feel inadequate.

- if you long to have Christ's peace, even in the midst of turmoil, so you can impart peace to others.

Candy's Other Books

FEELINGS: PRAYERS FOR WOMEN IN A WACKY WORLD

A TO Z EMOTIONS DEVOTIONS

Are your emotions soaring heavenward one minute and splashing for survival the next? This devotional will keep you anchored in Scripture so you can hear God's voice and heed His call, whether you're sinking or swimming. Each "feelings" page begins with "Lord, I feel _____," followed by a real-life situation, a relevant Scripture, and the Lord's perspective. Try it yourself. Half of the pages are lined for you to journal your own feelings.

MOURNING BREAKERS: A DAUGHTER'S REFLECTIONS ON HER MOM'S HOMEGOING

Tears may flow in the night, but joy comes in the morning (Psalm 30:5). If you are grieving the loss of a loved one or helping someone through their final days on earth, this brief personal experience devotional is a proven resource for caretakers who are seeking an anchor. Find your joy in the mourning.

Candy's Other Books

GAVIN GOODFELLOW:
THE LURE OF BURNT SWAMP

A SPIRITUAL FANTASY FOR YOUNG ADULTS

What do twelve-year-old dyslexic Gavin Goodfellow, prophetically-inclined Uncle Warney, mother-daughter witches from London, and a tattooed New Age guru have in common? Burnt Swamp—where flames from a mysterious underground fire have been smoldering for ten years. The battle is on for dominion of the swamp and possession of an ancient diary that holds clues to release or destroy the evil that dwells beneath the surface. Will Gavin respond to the Holy Spirit and embrace his God-given calling? Or will Bea Daark and her mum unleash forces that lure Gavin and the sleepy town of Ashboro deep into bondage?

Book One of the Burnt Swamp Trilogy

"Just when I thought the best fantasy-mystery-adventure books had already been written, I found *Gavin Goodfellow*. NOW you have the best! Not only is the story deliciously strange and can't-put-it-down intriguing, but Gavin and the challenges he bumps into are as real as you are. And at the center of it all, there's God—like you've never experienced God before. So follow Gavin and his cousins, Molly and Eric, into Burnt Swamp and be prepared for the journey of your life!"

—Nancy Rue, award-winning author
of youth and adult fiction

Candy's Other Books

MY 30-DAY PRAYER DIARY

This handy diary was created as a companion to *Fruitbearer: What Can I Do for You, Lord?* by Candy Abbott. It is patterned after the prayer diary by Catherine Marshall and Leonard LeSourd that Candy used in her journey to become better acquainted with the Holy Spirit. Come near to God, and He will come near to you (James 4:8) is a promise from His holy Word. By committing yourself to thirty days of prayer, you are intentionally drawing near to God, and you can do so in confidence, knowing that He is drawing near. Many of the topics addressed in this diary will be familiar, probably all of them, but each time these areas confront our spirit, we may be in a different frame of mind or circumstance. The blank portion, "My Prayer Requests" and "God's Answers" can be used to record your own personal spiritual journey or prayer concerns for others. If the Holy Spirit speaks to your heart, capture His words and date the entry so you can reflect on them later. The Word is alive in those of us who believe. Give the Holy Spirit freedom to search areas you may have resisted before.

SPIRIT FRUIT: A CANDID CALENDAR FOR FRUITFUL LIVING

This perpetual calendar will tickle your funny bone, make you think, and strengthen your spirit. A light and unexpected approach to biblical and everyday truths, *Spirit Fruit* will become your daily friend and be a good conversation piece for the whole family . . . year after year.

Order Info

**I've Never Loved Him More
And I'll Never Love Him Less**
and Candy's other books
are available from
Amazon.

For autographed copies,
visit www.fruitbearer.com
or contact Candy
at info@fruitbearer.com
302.856.6649

Fruitbearer Publishing LLC
P.O. Box 777, Georgetown, DE 19947

Made in the USA
Middletown, DE
24 February 2021

34307315R00188